KU-015-376

how to cook

hamlyn

First published in Great Britain in 2005 by
Hamlyn, a division of Octopus Publishing Group Ltd
2–4 Heron Quays, London E14 4JP

Copyright © Octopus Publishing Group Ltd 2005

All rights reserved. No part of this work may be reproduced or utilized in any form or by any means, electronic or mechanical, including photocopying, recording or by any information storage and retrieval system, without the prior written permission of the publisher.

ISBN 0 600 61273 2
EAN 9780600612735

A CIP catalogue record for this book is available from the British Library.

Printed and bound in China

10 9 8 7 6 5 4 3 2 1

MORAY COUNCIL
LIBRARIES &
INFO.SERVICES

20 16 12 85

Askews	
641.512	

Notes for American readers
Ingredients: equivalents and substitutions

UK	US	UK	US	UK	US
aubergine	eggplant	flaked almonds	slivered almonds	plain chocolate	bittersweet chocolate
back bacon	Canadian bacon	French bean	green bean	plain flour	all-purpose flour
bacon rasher	bacon slice	fromage frais	plain yogurt	polenta flour	cornmeal
beetroot	beet	full cream milk	whole milk	prawn	shrimp
belly pork	bacon	gammon steak	ham steak	ratafia biscuit	amaretti
bicarbonate of soda	baking soda	ginger nut	gingersnap	rocket	arugula
borlotti bean	cranberry bean	glacé cherries	candied cherries	runner bean	green bean
broad bean	fava bean	golden syrup	corn syrup	self-raising flour	self-rising flour
butter bean	lima bean	Greek yogurt	whole milk yogurt	single cream	light cream
cantaloupe	muskmelon	groundnut oil	peanut oil	soft brown sugar	brown sugar
caster sugar	superfine sugar	icing	frosting	soft cheese	cream cheese
chicory	endive	icing sugar	confectioners' sugar	soured cream	sour cream
cider	hard cider	King Edward potato	round white or red potato	sponge finger	ladyfinger
clear honey	honey	lamb fillet	boned rib of lamb	spring onion	scallion
coriander	cilantro	mangetout	snow pea	streaky bacon	bacon
cornflour	cornstarch	minced beef	ground beef	strong flour	bread flour
Cos lettuce	romaine lettuce	monkfish	angler fish	sultana	golden raisin
courgette	zucchini	muscovado sugar	brown sugar	swede	rutabaga
crème fraîche	sour cream	natural yogurt	plain yogurt	sweetcorn	corn
curd cheese	ricotta	pak choi	bok choy	tiger prawn	jumbo shrimp
digestive biscuits	graham crackers	Parma ham	prosciutto	tomato purée	tomato paste
double cream	heavy cream	passata	pureed tomatoes	treacle	molasses
eating apple	dessert apple	pepper,		vanilla pod	vanilla bean
endive	chicory	red/green/yellow	bell pepper	wholemeal flour	whole wheat flour

Approximate conversions

60 ml (2 fl oz)	¼ US cup
120 ml (4 fl oz)	½ US cup
180 ml (6 fl oz)	¾ US cup
240 ml (8 fl oz)	1 US cup
1 litre (1¾ UK pints)	4 US cups

Some standard equivalents
The following are the equivalent of 1 US cup:

125 g (4 oz) flour
225 g (8 oz) granulated or caster (superfine) sugar
125 g (4 oz) icing (confectioners') sugar
225 g (8 oz) butter
200 g (6 oz) rice

contents

1
where
to start **8**

2
mastering
the basics **60**

3
simple
techniques **136**

4
putting it
into practice **198**

Introduction

These days, when heating up a ready meal is often looked upon as cooking, it can be difficult for people to learn a real understanding of good food. Yet cookery skills are held in high regard – television chefs, for example, have become modern icons – and everyone loves homemade meals. People are truly impressed if you can bake bread, make a simple sauce or produce a great roast dinner. But successful cooking is within easy reach of everyone if you know where to start and take the right approach. If you master the basic principles it will provide a solid framework on which to build up your cookery skills and experience.

Learning the basics does not mean following lengthy, complicated methods – in contemporary cooking, the emphasis is on simplicity, speed and flavour, rather than on fancy culinary devices. This gives you the opportunity to cook with freedom, to follow your individual choice of ingredients and flavourings, without fear of doing things the wrong way. Cooking becomes a fun and fulfilling activity when you feel confident enough to experiment. From that moment on, you will never look back!

Getting organized Before you begin to cook in earnest, take a long, hard look at your kitchen and see how you can organize and free-up the existing space so that you have as much clear work surface as possible. Make sure that you have enough cupboard space to stock up on staples, such as dried pasta, rice; canned foods, such as tomatoes and beans; and a range of flavourings and spices. You will soon get to know which ingredients you use the most.

Where to start The first chapter in this book introduces you to the many ingredients on offer, to allow you to gain an understanding of the building blocks of cooking. It explains what the ingredients are and how to serve them, to give you confidence when shopping. There is also a section on Tools of the Trade to explain what you will need to get started. Of course you won't need all the gadgets described, but it will give you some idea of what is available.

Left Fresh fish with a simple sauce is so easy to prepare and yet is nutritious, delicious and impressive too!

Mastering the basics Confidence is really the
key to preparing good food, and this book is organized
in such a way as to encourage you to extend your
culinary expertise step by easy step. The chapter on
Mastering the Basics focuses in turn on a basic
ingredient or group of ingredients. It takes you
through choosing and buying your ingredients, how
to store them and then moves on to elementary
preparation advice and simple cooking instructions, so
you know how to deal with the food you have bought.
A number of mouth-watering recipes follow so that you
can put the skills you have learnt into practice.

Simple techniques Building on the information
so far, this section teaches some basic cookery
techniques, including making pastry, mastering batters
and simple soups. The techniques are carefully
explained in step-by-step sequences to give you
confidence. There are plenty of tips and advice for
achieving success every time. Each section goes on to a
selection of recipes to illustrate the technique and give
you something to practise on.

Above Presenting food beautifully isn't difficult and will impress
your guests when you're entertaining.

Putting it into practice Having covered all the
essential information, the next section, Putting it into
Practice, shows you how to do just that. It offers advice
on how to integrate your new-found skills into your
lifestyle – how to create great suppers after work, how
to produce mouth-watering meals on a tight budget,
and how to make sure you get a balanced diet. In
addition, this section gives you ideas and tips for
impressing family and friends when you entertain,
including shortcuts and cheats, in case you're short
of time and need to whip something up quickly.

Cooking terms explained The final section is
a glossary of cooking terms for easy reference. This
allows you to look up anything you don't understand
and offers a great resource to give you confidence in
your cooking.

The recipes Each section gives you a selection of
recipes that employs or builds on the basic skills you
have learned. There are classic recipes, drawn from
the popular cuisines of the world, that have stood the
test of time and changing food fashions. In addition,

there are inspiring modern dishes that bring together
ingredients in imaginative combinations.

While many of the dishes included in the book are
for everyday eating, there are definitive recipes for
those major culinary challenges when you really want
to make a special effort. To take the tension out of
entertaining, other recipes have been specially chosen
for their ability to impress, while being deceptively easy
to prepare. There are preparation and cooking times
with each recipe, so you can plan ahead and get a
realistic idea of how long it will take you to make each
dish. Many of the recipes also have fantastic colour
photographs to tempt you to try them out.

Your kitchen companion All in all, this book
offers everything you need in one volume to create
great dishes right from the word go. Use it as your
practical, everyday adviser in the kitchen, as well as a
source of inspiration for your cooking. You will derive
great pleasure not only from sampling the results of
your labours but from the satisfaction of having
produced something from scratch as well. So, with
no more ado, get cooking!

where to start

Vegetables

Season by season, the range of vegetables is always plentiful, not to mention colourful and delicious. Don't treat them as an afterthought – many vegetable varieties are exciting enough to take centre stage in a meal.

Artichoke (globe)
Available in summer. The base of this thistle-like flower is edible, as is the heart, which is highly prized. Cook in boiling salted water for 45 minutes, or until a leaf pulls away easily.
Serve hot or cold with vinaigrette or melted butter.

Artichoke (Jerusalem)
Available between October and March. A tuber with creamy-white flesh, similar to a turnip in texture. The flavour is sweet and musky. Scrub under cold water and put immediately into water with lemon juice added as the cut surfaces discolour quickly.
Serve boiled with butter, mashed, or fried in slices. Delicious in soups, vegetable bakes and stir-fries.

Asparagus
This is an expensive vegetable, but delicious. The tips are the most tender part and should be tightly closed and well formed. Local asparagus has the best flavour, but limited availability. Imported asparagus is available most of the year.
Serve steamed with melted butter, or in salads, soups or stir-fries.

Aubergine
The deep purple skin should be bright and shiny and the vegetable should feel heavy. Fry slices or chunks in olive oil, or barbecue or roast.
Serve in pasta dishes, ratatouille, or stuffed and baked.

Avocado
Avocados are available throughout the year, but are at their cheapest in midsummer. The creamy flesh is high in protein, vitamins and minerals. Once cut, brush the flesh with lemon juice to prevent discoloration.
Serve in salads, dips and sandwiches.

Bean (runner)
These large green pods have small beans inside and are flavoursome and delicious. They are generally only available in summer and autumn. The pod of the runner bean should be young and tender enough to snap in half. The beans should be topped and tailed before cutting them diagonally into thin pieces and either steamed or boiled until just tender.
Serve as an accompaniment, in tomato sauce, or in bakes or stir-fries.

Bean (French)
These beans should be bright to darkish green in colour, and no more than 10 cm (4 inches) in length. They are round in cross-section and smaller than runner beans. Treat and cook as for runner beans.
Serve as an accompaniment or in salads – the best known is Salade Niçoise – or add French beans to soups and casseroles.

Bean sprout
These are the sprouts of green mung beans, and are widely available. They are white, thin and very crunchy, and should be cooked or used on the day of purchase.
Serve in salads and stir-fry dishes.

Beetroot

A beautiful red-purple tuber, beetroot has a high sugar content, which gives the vegetable its distinctive flavour. It is sold raw or cooked; boil or roast the raw roots until tender.

Serve in salads, soups, risottos or bakes.

Broad bean (1)

Fresh broad beans are available from midsummer to early autumn. Remove the beans from the pods and boil for 2–5 minutes until tender, then slip the beans out of their skins.

Serve in salads, risottos, soups and pasta dishes or as a vegetable accompaniment.

Broccoli

Trim broccoli stems and cut each floret into even-sized pieces. Cook by steaming or boiling in salted water for 6–7 minutes until just tender – overcooking will spoil the flavour. The stems should be slightly crisp. Look out for purple sprouting broccoli which is a real treat.

Serve as an accompaniment, in pasta dishes, risottos, soups and bakes.

Brussels sprout

Brussels sprouts are an autumn and winter vegetable. To prepare, remove the outer leaves (if necessary) and cut a cross in the base of each sprout. Steam, or cook in boiling salted water for 8-10 minutes. They should still be crunchy.

Serve as an accompaniment or in a casserole.

Cabbage (2)

There are many varieties of cabbage, ranging from spring cabbage to spring greens, winter, red, white and Savoy. The best way to cook cabbage is to shred and steam it, or stir-fry it for a couple of minutes in butter.

Serve as an accompaniment, shredded into casseroles or raw in salads such as coleslaw.

Did you know?

Nutritionists recommend we eat at least five portions of vegetables or fruit each day to keep us healthy. Not only do they contain essential vitamins and minerals, but many vegetables protect us against serious illnesses like cancer. Try to eat as many different-coloured vegetables as you can to get the full range of protective benefits.

Chinese leaves

Oriental vegetables have become increasingly popular over the past few years and come in many different varieties, including pak choi, choi sum and Chinese cabbage. All can be briefly cooked or used raw.

Serve in stir-fries, soups and salads.

Carrot

Carrots are inexpensive and rich in nutrients, which include vitamin C, beta-carotene, minerals and fibre. All the vitamins are just below the skin, so it is best simply to scrub the carrots.

Serve steamed, boiled, stir-fried or roasted, or raw in salads, in batons or grated.

Cauliflower (3)

Cauliflower is much prized for its delicate flavour, which, if it is properly cooked, is delicious. Steam or boil until the florets are just soft and the stem still remains fairly crunchy.

Serve as an accompaniment, in bakes or curries, with cheese sauce, or raw with a dip.

Celeriac (4)

This large, knobbly white vegetable has a similar flavour to celery, though rather more delicate, but is grown for the swollen base of the stem rather than the tops. It is equally good served raw or cooked.

Serve puréed or in chunks as an accompaniment or in soups, stews or casseroles. Steam or boil the cubes for about 15 minutes until tender. Alternatively, peel and grate the raw tuber and serve in salads. It is especially good dressed with mayonnaise.

Celery

Celery is at its best during the winter months. It is the tall fleshy stems which are eaten, though the leaves can be used to flavour stocks.

Serve braised, added to stews and casseroles or made into soups, where it imparts a subtle savoury flavour. Also good raw as an addition to salads and, traditionally, with cheese at the end of a meal.

Chicory

This is a conical-shaped vegetable, rather like a tight, crispy lettuce head with the leaves packed closely together. The flavour is quite bitter, though it becomes less strong when cooked. It is particularly good as a foil for rich flavours, complementing cheese or fatty meats.

Serve braised in stock, grilled or roasted as an accompaniment, or separate the leaves and serve whole or shredded in salads.

Courgette (1)

Courgettes should be shiny and free from blemishes. They come in a range of different colours and sizes but green is the most common. They are versatile and can be steamed, baked, deep fried or boiled. Due to their high water content, cooking should be kept to a minimum.
Serve sliced and fried as an accompaniment, in pasta dishes or risottos.

Cucumber

Cucumbers should be very firm, free from blemishes and a good rich green in colour.
Serve in Oriental stir-fries and soups or, more usually, raw in salads and sandwiches, or with dips.

Endive

There are two varieties of this lettuce available, the curly Staghorn or the plain-leaved Batavia. The former is the most popular though it has a stronger flavour.
Serve in salads tossed with vinaigrette.

Fennel (2)

There are three main varieties of fennel: wild, common garden and Florence. The first is grown mainly for its seeds and leaves, while the others are cultivated for use as a vegetable. Fennel has a mild, sweet flavour, similar to aniseed.
Serve raw in salads, finely shredded and tossed in lemon juice. Alternatively, steam, poach or boil and use in risottos, bakes and pasta dishes.

TOP TIPS

- Leafy vegetables, such as spring cabbage, celery and lettuce, should have a fresh appearance, with no browning or wilting.
- Root vegetables, such as carrots, potatoes and swede, should be firm and have no sign of damp or shiny patches or any surface damage. Avoid potatoes with dry wrinkly skins or those that are turning green or beginning to sprout.
- French and runner bean pods should be young and tender enough to snap in half and free from blemishes; broad beans should be plump; pea pods should be round and full but not hard.
- Tomatoes, courgettes, peppers and aubergines should have firm, bright, shiny skins with no sign of bruising.

Leek (3)

Choose leeks with a long white section and fresh-looking leaves. Peel off the outer layer and slice the remainder, checking for earth between the layers.
Serve fried or steamed as an accompaniment, perhaps with white or cheese sauce, or in stir-fries or risottos. Baby leeks can be served whole, simply steamed.

Lettuce

Many types of lettuce are available, some with soft leaves, others more crunchy. Cos and Romaine are crisp and oblong, with long pointed leaves; the Webb has crinkled outer leaves and a firm heart. The Iceberg lettuce resembles a white cabbage, while the soft-leaf lettuce has floppy leaves and a crisp yellow heart.
Serve in salads, or shred and braise or add to soups.

Mangetout

A member of the pea family, cultivated for its pods, rather than for the peas. The pods should be crisp and fresh. To prepare, simply cut off the stems.
Serve steamed or lightly boiled in salted water, or in stir-fries or casseroles.

Mushroom (4)

Many types of mushroom are now available. Field and chestnut mushrooms have a better flavour than white or button mushrooms, and shiitake mushrooms are delicious in Oriental dishes. Some wild mushrooms are now also commercially available. To prepare, simply wipe the stalks and caps with kitchen paper.
Serve raw in salads, cook in melted butter or add to casseroles, stews, soups and risottos.

Onion (5)

There are several varieties, ranging from strong-flavoured white onions, large, milder Spanish onions, sweet red onions, mild shallots, small pickling onions and spring onions. Onions have firm but juicy flesh and many uses.
Serve raw in salads, or use in curries, stir-fries, pasta dishes, soups and casseroles.

Parsnip

These root vegetables have fibrous cream flesh and a distinctive sweet flavour. Choose small parsnips which will be more tender. Thinly peel away the skin, and roast, steam, boil or fry until tender. Although traditionally a winter vegetable, nowadays parsnips are available all year round.
Serve as an accompaniment to roast meats, in casseroles, or mashed with potatoes or carrots.

Pea (6)

Peas are available fresh, frozen or canned. They have a high sugar content, making them very sweet, and are at their best soon after picking. Young peas may be eaten raw in salads, or can be steamed or boiled until tender. **Serve** in soups, risotto, curries or casseroles, or as a vegetable accompaniment.

Pepper (capsicum) (7)

This brightly coloured vegetable (red, green, orange or yellow) should be firm and unblemished. It has a strong flavour when raw which becomes very sweet when cooked. To prepare peppers, remove the core and seeds. **Serve** either raw in salads, or stuff with rice or minced meat and bake. Also good in ratatouille, with pasta dishes or in risottos.

Potato (8)

An extremely versatile vegetable which can be a meal in itself. Use new potatoes for boiling, grating for rosti and for potato salad, and older potatoes for roasting, baking, sautéing, mashing and chips. **Serve** as an accompaniment or in salads or fishcakes.

Spinach

Baby spinach leaves have a sweeter flavour than the larger more mature leaves. Wash thoroughly to get rid of any soil, drain well and stir fry or steam. **Serve** as an accompaniment, raw in salads, in curries or in pasta dishes or risottos.

Swede

A winter vegetable with orange skin, yellow flesh and a rather fragrant flavour. Peel and dice before cooking, then steam or boil until tender. **Serve** mashed with butter as an accompaniment, or in soups, bakes or casseroles.

Sweetcorn (corn on the cob)

Sweetcorn should be yellow and firm, encased in white silky threads and light green leaves. Remove the leaves and silk, and boil for 10–15 minutes until the kernels are tender. Sweetcorn can also be barbecued. **Serve** the whole cobs hot with melted butter or the kernels in salads, casseroles and soups.

Tomato

Varieties range from tiny cherry tomatoes to large beefsteak tomatoes, and tomatoes now come in a range of different colours, including red, orange, yellow, green and purple. Plum tomatoes are best for cooking. **Serve** in salads, sauces and casseroles.

Fruit

Always refreshing and delicious, fruit plays an essential part in a healthy diet, providing energy, fibre, minerals and vitamins. The wonderful colours and sweet flavours of fruit add brightness to savoury and sweet dishes alike.

Apple (1)

Dessert apples are available throughout the year, cooking apples most of the year. Choose firm fruit without blemishes.

Serve apples in sweet dishes such as pies, flans, crumbles, jams and preserves. They also make a fine addition to savoury dishes, particularly those with rich meats such as pork and pheasant, and can be made into apple sauce to serve with roast meat.

Apricot (2)

Small, yellowish-orange stone fruit, with a slightly furry skin and juicy flesh. Available in summer.

Serve apricots raw or poach them for pies, crumbles, fools and jams. They can also be added to savoury dishes, including casseroles, Middle Eastern and Moroccan meat dishes.

Banana

Bananas are creamy in colour and mealy in texture. As the fruit ripens it becomes sweeter and softer.

Serve uncooked in fruit salads; alternatively, bananas can be fried, added to crumbles and pies, or barbecued in their skins for a delicious dessert.

Blackcurrant

These blackish-purple berries with a slight bloom to the skin are usually sold stripped from their stems.

Serve cooked with sugar to make pies, fools, mousses, ice creams and jellies.

Blackberry

These purplish-black soft berried fruits are usually cooked, unless they are very sweet. They are generally available from July to October. Cook by boiling or poaching gently with a little water or liqueur.

Serve in pies (especially with apples), flans, tarts, ice creams and sorbets, jams and jellies.

Cherry

Dessert cherries are sweet and available in the summer months. The morello cherry is slightly sour and ideal for casseroles, sauces and jams.
Serve in flans, pies, gateaux, ice creams and fruit salads, or in savoury dishes with rich meats.

Crab apple

These are small, bright red fruits touched with yellow. They have a very sharp flavour and are always cooked.
Serve in jams, jellies, pickles and chutneys.

Coconut

A large nut with a woody fibrous shell, enclosing succulent, pure white flesh and coconut juice. Puncture the three indentations at the top of the nut to pour out the colourless juice. Crack open the nut by hitting it with a hammer one-third of the way from the top. Use the flesh raw, or dried and shredded.
Serve in flans, cakes and biscuits.

Coconut milk is available in tins and is made by pulverizing the flesh with water. Coconut cream is the thickest part of the coconut milk and can be bought in a tin or block.
Serve in curries, noodle dishes and ice creams.

Date

Fresh dates are generally available in winter. They should have a shiny brown skin and sweet soft flesh.
Serve raw as a snack or after-dinner sweetmeat, or use in cakes and puddings.

Fig (3)

Figs come from Mediterranean-type areas. They have a deep purple, white or red skin and pinkish flesh, and are best from late summer to early winter.
Serve raw in savoury salads with ham or cheese, or in fruit salads. Dried figs are used in casseroles and cakes.

Gooseberry (4)

There are both dessert and cooking gooseberries, depending on their sweetness and the amount of pips they have. These green, hairy berries are available in the summer months.
Serve in pies, flans or fools.

Grapefruit

There are two types, those with yellow flesh and those with pink or red flesh. This is the largest of the citrus fruits and is available throughout the year.
Serve halved and sprinkled with sugar for breakfast, or in savoury salads with smoked chicken or fish.

Grape (5)

There are many varieties ranging from black to red, white, amber and green. The skin should have a whitish bloom.
Serve raw with cheese or in a fruit salad, or in savoury salads with fish, ham or smoked meats. Grapes are also used in flans and desserts.

Kiwi

This fruit resembles a large gooseberry, but with a brown hairy skin. Ripe fruits will give a little when gently squeezed, but should not be soft. The flesh is green with dark seeds around a light core. Peel before use with a sharp knife.
Serve peeled and sliced in desserts and ice creams or in fruit salads.

Kumquat (6)

These little oval orange citrus fruits have a very sharp flavour and are usually served cooked.
Serve in mixed fruit dishes or in sauces and casseroles as a foil for rich meats such as duck and lamb.

Lemon (7)

Choose smooth-skinned lemons if you want them for their juice, or knobbly, unwaxed lemons if you are using the rind. The skin should be unwrinkled and the fruit should feel heavy. Lemons are invaluable for both sweet and savoury dishes and have a multitude of uses in cooking.
Serve the finely grated rind as a flavouring for mousses, cakes, risottos and pasta dishes. Lemon juice is used extensively to add a little tang to fish dishes, salads and desserts. It is also used to prevent certain fruits, such as apples and avocados, from discolouring.

Lime (8)

A citrus fruit, similar in shape to a lemon, but much smaller. The flesh is green and the skin, which is quite thin, with little pith, is greenish yellow.
Serve in the same way as lemons. Limes are also used extensively in Thai and other Asian cuisines, for adding sourness to curries and other savoury dishes.

Loganberry

These juicy berries are long and deep red with a white central core. They have a tart flavour rather like a raspberry or blackberry. They are generally available in summer and autumn and are usually poached or stewed with sugar.
Serve in pies, tarts, crumbles, mousses, fools and preserves, either on their own or with apples.

Mango (1)

A large stoned fruit with a thick, yellow-green or orange-red skin. The flesh is deep orange with a distinctive, aromatic flavour. Choose fruit that gives a little when gently squeezed. Peel off the skin and slice the fruit off the stone.
Serve raw in fruit salads or savoury salads with ham or smoked meat. Can also be used in curries and other spicy dishes where it adds a delicious sweetness.

Melon

There are several varieties: honeydew melon has thick rough skin and yellowish-pink flesh; Ogen melon has thick green-striped skin, and sweet juicy flesh; Charentais melon is round and small, with yellow-green skin and dark orange, fragrant flesh. Cantaloupe melon is slightly flattened in shape with rough, green to yellow skin. Choose melons by smelling them. They will smell sweet and appealing if they are ripe.
Serve raw in fruit salads or as an accompaniment to ham, prawns or smoked meat.

Nectarine

A variety of peach, with a smooth, deep red skin tinged with yellow, and juicy, fragrant flesh.
Serve raw or cooked in sweet or savoury salads, or halved and baked with sugar and a splash of sweet wine. Nectarines are also delicious when used in tarts, pies and crumbles.

TOP TIPS
- Fruit that is firm, plump and unwrinkled will be fresh and its juice content will be good.
- The skins of fruit should not be split, broken or bruised in any way.
- There should be no insect damage.
- Don't be afraid to pick it up and smell it to see if it is ripe.
- Berries should look dry and full, with no signs of mould or wetness. Always check the base of punnets of wrapped berry fruit: there should be no sign of leaking juice or squashed fruit.
- Buy soft berry fruit for immediate consumption.
- Store fruit in a cool place, unless it needs to ripen – at room temperature it will quickly deteriorate.

Orange (2)

Two types are available, bitter or sweet. The bitter Seville orange is thin skinned and is best used for marmalade. Dessert oranges are sweeter and have thicker skins.
Serve the flesh in sweet and savoury salads, or in sauces with meats. Orange juice and grated rind are used to flavour drinks, cakes, desserts and meat casseroles.

Peach

Yellow peaches have a pink, furry skin flecked with yellow, and a pinkish-orange juicy flesh. White peaches have a pink skin and white flesh. Peaches are at their best in the summer months.
Serve in fruit salads, poached in wine, or halved and baked in the oven.

Pear (3)

Varieties of dessert pears include Conference, Comice and William, and they are available throughout the year, though they are at their best in autumn and winter.
Serve raw in fruit salads or with cheese, or poached in red wine or Marsala for a delicious dessert. Pears make a sweet, succulent filling for pies, tarts and crumbles.

Persimmon

Also called Sharon fruit, this is similar to a tomato in shape but is bright orange and has a leafy stem. The skin is thick and waxy and the flesh is very sweet, juicy and soft when ripe.
Serve raw in fruit salads.

Pineapple

A large oval fruit, with a rough, yellowish-orange skin, and dark green, prickly leaves at the top. The flesh is yellow and juicy with a thick core running through the centre. When ripe, pineapple will smell sweet and fragrant, and a leaf should come off easily when pulled.
Serve raw in fruit salads, or barbecued or griddled until golden brown. Pineapple is also used in Oriental stir-fries and curries.

Quince (4)

This large yellow fruit is a relative of the pear. It has a sharp but fragrant flavour and is usually served cooked.
Serve in jellies and preserves, poached in wine, or serve in crumbles and pies, with or without apples.

Raspberry (5)

A pinkish-red berry with a tart, fruity flavour. Do not wash before serving. Available in summer and autumn.
Serve plain with cream, or add to fruit salads, summer puddings, flans, ice creams, pavlovas or sauces.

Did you know?
A good way to select fruits is by smell. If they smell sweet, fragrant and appealing it usually means they are ripe and ready to eat. Fruit bought in supermarkets is often hard and tasteless, so try a good local greengrocer instead.

Redcurrant

A bright red, slightly translucent berry with a tart flavour, which is usually cooked by stewing or poaching, and is sweetened to taste with sugar. Available in the summer months.
Serve in pies, sauces, compotes, summer puddings, fruit salads, preserves and jellies.

Rhubarb (6)

This is really a vegetable but it is often treated as a fruit in sweet dishes. There are two types: forced or early rhubarb is available from early winter to early spring, and has thin pink stalks with yellow leaves. Maincrop rhubarb has thicker, reddish-green stems, with large, dark green leaves, and is available from mid-spring. Use only the stem as the leaves are poisonous.
Serve steamed, poached or stewed with sugar. Use in crumbles, fools, pies and tarts, although it is best covered with a top crust only as the excess juices will make the bottom layer of pastry soggy. Also delicious served with ice cream or made into jams, jellies and chutneys. Good in sauces with fatty meats.

Strawberry (7)

This bright, oval red berry is sweet and juicy, with a distinctive aroma. Strawberries are only really worth buying in the summer months when the fruit is completely ripe and a rich red colour all over. Use strawberries as soon as possible after purchase, since they soon start to deteriorate.
Serve raw with cream and sugar, or in flans, pies, cakes, tarts, summer pudding, pavlova, ice cream, sorbet or jams and jellies.

Watermelon (8)

This is the largest of the melon family, either round or oval, with a dark green or yellow skin. The bright pink, juicy flesh is studded with black seeds and has a fresh, fragrant flavour.
Serve cut into large chunks as a cooler, or use for ice creams or sorbets, fruit salads or smoothies.

Herbs

From sweet, pungent mint and spicy coriander to fresh, zesty parsley, the colours and flavours of fresh herbs will transform your cooking. It is often the herbs that characterize the great cuisines of the world: for example, coriander in Asia, mint in Morocco, oregano and rosemary in Italy.

Basil

Basil has a unique flavour and fragrance. The flavour is lost on prolonged heating, so add towards the end of cooking. Basil is the main ingredient in pesto.
Serve with eggs, soft cheeses, pasta, vegetable soups and creamy sauces, but basil's greatest partners are undoubtedly tomatoes and mozzarella.

Bay (1)

Bay leaves must be subjected to long cooking, when they release their musky flavour. Bay leaves form part of the classic bouquet garni.
Serve in stocks, casseroles, soups and pâtés where they will impart a very savoury quality.

Chervil

Chervil has a light, subtle flavour and is used most often in omelettes and sauces.
Serve in bland, creamy soups, with baked or scrambled eggs, pounded into butter to accompany grilled fish, or for flavouring sauces.

Chillies

Chillies are available in all shapes and sizes and are important ingredients in Mexican, Indian and Asian dishes. On the whole, the smaller the chilli, the more intense. Birdseye chillies are small and thin-skinned with a fiery heat, while Jalapeño chillies have a medium heat and are used in Mexican dishes.
Serve in curries, spicy soups and stir-fries.

Chives

Chives are the mildest of the onion family. They cannot stand heat and must be added to dishes after cooling. They make the ideal contrast to pale, creamy dishes and impart a light onion flavour.
Serve in leek and potato soup, scrambled eggs, quiches and sprinkle on salads and sliced tomatoes.

Coriander

Coriander looks much like flat leaf parsley, but the leaves give off a distinctive spicy smell when rubbed.
Serve the fresh leaves chopped and added to Indian curries and spiced dishes, North African, Thai and other Asian foods.

Dill

Dill resembles fennel with its soft feathery leaves, and has a similar aniseed flavour. It is widely used in marinades in Scandinavia, to make gravadlax and pickled herring.
Serve with poached or smoked fish, in soups or salads or with egg dishes.

Fennel

Fennel leaves have a strong aniseed taste and can be used in cold sauces and dressings. The stalks are often laid over barbecues to flavour fish.
Serve with poached or smoked fish, with chicken or in salads, soups or casseroles.

Garlic (2)

Garlic is probably one of the most well-known and widely used herbs. It is a member of the onion family and consists of a bulb made up of a number of different cloves. It is a basic ingredient in the cuisines of France, Italy, Spain, India, the Middle East and many Asian countries.

Serve crushed or chopped and added to sauces or inserted into meat to flavour it while it cooks. A peeled clove will flavour a vinaigrette and it is delicious used in garlic bread. The flavour becomes milder as it cooks.

Ginger

Fresh ginger is a knobbly root which should be shiny and firm to the touch. It is usually peeled and grated or finely chopped before use.

Serve in Oriental soups, stir-fries and curries, where it adds a hot, spicy flavour.

Lemon grass

These woody stalks have an intense citrus flavour and are usually sold trimmed. Lemon grass can be stored in a refrigerator for 2–3 weeks. Prepare by removing the outer leaves and finely chop or slice the remainder.

Serve in Asian soups, stir-fries and curries, or use to marinate meat for grilling.

Marjoram

Unlike many other herbs, marjoram dries well and keeps it flavour, so if you can't find fresh marjoram, use dried instead. It gives an authentic flavour to Provençal, Italian and Greek dishes and goes exceptionally well with tomatoes.

Serve in pizzas and Greek salads.

Mint

Spearmint is the mint most commonly used, for its vibrant, fresh and sweet flavour.

Serve in mint sauce and jellies, and add to the saucepan when cooking garden peas and new potatoes. Also delicious in Moroccan tagines and Middle Eastern dishes such as tabbouleh.

TOP TIP

If you need only a little at a time, buy herbs growing in pots in the supermarket.
Remove them from their plastic sleeves and keep them on the windowsill, watering from time to time and cutting as necessary.

Did you know?

A classic bouquet garni is made up of a bay leaf, a sprig of thyme and 2–3 parsley sprigs, which can either be bound together with string or tied into a small muslin bag. It is used to flavour stocks and soups.

Oregano

Oregano is wild marjoram, similar in taste but more powerful. It dries well and is essential in Italian dishes.

Serve in spaghetti bolognese and other pasta dishes, risottos, pizzas and salad dressings.

Parsley (3)

Parsley comes in two varieties: curly and flat leaf. Flat leaf parsley has a superior flavour and is widely used in Mediterranean cooking. Parsley has a bright, savoury taste which can lift stocks and soups. It is also delicious sprinkled over grilled meat, fish or pasta dishes.

Serve in parsley sauce, casseroles, soups, risottos and seafood dishes.

Rosemary (4)

Rosemary is a woody herb with evergreen leaves, dark green on top and silvery grey underneath. Its flavour is robust and can be overpowering, so use it sparingly. It adds a wonderful stringent flavour, which is a perfect complement to rich meats and other strong flavours.

Serve with lamb, monkfish, tomato sauces and game.

Sage

Sage has an extremely powerful flavour, so again, go carefully. It does not lose its taste, even after long cooking, and imparts a resinous, musky flavour.

Serve with fatty meats, such as pork, duck and goose.

Tarragon

French tarragon is one of the subtlest of herbs, and goes well with foods of delicate flavour. Add towards the end of cooking, so the flavour is not lost.

Serve in soups and sauces with eggs, fish and chicken.

Thyme

Thyme is a woody herb with a fresh, assertive flavour which withstands long cooking.

Serve with meat and game casseroles or roasts, sprinkle over roast chicken, or add to tomato sauces or well-flavoured seafood dishes.

Spices

The warm, fragrant scent of spices add a special aroma and flavour to all forms of cooking. For the best flavour, buy them whole, store in tinted glass jars away from sunlight, and grind just before you use.

Allspice (1)

Allspice berries are similar to large peppercorns, with a spicy flavour mingling the tastes of cloves, cinnamon and nutmeg.

Serve in smoked and pickled foods and traditional pork and game pies.

Cardamom

Three types of cardamom pods are available: black, green and white. In some dishes the whole pod is added, in others only the little seeds inside the pod are used. Cardamom is one of the essential spices of Indian cuisine, used in the spice mix garam masala.

Serve in biryanis, dhals and curries.

Cayenne

Cayenne is used as a milder alternative to chilli powder in Indian, North African and Latin American food, as well as some European dishes.

Serve with fish and seafood, cheese or eggs, where it will add a hot spiciness.

Chilli powder

Chillies are small, hot members of the pepper family, important in Latin American, Indian and South-east Asian cuisines. They are dried and ground to make chilli powder. Fresh chillies vary in their heat and the resulting chilli powders do too, coming in mild, medium and hot varieties.

Serve in curries, chilli con carne and spicy dishes.

Cinnamon (2)

Cinnamon is made from dried bark of the cinnamon tree and can be bought as whole curls of bark in stick form, or ground as a powder. It is generally used for sweet dishes in the West and savoury dishes in the East.

Serve in curries and kormas, spicy rice dishes, or in cakes, crumbles and pastries.

Cloves (3)

Cloves are both sweet and pungent, with an unmistakable aroma, but use them with restraint to avoid swamping other tastes. They can be used in both sweet and savoury dishes.

Serve in bread sauce or use to flavour ham dishes, apple pies and crumbles, and even curries.

Cumin

Cumin's spicy seeds are small, ridged and greenish-brown in colour. They have a strong, unmistakable aroma, sweetish and warming. Their flavour is similarly pungent and penetrating and should be used in moderation, in seed or powdered form. Always buy cumin as whole seeds and grind them when needed.

Serve in Indian curries, on grilled meat and in North African dishes.

Coriander seed (4)

Coriander seeds look like tiny, ridged brown footballs. They are milder than many other spices, so can be used in large quantities. The taste, fresh with a hint of bitterness, improves on keeping.

Serve in curries, pickles and on grilled meat.

Dill seed (5)

Dill seeds have a fresh, sweet aroma but a slightly bitter taste, not unlike fennel seeds.

Serve in pickles, vinegar, dressings and marinades.

Fennel seed

Fennel is best known as a vegetable or herb, but its seeds are also used in cooking, usually with fish.

Serve in marinades, sauces and stuffings, or in fish curries.

Ginger, ground

The fiery flavour of fresh ginger is diminished in the powdered form, which has a warmer, more earthy taste. Ground ginger is used in sweet and savoury dishes.

Serve in cakes and biscuits, with apples and plums, or in curries and spice pastes.

Did you know?

Most spices lose their flavour during storage, so buy them in small quantities which you will use up more quickly. It is better to buy whole spices and grind them yourself for a really fresh and pungent taste.

Mustard seed

Whole mustard seeds are the basis of all prepared mustards and of the pungent mustard oil, beloved in India. They are used primarily in Indian food and to flavour pickles. Dry-fried, they lose their heat and have a warm, nutty flavour.
Serve in curries and other spicy dishes.

Nutmeg

Nutmeg comes in the form of a large seed with a warm, sweetish taste. Grate directly over the mixing bowl or cooking pot to flavour a variety of sauces.
Serve in bread sauce, Christmas pudding, and spicy biscuits and cakes.

Paprika (6)

Paprika flavours a profusion of savoury foods, from goulashes to vegetables. The mildest kind is the most widely sold and imparts a reddish brown colour.
Serve with eggs, chicken and in goulash.

Pepper

Pepper is the most familiar spice of all. Black is stronger than white, and green peppercorns have a mild, fresh taste. Whole peppercorns are added to marinades and stocks, while ground pepper is used for everything else. It is better to grind your own peppercorns than to buy ground pepper, which soon loses its flavour.
Serve with scrambled eggs, curries, smoked salmon, or grind over just about any food as a seasoning.

Saffron (7)

Saffron is the world's most expensive spice. It imparts a distinctive aroma, a rich honey-like taste and strong yellow colour to food. It is available as strands (the dried stigmas of a crocus flower), and in powdered form, which is not as good, since it is not always pure saffron.
Serve in risottos, curries, paella and seafood dishes.

Star anise (8)

This pretty, star-shaped spice has an aniseed flavour. Available whole or ground.
Serve in Chinese and Indian dishes, such as stir-fries and biryanis.

Turmeric

Turmeric has a pungent aroma and imparts a rich yellow colouring to dishes. It is best known for its partnership with fish and rice.
Serve in kedgeree, curries, biryanis and pickles.

1

2

3

4

5

6

7

8

Beef and veal

Popular dishes such as Spaghetti Bolognese, Steak or Roast Beef are classics, but there are so many other ways of cooking beef. There is an abundance of different cuts which can be used to create a range of delicious dishes.

Buying beef

When you buy beef, the meat should be bright to dark red with the fat a creamy white. Small flecks of fat should be visible throughout the lean. Flesh that has a dark red colour indicates that the carcass has been well hung, essential if the meat is to have a good flavour and be tender. Bright red meat often indicates that it is very fresh or has not been hung long enough for the flavour to develop properly.

Aitchbone or top rump (1)

This is also known as thick flank. These are usually boned and rolled joints, but can also be bought on the bone. It has a layer of fat on the top, but has a good flavour and can also be salted. Best to pot-roast, braise or grill joints, but slices can be fried or grilled.

Brisket (2)

This has an excellent flavour but tends to be fatty, so always look for a lean piece. It can be cooked on the bone but is best boned and rolled as some of the excess fat is discarded. Use a long, slow method for cooking, such as braising or pot-roasting, and serve hot or cold. This cut is also available salted or pickled.

Minced or ground beef (3)

Various qualities of mince are available, some of which at the top end of the price market are almost fat free and can lack flavour. At the other end of the market is the cheapest quality, which does contain a lot of fat. The best way to remove any excess fat from mince is to begin the cooking by browning it in a pan without any extra fat. As it heats gently, the fat flows out and can then be spooned off.

Rib (4)

These come as wing rib, top rib, back rib and fore rib joints and they too can be bought on the bone or as boned and rolled joints. The flavour is particularly good when it is cooked on the bone and the best way to cook it is by roasting, pot-roasting or braising. This joint makes a most impressive centrepiece at a dinner party and is always every bit as delicious as it looks.

Silverside or round

This is a popular joint of beef, always boneless, which can also be bought salted to serve as the traditional boiled beef and carrots. It needs the long, slow cooking achieved by boiling or braising or, if preferred, pot-roasting.

Sirloin

This is a boned and rolled joint, with a good layer of fat to protect it, coming from the back of the animal. It is very suitable for roasting. It is also sold on the bone and can be bought with the 'undercut' on it (fillet). The joints can be cut to any size required. Usually it makes a round of about 18 cm (7 inches) across, but this can be larger or smaller depending on the size of the animal it is taken from. Steaks can also be cut from the sirloin.

Stewing meats

These include leg and shin, which are the cheapest cuts and need the longest and slowest of cooking to tenderize them, though the flavour is excellent. Neck and clod are also good for stews, but have less flavour and are less gelatinous than shin. Skirt and flank are boneless cuts which can be stewed, but are normally made into mince. Chuck and blade steak are the best cuts of stewing steak and they require less cooking. These cuts should not have too much thick fat on the outside, but the flesh of the meat should be well marbled or streaked with flecks of fat as this is what adds to the flavour. For all types of stewing steak, either stew, braise or casserole with flavouring ingredients such as onions and herbs. They can also be used in meat pies, and boiled for stock.

Topside or top round (5)

This joint is usually boned and rolled. As it is a very lean cut, with little or no fat of its own, a strip of extra fat is often tied around it by the butcher to prevent it from becoming too dry and tough when cooked. Topside can be roasted, although pot-roasting or braising often gives a better result as the liquid keeps it more moist.

Steaks

Steaks come in several different cuts, ranging from the more fatty cuts, which are cheaper to buy, to the leaner, more expensive cuts. All are suitable to grill or fry.

Chateaubriand

This is a thick slice taken from the end of the fillet, weighing from 375 g (12 oz) upwards, which can be grilled or roasted. It is an excellent cut and well worth trying for a special occasion. It is often offered in restaurants as a 2-portion serving.

Entrecôte

This is really the part of the meat between the ribs of beef, but a slice from the sirloin or rump, which is thin rather than thick, can also be termed an entrecôte steak. The flavour is good and the steak is very versatile, often used with a variety of sauces.

Fillet

Cut from the centre of the sirloin, fillet is probably one of the best known and most expensive cuts of beef, and steaks cut from it have no fat at all. It is very tender, but the flavour is not as good as that of rump.

Rump (6)

This is the joint next to the sirloin and one of the most usual cuts made into steaks and used for grilling and frying. The 'point' is considered the best part for flavour and tenderness – the flavour of rump is always good, but it may not always be that tender. There is a layer of fat all along the top edge of this steak.

Sirloin (7)

This is cut into two parts to give the porterhouse steak and the T-bone steak. The upper part is cut into thin steaks, called 'minute' steaks. Thicker slices cut from the sirloin joint resemble a large, boneless lamb chop. All these steaks have a layer of fat along the top edge.

Veal (8)

Veal is the meat from a calf or young cow. The flesh is pale in colour, and soft and moist with little fat. Many people find the traditional method of rearing veal calves in crates, where they have no space to move and only milk to sustain them, morally indefensible, and so veal has declined in popularity. However, it is now possible to buy veal that has been raised in a free-range environment (also sold as rosé veal). The most common cuts are chops, which can be grilled or fried, and escalopes, which are usually coated in breadcrumbs and fried.

Pork

Rich, succulent pork is a popular meat and is ideal for roasting, grilling, barbecuing, stir-frying and casseroling. It is also a commonly used meat for making into sausages and pâtés. Treating pork by using certain processes, such as salting and smoking, can produce gammon, ham and bacon, which produces quite a different flavour.

Buying pork

When selecting a joint or piece of pork, choose one that has a good layer of firm white fat, with a thinnish elastic skin around pale pink, smooth and fine-grained meat. It should not be brown or grey. A roasting joint should have a good rind that can be scored (cut into narrow parallel lines with a very sharp knife) to give a good crackling when cooked.

Belly (1)

Pork belly is cheap and fatty, but full of flavour. It can be used on or off the bone, either as a joint or cut into slices. Bone and roll it with a stuffing to roast or pot-roast; or use the slices to grill or fry, casserole or cook on a barbecue.

Fillet or tenderloin (2)

This is a prime piece of meat with very little fat. It is very versatile, and excellent for kebabs, escalopes, pan-frying and for grilling or frying. It can also be sliced lengthways and stuffed. Quite expensive, but it goes a long way.

Hand and spring (3)

This is the foreleg of the pig and is suitable for roasting, boiling, stewing and casseroling. It is relatively inexpensive and is the cut to buy if you want to mince pork to use for meatballs or pâtés.

Leg (4)

This is a large lean joint, often sold boned and rolled, although it is excellent when cooked on the bone. It can be cut into various sized joints, which are usually simply roasted.

Loin (5)

This is a prime roasting joint which can be bought on or off the bone. It sometimes includes the kidney and makes an excellent meal when stuffed and rolled. The loin is also cut into chops and sometimes boneless chops (or steaks as they are often called), which can be grilled or fried.

Shoulder (6)

Shoulder of pork is often divided into spare rib and blade. This is a tender cut, available on the bone or boneless. Roast, stuff, grill or casserole.

Spare rib (7)

Not to be confused with spare ribs, this joint comes from the shoulder. A fairly lean joint, but sometimes with more fat than other joints, it has an excellent flavour. Good to roast or it can be cut up to braise, casserole or stew.

Spare ribs

Taken from the belly, they are removed in one piece and then cut up into ribs with the meat left all around the bones. These are very popular and are usually barbecued, grilled, or casseroled.

Meat hygiene

- Wash your hands before and after handling raw meat. Wash knives and utensils between handling raw and cooked foods.
- Prepare raw meat on white non-porous boards, which can be washed in hot water with a little bleach.
- Carefully but loosely cover raw meat in a shallow container or, if pre-packed, leave it in the tray you bought it in and store it in the refrigerator.
- Avoid contact between cooked foods and raw meat during storage and preparation.
- Cool cooked meat intended to be eaten cold as quickly as possible, cover it and store it in the refrigerator for up to one week.
- Pork and chicken should both be thoroughly cooked through before eating. Test with the point of a sharp knife or a skewer: the juices should run clear. If the juices are pink, return to the oven and cook until the juices are clear.

Bacon, ham and gammon

Bacon and ham are the flesh of the pig that has been salted or cured in brine and then smoked. Green, or unsmoked, bacon is cured, but not smoked and is consequently less strong in flavour and will not keep for the same length of time as its smoked counterpart. Gammon is the bacon and ham cured as one piece.

Back bacon

Back bacon is taken from the back of the pig and is boned out ready to slice into rashers for grilling or frying. Short back rashers are the prime cut and are the most expensive. They can also be cut up to 2.5 cm (1 inch) thick when they are known as bacon chops. Back bacon should have a good eye of meat and a distinct layer of fat. Back bacon can also be rolled into a joint, with or without stuffing, to boil or bake.

Streaky bacon

These are narrow rashers which have lean and fat streaked together. They are taken from the belly of the pig. The amount of fat to lean differs widely. They have a good flavour, smoked or unsmoked, and can be fried or grilled, chopped and added to casseroles or minced for pâtés and terrines.

Collar

Prime collar from the shoulder, when boned and rolled, makes the best boiling joint, full of flavour and not too fatty. Joints vary from 500 g (1 lb) to 4 kg (8 lb) or more, and can be braised, baked or pot-roasted.

Gammon or ham (8)

Gammon is the hind leg of the pig, which is cured on the side of bacon; if the leg is then cut off and cooked and served cold, it is known as ham. A true ham, however, is the hind leg of the pig, detached before curing, which is then cured, salted, matured, hung or smoked, depending on the manufacturer's process. Many countries produce different types of ham, each with its own properties and flavour.

Did you know?

Good fresh bacon should have a pleasant aroma, firm white fat and pink-coloured lean, which is firm, with a good bloom. The rind should be a good pale cream colour if unsmoked or green; or light to dark golden brown for smoked bacon.

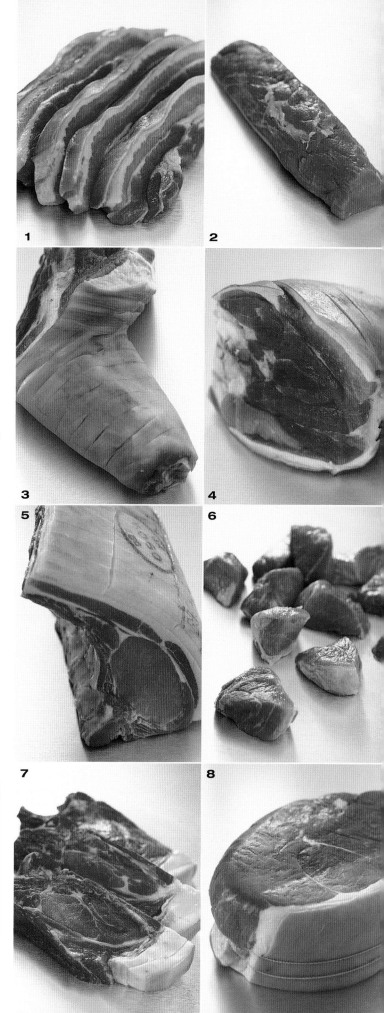

1 **2** **3** **4** **5** **6** **7** **8**

Lamb

Lamb is one of the most versatile of meats, with a distinctive, assertive flavour and rich juiciness. It is a popular meat all over the world, from a traditional crisp-skinned roasted leg of lamb or char-grilled chops with rosemary butter, to rich curries, spicy stir-fries and tender, herb-scented kebabs.

Buying lamb

When you buy lamb, the age of the animal is indicated both by its weight (the heavier a joint, the larger and older the animal), and by the colour of the lean meat. Pale pink flesh denotes young lamb, and this turns to light red as the age of the animal increases. Mutton is from an older animal and is not as tender, so it requires a different method of cooking. Lamb is generally from an animal under a year old, mutton from an animal under 2 years, but more often mutton is defined as coming from an animal weighing over 36 kg (79 lb). However, if you can find it, the flavour of mutton is distinctive and extremely good.

Cuts of lamb

Because lamb comes from a young animal, almost all the cuts are extremely tender, making them suitable for frying and grilling.

Best end of neck (1)

This is a prime roasting joint, either on the bone or boned and rolled. It is from this joint that the spectacular crown roast of lamb and guard of honour roasts are made. It can be cut into cutlets, which are left as they are or can be trimmed.

Breast of lamb (2)

This versatile and cheap cut of lamb is very tasty, but also very fatty. It is ideal for casseroling, but should be cooked the day before required so that it can be cooled and the resulting layer of fat on the surface removed before the dish is reheated. It can be boned, stuffed, rolled and slow roasted or pot-roasted with great success. Breast of lamb is also good cut into pieces, or 'riblets', still on the bone to bake in the oven

or on a barbecue: the fat pours out of the meat, leaving crunchy brown morsels of lamb.

Leg (3)

This is a prime joint which is quite large and always rather expensive. It is often cut in half and sold as half legs. The fillet (top) half is sometimes boned out and is good for kebabs and for casseroling; it can also be cut into leg steaks. Lamb shanks are the bottom halves and are delicious when slow-cooked in wine. Leg of lamb, whether whole or in halves, is usually roasted, although it can be pot-roasted with great success.

Loin (4)

This is a prime cut which is usually roasted on the bone or boned and rolled, with or without a stuffing; it can also be pot-roasted. This part of the animal can be cut up and made into an assortment of chops.

Middle and scrag end of neck (5)

These are the cheap cuts, with a rather high percentage of bone and some fat, but again with a good flavour. Well worth using for casseroles. Chops can be cut from the middle neck.

Shoulder (6)

This is one of the sweetest and most tender parts of the animal but it does have a fair amount of fat and is one of the most difficult of all joints to carve. It is always succulent and is most often roasted, either on the bone or boned and rolled, when some of the fat can be discarded. Boning also leaves a pocket which can be filled with stuffing. Shoulder of lamb can also be pot-roasted and boiled to serve with caper sauce. It is a cheaper joint than the leg and again can be cut in half. Shoulder meat can also be boned to use for kebabs, casseroles, curries and mince when excess fat can be trimmed off before cooking.

Did you know?

Legs and shoulders of lamb should be plump with a thin layer of fat covering the flesh; this fat should be white to pale cream, not a dark yellow. If you buy frozen lamb, take time to thaw it out very slowly so that the meat is in prime condition when you cook it. If it is thawed fast, the flavour will deteriorate and more often than not the meat will be tough when cooked.

TOP TIP

Lamb joints, chops and cutlets, which are roasted or grilled, are often served rare: that is, while the meat is still a little pink in the middle. This results in juicy, succulent meat and ensures it does not dry out. When overcooked, lamb can be tough.

Chops and cutlets

All chops and cutlets of lamb are tender and are ideal for grilling, frying or barbecuing. Because of the layer of fat they need very little extra fat added for cooking and stay moist and juicy. Lamb chops and cutlets can also be pan-fried, braised and used in casseroles, as in the traditional Lancashire hot-pot of onions, potatoes and lamb chops.

Boneless chops (7)

These include noisettes, which are taken from a boned-out best end of neck (or sometimes a small loin). The meat is rolled up tightly and secured with cocktail sticks or string and then cut into slices that have a layer of fat all around the outside and with an eye of meat in the centre. Sometimes a kidney or some herb stuffing is rolled into the centre of the meat for extra flavour. These are succulent morsels and can be grilled, fried or pan-fried. They can also be browned on both sides in a hot frying pan, then roasted in the oven to finish off the cooking. Don't overcook or they will be spoiled.

Chump chops

Taken from between the loin and the leg of the lamb, these are the largest and leanest of the chops.

Cutlets

Cut from the best end of neck, cutlets have a small eye of meat and a long bone, which can be left with meat on it or be trimmed.

Leg chops (8)

These are slices taken straight across the leg joint and have an 'eye' of bone in the centre, surrounded by tender flesh.

Loin chops

These contain part of the backbone of the lamb, and are cut from the loin as single or double loin chops (also known as butterfly chops).

Offal

Offal is relatively inexpensive but quite delicious and nutritious. Think liver and bacon with onion gravy, rich oxtail stew, pan-fried liver with sage, devilled kidneys or a sumptuous rich pâté. There is very little waste on offal and most of it is quick to cook and easy to prepare.

Buying liver

There are several types of liver and all are good value. They vary in flavour and texture and require different types of cooking to be at their best. Whatever the type, liver should be smooth and glossy, and it should not have a strong smell. Always wash it to rinse away excess blood and cut out any tubes or membranes. Take care not to overcook liver or it can become hard and dry.

Calf's liver

The finest and most expensive of all the livers, it is not always easy to obtain. It is very tender with a delicate flavour. Serve simply, lightly fried in butter, grilled, or pan-fried with various flavourings.

Chicken livers (1)

These are very tender and are usually sold frozen in small plastic tubs. To prepare, rinse well and remove any pieces of white membrane. Serve in pâtés and terrines, for stuffings, use to top bruschetta or toast, or pan-fry and serve over lettuce as a warm salad.

Lamb's liver (2)

This is probably the most popular of the livers, with a good flavour which is not as strong or pronounced as pig's or ox liver. Although not as tender as calf's liver, it is much cheaper. Serve as liver and bacon, pan-fry with butter and sage, or grill.

TOP TIP

Liver is extremely nutritious, containing a whole host of minerals and vitamins, particularly iron, and vitamins A and B.

Ox liver

This is the cheapest of the livers, has a strong flavour, and can be tough because the texture is rather coarse. It needs to be soaked or blanched before cooking to help remove some of the strong flavour. Choose a slow cooking method such as braising or casseroling as this will make it more tender.

Pig's liver (3)

This is fairly cheap and has a distinct and rather strong flavour with a much softer texture than some of the other livers. It is possible to remove some of the strong flavour prior to cooking by soaking in milk for about 30 minutes. Serve fried or grilled, or better still braised or casseroled. Use for making pâtés and terrines.

Buying kidneys

Kidneys are sometimes sold still in their casing of suet which must be removed. They should smell mild, be smooth and shiny with no discoloured patches, and be soft to the touch. All kidneys are covered in a thin transparent skin which must be removed before cooking, as must the fatty core. It is best to snip out the core with a pair of scissors. Prepared kidneys can often be bought from a supermarket or butcher. Kidneys can be grilled or pan-fried, as well as being added to casseroles and pies along with other meats, or to stuffings and risottos. They should not be overcooked, though, as they are virtually fatless and therefore shrivel and dry out easily.

Calf's kidney

Similar to ox kidney, but much smaller and paler in colour. It is more tender and more delicate in flavour. Pan-fry or grill and serve with herb butter.

Lamb's kidney (4)

Usually the best and most popular of all kidneys. They are small and well flavoured but do not have a harsh or overpowering taste. The flavour blends well with many other foods and is enhanced by the addition of wine, herbs and citrus flavourings, among others. Do not overcook or they become tough and dry. Cook whole or halved, by frying in butter or grilling. Serve in a cooked breakfast, devilled in a spicy sauce, or in a hotpot or casserole.

Ox kidney (5)

This is the largest and cheapest. It has a fairly strong flavour and needs a little more cooking than the smaller kidneys. Ox kidney is often sold cut up in pieces by butchers to suit your needs. Serve in steak and kidney pudding or pie.

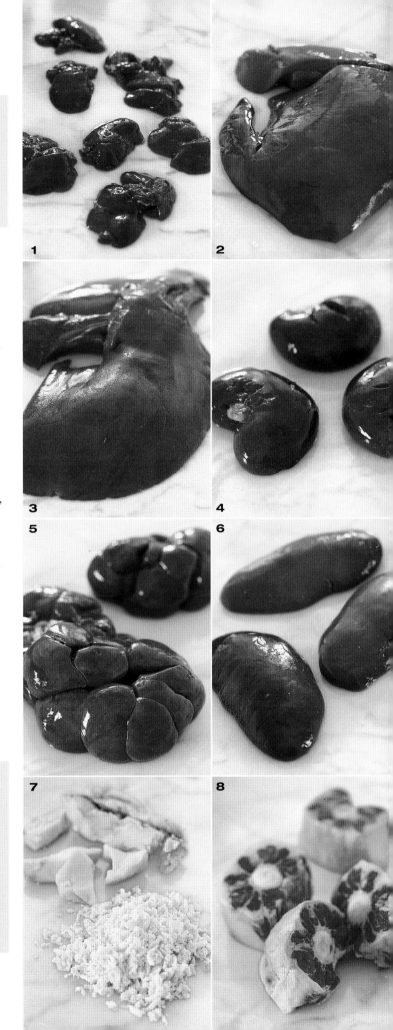

Did you know?

The word offal means, literally, the 'off-fall' or off-cuts from a carcass. The name doesn't sound particularly appealing, so it puts many people off even trying these delicious off-cuts of meat.

Pig's kidney (6)

Pig's kidneys are larger than lamb's kidneys, more elongated in shape and slightly lighter and more orange in colour. Pig's kidneys are also stronger in flavour, but can still be fried or grilled. Serve diced in casseroles for flavour, as part of a cooked breakfast, or in a pie or savoury pudding.

Suet (7)

This is the hard fat from around sheep or ox kidneys. Beef suet is better flavoured and more often used in cooking. Fresh suet used to be an important ingredient, but nowadays it is usually bought ready shredded in packets. However, fresh suet still has the best flavour. Serve in sweet and savoury suet puddings, roly poly pudding or dumplings.

Oxtail (8)

This part of the animal has an excellent flavour. It has a high proportion of bone and is usually rather fatty, some of which can be trimmed off before starting to cook. It should look fresh and bright when bought, with good red flesh and creamy white fat. It best suits long, slow cooking to bring out the flavour and to really tenderize the meat; for preference, it should be cooked the day before it is required so that a layer of fat can form on the surface and then be removed before reheating to serve. Oxtail is delicious in casseroles, stews and soups.

Storing offal

Offal is perishable and should be bought and eaten on the same day if possible, or kept in the refrigerator. Offal can be bought and frozen, provided it is fresh and has not already been frozen; it will keep for up to two months in the freezer. As with all meats, it is best thawed out slowly and then cooked as soon as possible.

Poultry

Poultry are domestic birds that are reared for the table; they include chicken, duck, guinea fowl, turkey and goose. These are popular meats which lend themselves to a whole host of treatments, from grilling and barbecuing to casseroling and currying. It is important to choose a good free-range bird for maximum flavour.

Chicken (1)

Chickens are usually sold ready for the oven, either fresh or frozen, with or without giblets. They can even be bought ready-stuffed or covered with herbs and butter. The weight range is about 1.5–3.2 kg (3–7 lb). The giblets, when packed with the bird, are usually placed in a bag in the body cavity. They include the neck and offal (such as heart, liver and gizzard) and make wonderful gravy. If the bird is sold with giblets, remember to remove them before cooking as they often come wrapped in plastic.

Chicken portions (2)

Boned or part-boned, with or without skin, these are convenient for a wide variety of cooking. Chicken quarters include drumstick and thigh (which tend to have a lot of meat on them) or wing and breast. They are useful single portions for braising or roasting. Smaller joints, including drumsticks, thighs, breasts and wings, can be braised, grilled and fried. Stir-fry strips and minced chicken are also available.

Corn-fed chicken (3)

These birds are fed on maize, which gives them their characteristic yellow skin and yellow-tinted flesh, with a rich flavour. They are cooked in the same way as ordinary chicken but the flavour is slightly different.

Poussins (4)

These are four-week-old chickens, weighing 500–750 g (1–1½ lb). They are very tender and ideal for roasting. Each bird will serve one person. They can also be spatchcocked, or opened and flattened out, which makes them perfect for grilling and barbecuing as they cook more evenly.

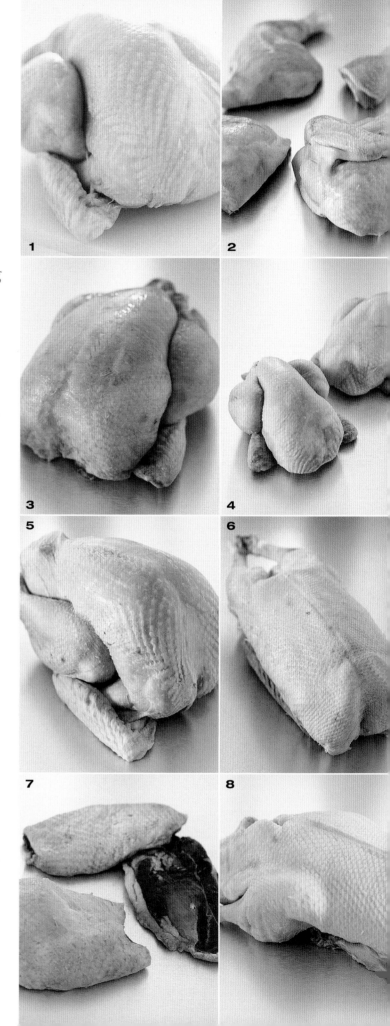

Turkey (5)

This is probably the most versatile and economical of all the various kinds of poultry. Although large, it can be cooked in many different ways apart from the traditional roast. It is now also available in many different cuts – wings, thighs, drumsticks, escalopes, fillets and steaks, as well as rolled, boned roasting joints. Free-range bronze turkeys have perhaps the best flavour of all. Be sure not to overcook turkey as it can easily become dry.

Turkey is available all year round, although the larger fresh birds are more readily available at Christmas, Easter and around bank holidays. The size of whole turkeys varies enormously from the mini birds of around 2.25 kg (5 lb) up to the very large ones of 13.5 kg (30 lb). An average domestic oven can handle a turkey of about 10.5 kg (23 lb), but not much more. A 3.6–4.5 kg (8–11 lb) bird will give 10–15 servings. Always buy the giblets with a whole bird. As with chicken, choose the best turkey you can afford as you really will notice the difference in flavour and succulence if the bird has been reared in a traditional manner with space to move around.

Duck (6)

Duck has dark meat with a good rich flavour, a thick skin and plenty of fat. Duck or duckling is available all year round, both fresh and frozen, as a whole bird and as portions. There is always less flesh on a duck than it might appear, so allow at least 500 g (1 lb) per portion. An average duck will weigh 1.75–2.25 kg (4–5 lb) and, in general, one duck will not feed more than four people. Fresh ducks, like chickens, are always better than frozen ones.

It is not traditional to stuff duck for roasting, although some cooks like to add a sage and onion stuffing to the duck rather than cook it separately. A stuffing will absorb a lot of fat. It is quite usual, though, to put a quartered onion inside the cavity of the duck before roasting.

Did you know?
For the best flavour, all types of poultry should be hung for 2–3 days after killing before it is drawn and put on sale. This helps develop the flavour and tenderizes the flesh of the bird. This is one reason why fresh birds are generally considered superior to frozen where the speed of the killing, chilling and freezing processes allows no time for hanging.

Duck portions (7)

Boneless duck breasts are readily available, with or without skin on. They make a substantial meal, one per person, and can be grilled, pan-fried, stir-fried or roasted. Duck quarters and legs, on the bone, are also sometimes available.

Goose (8)

This is a rather expensive bird which is becoming much more readily available, both fresh and frozen. It is a large, bony bird with a low meat to body size ratio. The flesh, though, has a fine flavour and texture. It is usually tender, although it is very fatty, and should always be pricked all over with a skewer and then stood on a rack to cook so that it doesn't stew in its own fat.

An oven-ready goose should weigh about 4.5 kg (10 lb) and will feed 6–8 people only.

A goose for roasting – the best way of cooking one – can be stuffed with a sage and onion stuffing, but the stuffing is more often cooked and served separately. A prune or apple stuffing is good with goose, as is a stuffing containing the liver of the bird. A quick and simple way of cutting down on richness and adding flavour at the same time is to put some peeled and cored sour or cooking apples into the cavity of the goose before roasting.

TOP TIP
It is worth spending money on the best poultry you can afford. Animal welfare issues aside, a free-range, organically-fed bird will have a far better flavour and texture than a cheaper, mass-produced one. You will really notice the difference, especially if the meat is simply roasted.

Poultry giblets
Always make sure you are given the giblets when buying poultry. These include the heart, liver, neck and gizzard, and can be used to make an excellent stock for the gravy, or can be chopped and added to the gravy, to stuffings or casseroles. Wash them thoroughly before use.

Game

Game is becoming popular once more as interest grows in naturally reared meats and food produced with flavour in mind. The term game refers to wild birds and animals that are hunted for food, including grouse, pheasant, partridge, quail, wild duck and wood pigeon. Deer, hare and rabbit are also game animals. However, many types of game are now farmed, including pheasant, quail, rabbit and venison but the quality is still good.

Grouse (1)

There are several species of grouse, the best known being the red grouse, which is, to many, the finest of all game birds. They are usually only available fresh and are best roasted. Older birds can be marinated and casseroled, or made into pâtés or pies. One grouse will usually serve only one person, although sometimes the larger birds will serve two.

Roasted grouse should be cooked until only just done. The liver is considered such a delicacy that it is generally fried lightly, mashed and spread on an oval slice of bread. This is slipped under the bird towards the end of cooking time and it absorbs many of the delicious juices.

Did you know?
Most game can only be killed at certain times of year to protect the animals and ensure that they continue to breed. Frozen birds may be available all year, but if you are buying fresh, the seasons are as follows:
Pheasant – 1 October to 1 February
Partridge – 1 September to 1 February
Wild duck – 1 September to 31 January
Pigeon and quail – available all year
Rabbit and hare – available all year
Venison – some types of venison are available all year round.

Serve in casseroles, pies and terrines, or young birds can be roasted whole and served with a thin gravy made from the giblets.

Hare and rabbit (2)

Rabbit is mainly farmed, though wild rabbit is available from local butchers. Rabbit is a mild-flavoured, pale meat. Serve braised, casseroled, roasted, grilled or fried. Hare is quite different from rabbit. It is a dark, full-flavoured meat and the animal is much larger.
Serve casseroled, in pies and pâtés, or slow-roasted.

Partridge (3)

These are small game birds that will serve only one person. The flavour of partridge is delicate and natural, and the birds are thought to be at their best in autumn. They are available fresh and frozen. Young plucked birds weigh up to 400 g (14 oz). They are best roasted, but are also good when spatchcocked to cook under the grill or on a barbecue. Older birds will weigh up to 450 g (1 lb) or more.
Serve in game stews, casseroles, pies and terrines, or the young birds roasted whole. The breast can be covered with bacon to retain moisture.

Pheasant (4)

This is probably the best known and most popular of all the game birds. It is available fresh and frozen and can often be found in larger supermarkets, as well as in butchers and game dealers. Birds are often available – and are cheaper – by the brace, meaning a cock and a hen. The cock is larger, with brightly coloured plumage, while the dull brown hen is plumper and more succulent, and generally considered better for eating. Young birds are best roasted, but more mature birds, which have a better flavour, will be tougher, so need the longer cooking of casseroling, braising or pot-roasting to ensure that the meat is tender. One pheasant will serve two to three people when roasted, and larger mature birds may serve up to four when casseroled with other ingredients.
Serve in casseroles, stews, pies and terrines, or young birds can be roasted whole.

Pigeon (5)

Wood pigeon are in season all year, but are best from early spring to late summer, when birds are young. If plump and young, one bird will serve one person; an older bird will serve two people if casseroled. A roasted bird needs to be covered with streaky bacon to keep it moist.
Serve in casseroles, stews, pies and terrines, or young birds can be roasted whole.

TOP TIP

Game is mainly available fresh, and is displayed by butchers and game dealers when in season. It is always hung before it is prepared to tenderize the meat and to improve the characteristic flavour associated with game. The longer it is hung, the more intense the flavour.

Quail (6)

These are the smallest of the game birds, like tiny partridges. As they are so small, two can be served for a good portion, but one is usually enough, and eating them with the fingers is almost obligatory. Quails must be eaten really fresh. Their meat is soft and tender, with more flavour than chicken.

Serve roasted whole, or the breasts pan-fried.

Venison (7)

Venison comes from deer of different breeds and ages, male or female. The seasons for wild deer vary according to the particular animal. Farmed deer now account for most of the venison available in supermarkets. This meat is suitable for roasting, braising or stewing, according to the cut. It is sold as joints, steaks, cubed or minced. Similar to beef, but slightly stronger and richer in flavour, venison can be very dry if overcooked, and requires moist cooking or marinating and basting.

Serve in casseroles, stews, meatloaves and pies.

Wild duck (8)

All wild duck have very dry flesh because they are virtually fat-free. For this reason, when they are roasted, the skins should not be pricked like that of domestic ducks; instead cover it liberally with fat to prevent the bird drying out.

Roast wild duck should be served just barely done, sometimes slightly underdone (unless you've acquired a tough old bird which would have been better braised). Timing is important: if the birds are too underdone they will be inedible, and if overcooked they will be dry and tasteless. A mallard or large wild duck should serve two people, while smaller birds will serve only one portion.

Serve wild duck roasted with a thin gravy made by using the giblets and pan juices and flavoured with orange and port.

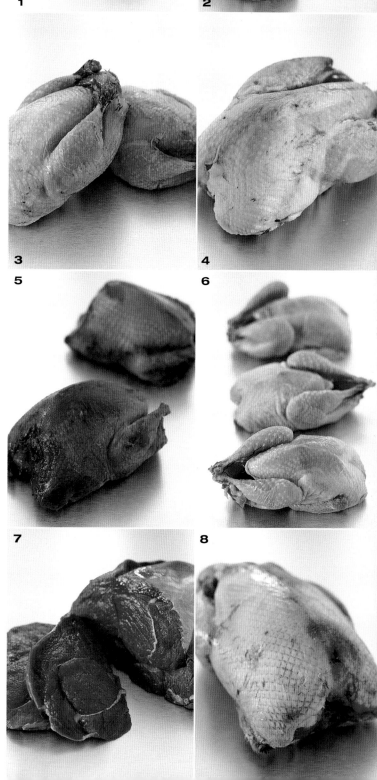

Fish

Fresh fish requires very little cooking, making it a quick, easy and delicious meal. Buy fish from a fishmonger, since it will probably be fresher and you will have more choice than in a supermarket. Talk to your fishmonger as he will advise you on what and how much to buy, how to prepare it and the best way to cook it.

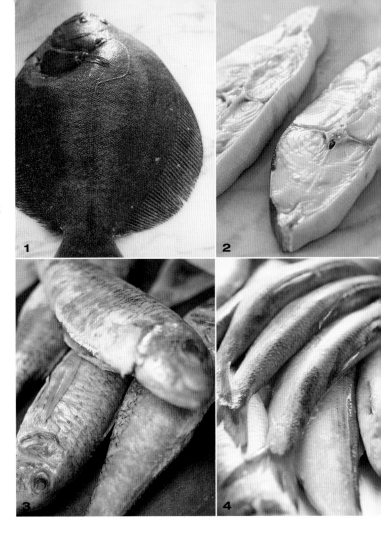

Bass (Sea)
A round fish, silver in colour. The flesh is white with a delicate flavour and texture. Much sea bass is now farmed, so it is cheaper than it used to be. Sold whole. **Serve** baked, steamed, poached or grilled. Good with buttery or creamy sauces.

Bream (Sea)
A round fish with very coarse, big scales; it is identifiable by a black spot behind the eye. The flesh is pink and delicate. Sold whole or in fillets. **Serve** steamed, baked or fried. Good steamed with herbs.

Brill (1)
This saltwater flat fish is similar to turbot in appearance but smaller, with a brownish yellow skin and small scales. The flesh is creamy white, and delicate, breaking up easily. Sold whole or filleted. **Serve** baked, steamed, poached, fried or grilled. Good with cheese sauce.

Cod
This is a very large, round saltwater fish with a silver-grey skin with small yellow and brown spots. The flesh should be pure white and firm with a coarse texture. Available fresh, as steaks or fillets, and salted, smoked and dried. **Serve** grilled, fried, poached, stir-fried, steamed, or in pies. Good with parsley, eggs or cheese sauce.

Coley
A round saltwater fish with very dark charcoal-grey skin and greyish pink flesh that turns white when cooked. Sold in fillets and a good alternative to cod. **Serve** fried, baked, or in soups and pies.

Dogfish (Huss, Rock salmon)
This saltwater fish is related to the shark family. Always sold skinned and split through, it has a white flesh which is soft and a little oily in texture. **Serve** deep-fried, in seafood stews, soups and pies.

Haddock
This is a round saltwater fish, related to the cod family. It has greyish silver skin with a dark line running along both flanks. The white flesh is firm and tasty, but coarse in texture. Available whole, in fillets and cutlets. **Serve** grilled, fried, poached or baked.

Halibut (2)
This is the largest flat saltwater fish. The flesh is firm, coarse and white. Available in steaks, fillets and whole when small. **Serve** grilled, poached, fried, baked or steamed.

Herring
A fairly small fish with silvery blue skin and a brownish white, oily flesh. The skin should be shiny. Very bony, but delicately flavoured. Sold whole or filleted. **Serve** grilled, fried with bacon, or baked.

Mackerel

A silver-skinned oily fish with blue and black stripes from the head to the tail. The firm flesh is pinkish brown, the flavour is fairly rich. Sold whole or filleted. **Serve** grilled, fried, barbecued or baked; best with a tangy sauce or a wedge of lemon.

Monkfish

This deep-sea fish has such an ugly head that usually only the tail is sold. The skin is blackish; the flesh is white, firm and succulent. Monkfish is good in fish stews and as kebabs because the flesh does not flake and fall apart. **Serve** roasted, poached, steamed, fried or grilled.

Mullet, Grey

A saltwater fish with large scales and a grey skin. The flesh is greyish white, firm and rather fatty. Sold whole. **Serve** steamed, baked, poached or grilled.

Mullet, Red (3)

A small saltwater fish with pinkish red skin and large scales. The flesh is white and firm. Sold whole. **Serve** grilled, fried or in stews and soups.

Plaice

A flat saltwater fish with a brownish grey upperside with bright orange spots; the underside is cream. The flesh is white but a little bland. Sold whole or in fillets. **Serve** fried, poached, steamed, baked or grilled, preferably with a sauce.

Salmon

Today, most salmon is farmed. The wild fish matures in the sea, but spawns in fresh water. The skin is silvery, the flesh pink to dark red and close textured, with a delicate flavour. Sold whole or in steaks or cutlets. **Serve** poached, steamed, pan-fried or grilled.

Sardine (4)

A silver-skinned, small salt-water fish, which is a young and immature pilchard. Make sure sardines are very fresh as they taste stale and oily when they have been stored for some time. **Serve** barbecued, fried or grilled.

Skate

This flat, saltwater fish is shaped like a ray. Only the wings are sold, which have firm pinkish-cream flesh on either side of the cartilage bones. **Serve** fried, poached or grilled. Cut into chunks and serve in fish stews and soups.

Sole, Dover

A flat saltwater fish with an oval body and fairly small fins. The skin on one side is brownish-grey, the underside is creamy white. The flesh is fine textured with a delicate flavour: it is the finest of the flat fish. **Serve** poached, fried, steamed or grilled.

Sole, Lemon

Considered inferior in flavour and texture to Dover sole, but cheaper and enjoyable all the same. It is wider, with a more pointed nose. Sold whole or filleted. **Serve** poached, fried, steamed or grilled.

Trout (Rainbow)

Most rainbow trout are farmed. This is a silver-skinned freshwater fish with a rainbow-coloured body. The firm flesh is pink or creamy white; sold whole or filleted. **Serve** grilled, fried, poached or baked.

Trout (River, or brown)

This is a brown-skinned freshwater fish with dark spots. The flesh is finer than that of the rainbow trout. **Serve** grilled, fried, poached or baked.

Trout (Sea, or salmon)

A freshwater river trout that has spent a season or more at sea. It has a silver skin, with silvery scales, and pale pink flesh with a flavour similar to salmon. **Serve** grilled, fried, steamed, poached or baked.

Tuna

This large fish is sold in steaks or as a large piece. It has dense, flavoursome pink flesh. **Serve** grilled, baked, in seafood stews or with sauces. Good seared in a hot pan and served raw inside.

Turbot

A large, flat saltwater fish, with a dark brown or black skin; the underside is white. The flesh is firm and white with a delicate flavour. Sold whole, in cutlets or filleted. **Serve** baked, steamed, poached, fried or grilled.

TOP TIP – Smoked fish

Fish can be hot- or cold-smoked to preserve it and give it a distinctive flavour. Some, such as smoked haddock and kippers, need to be cooked. Others, such as smoked salmon and mackerel, can be enjoyed as they are.

Seafood

This is the term loosely used for shellfish. There are two types of shellfish, those like mussels which have soft bodies and live in a hard shell are called molluscs; octopus and squid belong in this group although they have no shells. The creatures that have a hard, jointed outer shell, like crabs, are known as crustaceans.

Clam (1)

Clams are like large cockles with a greyish thick, very tightly fitting shell. Several different types are available, and they are usually sold live. Soak them in a bucket of saltwater for at least one hour before cooking to remove the sand. Scrub the shells before cooking.
Serve in soups such as chowders, fish stews, salads, rice and pasta dishes.

Cockle

A tiny shellfish enclosed in a whitish fluted shell. Cockles are usually sold cooked, but if you can find them fresh, soak them in a bucket of saltwater for at least one hour before cooking to remove the sand. Scrub the shells before cooking. They can be eaten raw or cooked.
Serve in fish soups, pies, salads or as a starter.

Crab (2)

Crab is pinkish brown when alive, the shell turning to orange-red when cooked. As with lobster, it is better to buy crabs live so you know they are fresh and will taste delicious. However, dressed crabs are very convenient, and many fishmongers sell whole crabs that have been freshly cooked and prepared.

The body contains soft brown meat; the white meat comes from the legs and claws. The male crab has larger claws than the female, but the female, or hen crab, is generally considered superior. Allow one large crab for two people, or one small to medium crab per person for a main course dish.
Serve freshly cooked and dressed, or cold with mayonnaise. Crab may also be grilled with butter and breadcrumbs on top. It is used in soups, pâtés, mousses, fish dishes, or in sandwiches or salads.

Langoustine (Dublin Bay prawn)

These large prawns are about 10 cm (4 inches) in length and have spiny shells and long claws like a lobster. The shell is pale pink when live, turning to a deeper pink when cooked. Sold fresh or frozen.
Serve cold with mayonnaise, in soups, stews and rice dishes, grilled or barbecued.

Lobster (3)

This crustacean is blue-black when live, and cooks to a bright red. The male, although smaller than the female, has larger claws. The flesh of the female is finer than that of the male, and the body contains the coral, or roe, which is bright orange when cooked. It is highly prized and is used as a garnish or to make sauces.

It is best to buy lobsters live and cook them yourself so you know they are fresh. However, some fish shops sell freshly boiled lobsters. Once cooked, lobster flesh loses its wonderful flavour quickly. Avoid lobster with white blemishes on the shell; these are a sign of age.
Serve boiled with mayonnaise, in salads or soups. Lobster can be grilled, barbecued, or stir-fried.

Mussel (4)

These shellfish have deep blue-purple to black shells. They are usually sold live in the shell. Soak in a bowl of saltwater for one hour before cooking to remove any sand or grit. Wash well, scrub the shells, and pull off the beards. Discard any shells that are broken, or do not close swiftly when tapped. Discard any that have not opened during cooking.
Serve boiled in wine sauce, in rice dishes, pasta dishes, fish stews, soups and tartlets.

Octopus

Rather like a squid, but with eight large tentacles covered with suckers. Octopus is tougher than squid and needs long, slow cooking. The flesh is pinkish white and very tender when cooked.
Serve boiled, stewed or roasted. The edible black ink is used to flavour and colour rice and pasta dishes.

Did you know?
Frozen shellfish, such as scallops, prawns, mussels and bags of mixed seafood cocktail, usually comes covered with an ice glaze. Defrost well before using to get rid of the excess moisture and pat the shellfish dry with absorbent kitchen paper before use.

Oyster (5)

The most prized of the molluscs. The shells should be tightly closed when they are bought. Oysters are usually served raw, although they are sometimes very lightly cooked. The shell should be opened just before the oyster is eaten.

Serve raw in the half shell on a bed of crushed ice with pepper, lemon or Tabasco sauce. Allow 6 per person as a starter. Add to steak pies, or serve in creamy sauces. Oysters are delicious when covered with a little cream or cheese sauce and grilled.

Prawn (6)

A grey-shelled sea creature that turns pink when cooked. Only the body and tail are edible. To prepare, pull off the head and legs, and carefully peel away the shell on the body and tail. Prawns are usually sold cooked, either peeled or still in their shells.

Serve in salads, prawn cocktails, stir-fries, fish stews, soups, pies and risottos.

King prawn (tiger prawn)

The largest of the prawns, these may measure up to 15 cm (6 inches) in length. The pinkish-orange shell encloses fine pink flesh. Imported frozen, they are sold frozen or defrosted, either cooked or uncooked. Uncooked prawns will give a better flavour to a dish.

Serve stir-fried, cooked in garlic butter, in salads, fish stews, pasta, rice dishes and curries.

Scallop (7)

The scallop lives in a large, flat, fan-shaped shell. It is a creamish white nugget of firm flesh with a bright orange coral (roe) and a delicious sweet flavour. Fresh scallops should look plump and firm; they are also available frozen, usually without their roe, but they are often very wet and a bit mushy when defrosted. Scallops require very little cooking, since the flesh becomes tough if it is overcooked.

Serve pan-fried, stir-fried, baked or grilled. Also good in soups and casseroles. Often served in the shell in a creamy sauce with a piped border of creamed potatoes.

Squid (8)

A strange-looking sea creature covered with a fine purplish membrane, which must be removed to reveal the white flesh. The body and tentacles are edible. The ink sac, found inside the body, can be used to colour and flavour the cooking liquid.

Serve cut into rings and fried, stir-fried, barbecued, or in pasta and rice dishes. Large squid can be stuffed with herbs and breadcrumbs.

1   2   3   4   5   6   7   8

Dairy products

Dairy products – including milk, cream, butter and cheese – add a rich creaminess to sauces, soups, curries, sweet and savoury mousses, soufflés and other desserts. Many of them, including cream and crème fraîche, can also be served as an accompaniment to desserts of all kinds.

Butter
Butter is available salted or unsalted. Unsalted butter has a delicate sweet taste and is better suited to making cakes and biscuits than salted butter. Salted butter burns at a lower temperature than salted butter therefore unsalted butter is better for frying. Salted butter keeps longer as the salt helps to preserve it.
Use in cakes, biscuits, sauces, pastry, or for spreading.

Crème fraîche
Like sour cream, this is made from fresh cream that has had a culture added, however, the flavour is not as sharp. Crème fraîche has a creamy flavour and a silky texture.
Use in soups and sauces, and with fruit and desserts.

Double cream
Double cream has a high fat content (48 per cent) and is thick and rich. It can be whipped to fill or decorate cakes and puddings, but care must be taken not to overwhip it; aim to stop whipping when soft peaks form, otherwise it may turn granular.
Use to spoon over fruit and to thicken sauces, soups and curries.

Single cream
The fat content of single cream is 13 per cent, so it is not suitable for whipping. This cream is thinner than double and whipping cream.
Use to enrich soups and sauces and for pouring over all kinds of desserts.

Soured cream
This cream has had a culture added to it to give it a sour flavour. It should never be boiled and should be added to hot dishes towards the end of cooking.
Use mainly in savoury dishes, especially soups, stews and sauces, or as an accompaniment.

Whipping cream
This has a fat content of 35 per cent and is not as rich as double cream. It should be whipped with a balloon whisk until it doubles in volume.
Use in ice creams, soufflés and mousses.

Milk (1)
Most of the milk we buy is pasteurized cows' milk. Fresh milk is available as whole milk, which usually has a layer of cream at the top if left to stand. Skimmed milk has had the cream removed to give a virtually fat-free product; semi-skimmed milk has had about half of the cream removed; and homogenized milk has been treated so that the cream is evenly distributed throughout the milk. Goats' and sheep's milk are now increasingly available and are ideal for those with lactose intolerance.
Use in sauces, soups and desserts.

Yogurt (2)

A fermented milk product which is available in full-fat and low-fat forms. Natural yogurt must be heated gently to prevent separation. Greek yogurt is full-fat natural yogurt that has been strained to make it thicker and creamier.

Use as a marinade, in sauces and desserts.

Buying and storing cheeses

Avoid cheese that looks dry, sweaty or has blue mould on the surface. When choosing soft cheeses such as Brie and Camembert, press the top surface lightly with the fingertips. The cheese should yield slightly. It should be creamy in texture throughout, without any chalkiness in the centre. Cheese should be stored in a cool, draught-free larder – a refrigerator is the next best thing. Wrap in waxed or baking paper for best results.

Brie

A soft, whitish cheese, made from cows' milk, with a white crust. It is smooth and creamy inside and has a mild flavour. It should be soft throughout, without any chalky solid centre. Smoked Brie is also available, as well as a variety with a thickly peppered crust. Generally, Brie is eaten uncooked, but it may be melted into pasta dishes and bakes.

Use with the rind removed in tarts and flans.

Blue Brie

This is generally a thicker cheese than plain Brie, with blue veining throughout.

Use as for plain Brie.

Caerphilly

A hard, crumbly Cheddar-like cheese with a sharp taste and pale, almost white colour. Caerphilly is made in Wales and Somerset. It is a flavoursome addition to an after-dinner cheeseboard.

Use in place of a basic Cheddar in sauces, gratins or other cooked dishes. It melts well and gives a tangier flavour than Cheddar.

Camembert

This is a soft cheese that is similar to Brie, but stronger-flavoured. It is pale yellow in colour and has a white furry skin with brown flecks. Camembert should bulge but not run when the top surface is lightly pressed. It is normally about 2.5 cm (1 inch) thicker than Brie, and comes in large or small flat disks, packed in wooden boxes.

Use uncooked with bread, biscuits or salad, or deep-fried with a crisp coating and served with redcurrant jelly or other tangy sauce.

Cheddar

Probably the most popular of British cheeses. Its flavour ranges from very mild to a fully matured, strong, almost nutty taste.

Use for eating with bread or biscuits and pickles or chutney, or with fruit. Ideal for grating and cooking in all kinds of dishes.

Cottage cheese

This is a mild-flavoured cheese, very low in calories, since it is made from skimmed milk curds and is low in fat. It can be flavoured with herbs or fruit.

Use uncooked, but it may be used for flans, cheesecakes and some sweet or savoury dishes. It is sieved when used in cheesecakes to give a smoother texture without the lumps.

Cream cheese

Usually a full-fat cheese, although it is available in low-fat varieties. It has a creamy flavour which is rather bland.

Use cooked or uncooked. Ideal for savoury and sweet dishes, including cheesecakes, desserts and icings, sauces, pâtés and bakes.

Curd cheese

A soft, unripened, slightly grainy cheese, with a clean acidic, bland taste.

Use generally for cooking, in both sweet and savoury dishes; it is often added to cheesecakes.

Dolcelatte

A creamy white Italian cheese with bluish-green veins, a robust yet creamy flavour and a creamy, moist texture.

Use uncooked as a rule, but also for cheese sauces, especially with pasta.

Edam (3)

Made from partly skimmed milk, this yellow cheese is made in the shape of a large ball with a yellow or red waxed coating. The semi-hard pressed cheese is firm but rubbery in texture. It has a mild, creamy flavour and is relatively low in calories.

Use uncooked in sandwiches and salads – it slices very easily. Edam is also suitable for cooking in sauces, with pasta and risottos, in pies and flans.

Emmenthal (4)

This buttery-yellow Swiss cheese with large holes is slightly rubbery in texture and has a mild to strong, sweet nutty flavour.

Use in fondues, since it melts well. Also good uncooked.

Feta

A semi-soft curd cheese made from sheep's milk. Brilliant white in colour, with a crumbly texture, it has a salty, bland flavour.
Use uncooked in salads or in cooked dishes. It is best known for its use in Greek salads.

Fontina

An Italian straw-coloured, soft full-fat cheese, with a few holes. It has an orange rind and the flavour is nutty and delicate.
Use uncooked or for cooking. It melts easily and is perfect for making sauces.

Fromage frais

Fromage frais is a smooth, creamy-textured cheese made from either skimmed or whole cows' milk that has had a culture added to it. You can buy virtually fat-free fromage frais or one that has about 8 per cent fat, making it a healthier accompaniment to desserts.
Use instead of cream or yogurt in cooking, since it is less liable to curdle, or serve simply with fruit. Fromage blanc is similar but smoother in texture.

Goats' cheese

Cheeses made from goats' milk come in a wide range of flavours, textures and types. Some hard varieties are available, but most continental goats' cheeses are soft. Mature continental goats' cheeses have a blue mould rind or a thick white rind; they are sometimes coated in ash. Some of the most popular goats' cheeses are the French log-shaped ones that have a thick, fluted white rind and are often sold in slices. Fresh goats' cheeses are soft and chalky and should be eaten young.
Use uncooked in salads, or toasted under a grill.

Gorgonzola

A strongly flavoured, pale yellow Italian cheese, with bluish-green marbling and a coarse brown rind. It is a semi-soft cheese and should be delicate and creamy. It has a distinct smell and can have a mellow, strong or sharp flavour.
Use uncooked, but it is also delicious if lightly melted into sauces and risottos.

Gruyère

A pale yellow cheese with small holes, similar in texture to Emmenthal. It has a rich, nutty, full flavour with a little sweetness.
Use uncooked. It is also an excellent cooking cheese as it melts well, and in France is often served grated on top of fish soup.

Haloumi

Haloumi is a goats' or sheep's cheese from the Middle East and parts of Europe. It is quite salty and may need rinsing before consuming to remove some of the saltiness. It has a rubbery texture and mild flavour.
Use as it is, or marinated, grilled, barbecued or fried, when the surface becomes crisp and the inside melts. It is delicious grilled and served with salad.

Mascarpone

A rich, creamy cheese made from cows' milk, mascarpone has the consistency of soft butter and a delicate dairy flavour.
Use to replace cream in many recipes, such as pasta sauces and desserts, where it gives a really creamy texture and flavour. Mascarpone can be served on its own as an accompaniment to desserts instead of cream. It is particularly good with baked peaches or warm pears in wine. It is also used to make the Italian dessert, tiramisu.

Mozzarella (1)

A soft, compact curd cheese, usually moulded into a ball or egg shape. It is also sold in oblong blocks, sealed with plastic, although this type is not recommended as the texture and flavour can be rubbery. It forms long strands during cooking and becomes rather hard if it is overcooked.
Use raw in salads, where it has an affinity with tomatoes and basil, or in pasta dishes. Perhaps best known as a topping for pizza.

Panir

An Indian curd cheese with a rubbery texture and bland, salty flavour, used in many sweet and savoury dishes, particularly vegetarian curries. It is now more commonly available in larger supermarkets and Asian shops.
Use cut into cubes and fried to form a golden crust with a slightly softened middle, before adding to a moist dish such as curry.

Parmesan

A very hard Italian cheese, made from skimmed cows' milk, mixed with rennet and cooked for 30 minutes. Parmesan is yellowish in colour and fairly grainy with a strong, fruity flavour. It should be grated just before it is required. This cheese is principally used grated in cookery, for soups, pastas, soufflés and gratins.
Use in cooking or serve grated and sprinkled over pasta and soups: the mature, three-year-old cheese is best for this.

Pecorino

A whole family of sheep's milk cheeses come under this name, the best known being Pecorino Romano. They have a pronounced piquant flavour with a white, cream or straw-yellow centre, depending on the degree of their maturity. Fresh Pecorino goes particularly well with country bread and more mature Pecorino is used as a condiment like Parmesan cheese.

Use as a table cheese when fresh or grated in the same way as Parmesan when mature for many regional Italian dishes. It is one of the main ingredients of traditional pesto.

Pont l'Eveque

A semi-soft, pale yellow French cheese with a yellow crust. It has a rich, creamy flavour, stronger than that of Camembert.

Use with soft, crusty bread as part of a cheeseboard.

Port Salut

A French cheese with a thin orange rind. It is semi-hard, with a rubbery texture, and has a creamy, bland flavour that becomes stronger when it is fully ripe.

Use for a cheeseboard and for cooking.

Quark (2)

Quark is a type of skimmed milk curd cheese made in Germany. Slightly acidic in flavour, it has a low fat content. It is rarely served by itself.

Use for savoury dips or spreads, or mixed with fruit purées or made into desserts. It is a good substitute for whipped cream to accompany sweet pies and flans or stewed fruit dishes.

Ricotta (3)

An Italian curd cheese made from cows' or sheep's milk, ricotta has a mild flavour, soft texture and a low fat content.

Use mixed with spinach and cooked potato and made into gnocchi or use as a filling for ravioli and cannelloni. It is also delicious served as a dessert blended with Marsala or as a filling for a cheesecake.

Did you know?

Quark cheese makes a great topping for carrot cake just as it is. Its slightly tart flavour off sets the richness of the cake perfectly. Simply spread it over the cake and top with walnut halves.

Roquefort

A French cheese made from sheep's milk curds. A crumbly, semi-soft cheese with a strong, salty flavour, it has bluish-green veins and is one of the best of the blue cheeses in terms of flavour and texture.

Use cooked or uncooked. Perfect for flavoured butters, sauces and salad dressings or crumbled over salads with nuts and croûtons. Roquefort is also commonly used in a number of recipes such as soufflés, pancakes, puff pastries and soups.

Stilton (4)

This salty, English blue cheese is perfect for serving after dinner with a glass of port or Burgundy, together with fresh walnuts or grapes. It should be very creamy and not dry in texture, and the blue veining should be evenly distributed throughout the pale cream-coloured cheese. If the cheese is white in colour, it is a sign of immaturity.

Use in flans or sauces to add a rich, creamy blue-cheese flavour – not much is required. Stilton is perhaps best enjoyed simply with bread or biscuits. To revive a slightly drying cheese, simply wrap it in a moistened cloth and leave until the creamy consistency has been restored.

Rice and grains

Along with pasta, rice and grains are among the most useful ingredients in the kitchen. They need little preparation, cook quickly, are adaptable, go well with a variety of dishes and are very nourishing. They can be served as a meal in themselves or as an accompaniment to moist casseroles and stews.

Rice

Rice is simple to cook, but there are numerous different types of rice, so to achieve perfection every time, be sure to match the method to the purpose.

Basmati rice (1)

This very long grain has a delicate aroma and flavour.
Use for Indian dishes, such as pilau and biryani.

Camargue red rice

An unusual short-grain rice grown in the south of France. It has an attractive russet-red colour, with a nutty flavour and chewy texture.
Use as you would brown rice, whose flavour and texture it resembles.

Easy-cook rice

Either white or brown rice that has been steamed under pressure before milling to harden the grain, ensuring that it keeps its shape well during cooking and that the grains stay separate.
Use in salads and stir-fries.

TOP TIP
To prevent rice grains sticking together, wash white and basmati rice in a sieve under cold running water before cooking to remove some of the starch.

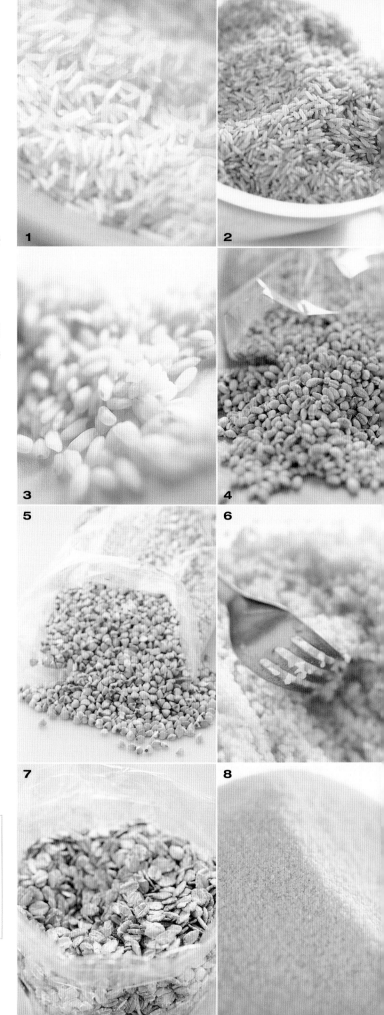

Glutinous rice

A round, pearly grain which becomes sticky when cooked and has a slightly sweet flavour.
Use especially in Chinese cuisine: the grains stick together and are easy to pick up with chopsticks.

Jasmine rice (Thai fragrant rice)

An aromatic rice with a delicate flavour. The cooked grains combine a soft, slightly sticky outer texture with a firm bite.
Use for Thai and South-east Asian dishes.

Long-grain brown rice (2)

A wholegrain rice, milled only enough to remove the outer husk, but still retaining the bran layer. This gives a distinctly nutty flavour and chewy texture.
Use instead of white long-grain rice in most dishes.

Long-grain white rice

Slim, long grains, which have been milled to remove the husk and bran layers.
Use for most savoury dishes, especially American, Mexican, Spanish and Caribbean recipes. It can also be used in Chinese dishes.

Pudding rice

The short, plump grains of this rice cling together when cooked.
Use for rice puddings and sweets.

Risotto rice (3)

This is a medium-grain rice, the main varieties being Arborio and Carnaroli, which absorbs up to five times its weight in liquid during cooking.
Use for risottos. Starch released from the grains during cooking gives classic risottos their characteristic creamy texture.

Sushi rice

Different varieties of Japanese rice are used for sushi and expert chefs have their favourite. The grains remain separate and firm, but they hold together when cooked.
Use for sushi.

Did you know?

The world total of rice varieties is said to be more than 7,000, with more than a thousand in India alone. Rice is a staple food for over half the world's population.

Wild rice

This is not actually rice, but an aquatic grass which was a traditional food of the American Indians. It has a firm texture and a full, nutty flavour.
Use mainly in savoury dishes; it is often mixed with white rice to add a contrast of texture and flavour.

Grains

Grains are rather bland in flavour, so they combine well with many other types of sweet and savoury foods, and make a good accompaniment to richly flavoured dishes. Many make a good base for salads and take on the flavours of the herbs and spices used with them.

Barley and Pearl barley (4),

These wholegrains add substance to savoury dishes.
Use in soups, stews and casseroles.

Buckwheat (5)

Roasted buckwheat is also known as a kash. It cooks quickly and can be served as an alternative to rice.
Use as rice or use the flour to make bread and crêpes.

Bulgar wheat

This is a cooked wheat which has been dried and lightly crushed. Bulgar needs only soaking or light cooking.
Use as a nutty-flavoured accompaniment to savoury dishes and as a base for salads, such as Tabbouleh.

Couscous (6)

This is made from wheat semolina which is steamed and rolled to give a small, cream-coloured grain. Instant couscous requires short soaking, making a quick and easy accompaniment for savoury dishes.
Use with Moroccan-style stews or as a base for salads.

Millet

Rich in iron and protein, these fine grains cook quickly to make good pilau.
Use particularly with Indian and African dishes; it is also good in burgers.

Oats and Rye (7)

Staple grains that can be used in sweet and savoury dishes.
Use for porridge, crumbles, bread and flapjacks.

Polenta (8)

A fine, granular cornmeal which is a staple food in Italy. It can be served wet, rather like porridge, or allowed to set then sliced and fried. Instant polenta is quick to cook.
Use cold or hot as an accompaniment to moist meat and vegetable dishes, sliced, fried or grilled.

Pasta and noodles

Pasta comes in hundreds of types, shapes, sizes and colours, both fresh and dried. Dried pasta is extremely convenient and is in no way inferior to fresh pasta. Noodles are the Asian version of pasta and fulfil a similar role in a meal.

Pasta

A dough made from durum wheat, semolina, water, and often eggs, pasta is shaped in different ways and sometimes flavoured.

Filled pasta (1)

Filled pasta comes in many shapes and sizes, with an infinite choice of fish, meat, vegetable or cheese fillings. Ravioli is, perhaps, the most familiar; smaller ravioli is known as ravioletti or raviolini. Agnolotti are small circles, filled and folded into crescent shapes; cappelleti look like pinched, three-cornered hats; and tortellini are round shapes, with the larger version known as tortelloni.

Flat pasta (2)

Pasta dough is rolled and cut to various widths to make ribbon or flat pasta. The narrowest type is linguini, followed by slightly broader fettuccine and tagliatelle, then broad-cut pappardelle and sheets of lasagne. The thicker ribbon pastas are ideal for egg-based sauces, such as carbonara, as the larger smooth surface area of hot freshly cooked pasta helps to set the lightly cooked egg quickly. Wide noodles are also good with tomato, cream or Bolognese-type sauces; the finer ones, such as linguine, are best with pesto or light tomato sauce.

Long round pasta (3)

This includes spaghetti, bucatini and macaroni, which are made by extruding long strands of the dough. These pastas are traditionally served with meat sauces, ragu and tomato-based mixtures. Ziti or zitoni is the broadest of these and is useful served with rich meaty sauces. The finest, traditionally gathered and dried into nests, is capellini (fine hair) or *capelli di angelo*, angel's hair pasta, which should be used with light sauces or in broths.

Short pasta (4)

This group includes familiar shapes such as penne, farfalle, conchiglie and fusilli. They are best served with tomato or meat sauces as their shapes trap the sauce well.

Very short pasta, or 'pastina'

These are the very small, quick-cooking pasta shapes. They are traditionally used in soups and broths in Italy. They include lumachine (little snails), stelline (stars) and ditalini (thimbles).

Speciality pastas (5)

There is a huge array of imaginatively shaped, coloured and flavoured pastas available. Green pasta (verde) is made by adding spinach purée; red (rossa) has tomato purée or beetroot added to it; and pasta nera, the black pasta, has squid ink added to the dough. These pastas have distinct flavours as well as colours. Three-colour (tricolore) with green, red and plain pasta shapes add variety to the simplest dishes and are always popular with children.

There are also many types of pasta flavoured with mushrooms, truffles, herbs and spices. You can even buy chocolate pasta with added cocoa, which makes an unusual and surprisingly tasty dessert!

As well as the flavoured doughs, there are many traditional types of pasta made from ingredients other than wheat flour. Buckwheat pasta, corn- and rice-based pasta are all readily available.

TOP TIP

Look for pasta made with 100 per cent durum wheat (*pasta di semolina grano duro* in Italian) as it has a good, firm texture. Some dried pastas include eggs (*pasta all'uova*), but eggs are more commonly used in fresh pasta doughs.

Noodles

Noodles are used extensively in Asian cookery and are made, most commonly, from flour, eggs and water.

Cellophane noodles (6)

These transparent noodles are made from mung beans, which are cooked and puréed, dried into sheets, then cut into noodles. Soak for a few minutes then add to stir-fries or soups, or dry well and deep-fry until crisp.

Chinese egg noodles (7)

These are made with wheat flour and eggs, and are widely used in Chinese and Thai cookery. They are usually dried and packed in rectangular sheets, but some specialist shops do sell them fresh. Simply serve them boiled, or boil then either shallow or deep fry.

Japanese noodles

There are several types of Japanese noodles. Soba noodles are thin noodles traditionally made from buckwheat flour. Udon are thicker, white noodles made from wheat flour. Somen are thinner wheat noodles. Japanese noodles are usually boiled or soaked and served with dipping sauces or in a light broth or soup.

Rice noodles (8)

There is a wide variety, including rice sticks. These are fine, brittle noodles made from rice flour. They may be soaked and drained, then added to soups and other dishes, or deep-fried straight from the packet.

Short pasta shapes

Short pastas come in a wide variety of shapes, each traditionally served with a specific type of sauce:

- Penne – pens or quills
- Rigatoni – wide ribbed tubes
- Farfalle – bows or butterflies
- Conchiglie – shells
- Conchigliette – small shells
- Fusilli – spirals
- Macaroni or elbow macaroni – smooth tubes
- Bucatini – wide, short, smooth tubes
- Ruoti – cartwheels
- Spirale – spirals
- Fiorelli – flowers
- Lumache – snails
- Orecchiette – ears

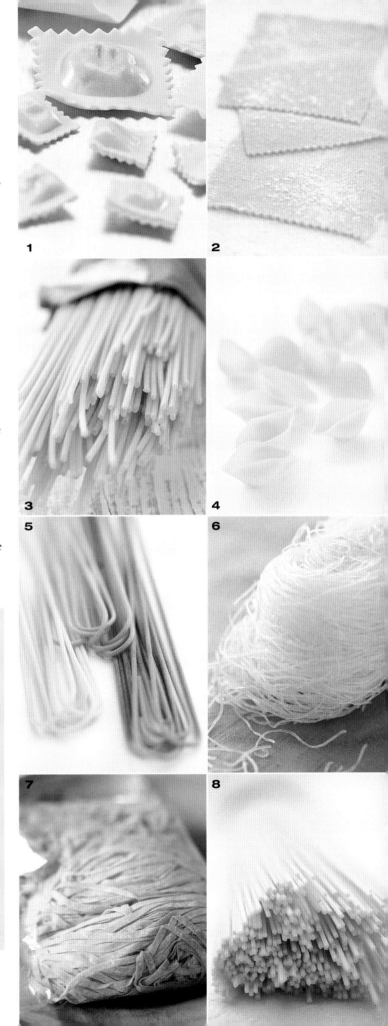

1
2
3
4
5
6
7
8

Beans and pulses

Beans and pulses are a useful source of protein and an excellent alternative to meat. They're also a good form of carbohydrate, with slow-release sugars. They will provide a constant source of energy throughout the day and will have a steadying effect on blood sugar levels.

Advaki bean (aduki)

This small, dried, dark red starchy bean is particularly popular in Japanese and Chinese cooking and can be purchased whole or powdered in Asian food stores. **Serve** in burgers, soups or Oriental confectionery; its flour is also used for making cakes and pastries.

Black-eyed pea (1)

This small whitish-beige bean with a distinctive spot of black at its inner curve is also called the black-eyed bean or cowpea. It is generally sold dried. **Serve** in salads, rice dishes and dips.

Borlotti bean (2)

A dried or fresh bean from the haricot family, which is very popular in Italy. The bean is light brown or pink and speckled with deeper red. It resembles the pinto bean in appearance and is also sold canned. **Serve** in Italian stews and soups.

Chickpea

Although not actually a bean, this small round legume with its firm texture and mild, nutty flavour, is used in similar ways. Chickpeas are used extensively in the Mediterranean, India, and the Middle East. They can be ground to produce gram flour, or besan, which is used in Indian cooking. Available canned or dried. **Serve** in salads, soups and stews or use to make hummus.

Fava bean (3)

This flattish bean, also called the broad bean, resembles a very large lima bean. Fava beans are available fresh, dried, canned and frozen. The pods of

very young fava beans are edible and simply require topping and tailing; they can be eaten raw. Old fava beans tend to have a tough skin, which should be removed by blanching before they are cooked.
Serve them in a variety of ways; falafel is a well-known Middle Eastern favourite, while in Europe fava beans are traditionally served stewed with ham or bacon.

Flageolet bean (4)

Usually white or pale green, this tiny, tender French haricot bean has a creamy, delicate flavour. It is available fresh, dried, canned, and sometimes frozen.
Serve with lamb or ham.

Haricot bean

Varieties include certain green beans, kidney, pinto and pink beans, and flageolet (see individual entries). Haricot beans (as opposed to the pods) are sold either fresh or after being dried in their pods.

In France and Britain, 'haricot' bean generally refers to small, smooth, white dried beans, which are oval rather than kidney-shaped. In the US such haricots are called white beans. Varieties include the navy (or Yankee) bean, used as a staple by the US navy since the mid-1800s, and the pea bean.
Serve in Boston baked beans, stews and soups.

Kidney bean

The red kidney bean is a type of haricot bean – firm, with a dark red, glossy skin and cream flesh. It is readily available dried or canned. The black kidney bean, also called the turtle bean, has the same uses as the red kidney bean. White kidney, or cannellini, beans are less flavoursome and are available dried or canned.
Serve red and black kidney beans in Latin American dishes, notably *feijoada* and in the classic chilli con carne. They are also popular in West Indian cooking and Spanish dishes. Serve white kidney beans in Italian cooking, particularly in salads, casseroles and soups.

Lentils (5)

Available both whole and split, dried lentils are popular in Europe and are a staple throughout the Middle East and India. They require no soaking and soften after cooking. The most familiar varieties include the small reddish-orange split lentil, originally from India; the large, flat, green-brown Continental lentil; and the tiny, grey-green Puy lentil. They are usually boiled but are also delicious cooked slowly in stock until all the liquid has been absorbed.
Serve puréed or whole and combined with spices, herbs or vegetables, in salads, soups and stews.

Lima bean (6)

There are two distinct varieties – the fordhook and the baby lima. Popular in the US, they are usually sold shelled and frozen, or fresh in their pods. Although young beans do not require shelling, they usually are shelled just before cooking to reveal plump, pale green seeds with a slight kidney-shaped curve. Lima beans are also available canned and dried. Sometimes dried lima beans are referred to as butter beans. The large European butter bean, or Madagascar bean, is a close relative and is often available canned or dried.
Serve in casseroles, bean salads and mashed with herbs as an accompaniment to a main course.

Mung bean

A small cylindrical bean, most commonly olive-green in colour with a yellow interior, but brown and black varieties exist. Widely used in Asian cooking. They are often sprouted to produce the long, white bean sprouts.
Serve in soups, stews, and pilafs.

Pinto bean (7)

A variety of haricot bean grown in Latin America and the southwest US, this pale pink bean is streaked with reddish-brown. It can be used interchangeably with the pink bean. Pinto beans are available in dried form.
Serve in Tex-Mex cooking and Mexican bean dishes.

Salted black bean (8)

This is a small soya bean, which is fermented and salted. Salted black beans have a strong flavour. They are available dried and canned.
Serve in Chinese cooking as a savoury seasoning.

Soya bean

There are over a thousand varieties of soya beans, ranging in size and colour. They are very nutritious and are used to produce many products – tofu, soya flour, soya milk, textured vegetable protein (TVP), fermented black beans and bean pastes, and soy sauce. Soya beans can be soaked and cooked like any other dried beans.
Serve in soups, stews, and casseroles. They can also be sprouted to produce bean sprouts and used in salads or as a cooked vegetable.

TOP TIP
Beans are full of minerals, including iron, potassium, selenium, calcium, manganese, magnesium and folic acid.

Nuts and dried fruits

Nuts and dried fruits are useful store cupboard ingredients that are delicious in both sweet and savoury dishes. They are often used in traditional Christmas fare since in days gone by they were among the few ingredients available in the winter months. They are also widely found in Asian, North African and Middle Eastern cuisines.

Almond (1)

This is the seed of a tree that is a member of the peach family. Almonds come in two varieties, bitter and sweet. They are oval in shape and off-white in colour. They are available whole, blanched (with the brown skins removed), slivered (fairly thickly sliced lengthways), flaked (shaved into paper-thin slices), or ground.
Serve in both sweet and savoury dishes in baking, confectionery, salads, stuffings and rice dishes. Ground almonds may be used in marzipan, pastry or cakes.

Cashew

Cashew nuts are the seeds of a native South American tree. They are kidney shaped and have a sweet flavour and soft texture.
Serve in cakes, biscuits and puddings, or savoury dishes like nut roasts, stir-fries and curries.

Chestnut

A sweet-tasting, starchy, low-fat nut, chestnuts can be used in both sweet and savoury dishes. Whole chestnuts are available canned or dried. Sweetened or unsweetened purée is also available.
Serve in soups, stuffings and stews. Sweetened purée is used in desserts, especially with chocolate.

Hazelnut (2)

These are also called cobnuts. They are the small, round nut of the hazel tree found in Europe and North America. To prepare, they should be shelled and then they can be eaten whole, chopped or ground. The flavour improves if the nuts are roasted in a medium oven for 10 minutes.
Serve in cakes, biscuits and stuffings.

Peanut

Also known as a groundnut, the peanut is the seed of a pulse found in the tropics. As well as being a popular snack, peanuts are used in peanut butter and can be found in Thai and West African cooking.
Serve in stuffings and stews.

Pecan

Closely related to the walnut, the pecan nut is native to the United States.
Serve as a snack or use in pecan pie, ice cream and cakes or in savoury stuffings for poultry.

Pine nut

Also called pine kernels, these are the kernels from the cones of pine trees common in the Mediterranean. They are small, with an off-white colour. They may be chopped or ground, toasted or eaten raw.
Serve in salads, risottos and pilafs, or to make pesto.

Pistachio (3)

Pistachio nuts are native to Syria but are grown in other warm areas. They have a cream shell that splits at one end. The nut inside is green. They are often available salted as snacks, but have other uses.
Serve in ice creams, add to cakes and fruit salads, or use to make praline.

Walnut (4)

Walnuts are enclosed in a hard, wrinkled shell. They can be eaten whole on their own, or in sweet or savoury dishes, halved or in chopped or ground form.
Serve in salads, cakes, pasta sauces and stuffings.

Candied peel

Candying is a slow process that involves saturating fruit or peel with a sugar solution. Long strips of candied orange, lemon, citron and grapefruit peel have a superior flavour to the chopped variety.
Serve in mincemeat or in baking, such as tarts and Christmas cakes.

Currant

Currants come from a smaller, bushier vine than that of raisins or sultanas. They are seedless, small and sweet.
Serve as a snack or use in cakes, puddings, kedgeree, curries and stuffings.

Dried apricot (5)

Dried apricots have a sweet flavour with a hint of sharpness. They may be reconstituted by soaking in cold water overnight or for 30 minutes in boiling water.
Serve in sweet or savoury sauces, add to fruit salads, muesli, cakes and sweet breads, or North African and Middle Eastern rice dishes and stews.

Dried date

The date is the fruit of the date palm. Dates are either sun-dried or dried in hot-air tunnels. Top-quality dessert dates are amber coloured and are soft and fleshy in texture. Cheaper dates, used mainly for cooking, are dark and short and have a coarser texture.
Serve in cakes, puddings, preserves or savoury dishes.

Dried fig (6)

Dried figs are an excellent source of dietary fibre and contain minerals and vitamins.
Serve in cakes, puddings, breads and savoury dishes, including stuffings. Dried figs can be soaked and poached and eaten by themselves, or combined with other fresh and dried fruits in a compôte.

Prune (7)

This is a dried purple-skinned plum. Prunes have a naturally sweet flavour and soft, juicy texture.
Serve as a snack or add to fruit salads; they may also be stewed. Use chopped in breads, cakes and savoury dishes.

Raisin (8)

Raisins are dried white or black grapes. They come in a variety of colours, flavours and sizes, depending on the variety of grape. Muscat raisins are very sweet and succulent with a pronounced flavour.
Serve in cakes and puddings, salads, savoury dishes or pickles and chutneys.

Sultana

Sultanas are dried seedless white grapes and are golden brown. They are very sweet and succulent.
Serve in the same way as currants and raisins.

TOP TIP

Many dried fruits, including apricots, figs, and raisins, make a great addition to spicy stews and rice dishes. They add a mellow sweetness and depth of flavour, which will counteract the richness of meat and poultry.

1
2
3
4
5
6
7
8

Cooking fats and oils

Fats and oils are used in the kitchen for deep or shallow frying; for adding a rich flavour and smooth texture to sauces; for making dressings for salads and vegetables; for basting meat during cooking; and for making cakes, biscuits and rich pastries.

Corn oil
Corn oil, also called maize oil, has a distinctive golden yellow colour and is crushed from the germ of corn kernels. It can be heated to a very high temperature and is very economical. Corn oil is high in polyunsaturates, making it a good choice for low-cholesterol diets.
Use for deep-frying.

Ghee (1)
Ghee is unsalted butter from which all the water and milk solids have been removed. The result is a clarified butter that can be heated to very high temperatures without burning. This means it can be used for frying at temperatures at which normal butter would burn. It is a traditional ingredient in Indian cooking.
Use in Indian cuisine to give a rich, buttery flavour to both sweet and savoury dishes.

Groundnut oil (2)
Also known as peanut oil, groundnut oil is valuable to the cook since it is relatively flavourless, making it suitable for many different dishes.
Use for stir-frying, for which it is ideal because it can be heated to a very high temperature.

Hard white fat
Made from vegetable oil, hard white fats give a similar result to lard, but they are preferable for health reasons and are the obvious choice for vegetarians.
Use for frying and pastry-making to give a very light and flaky texture.

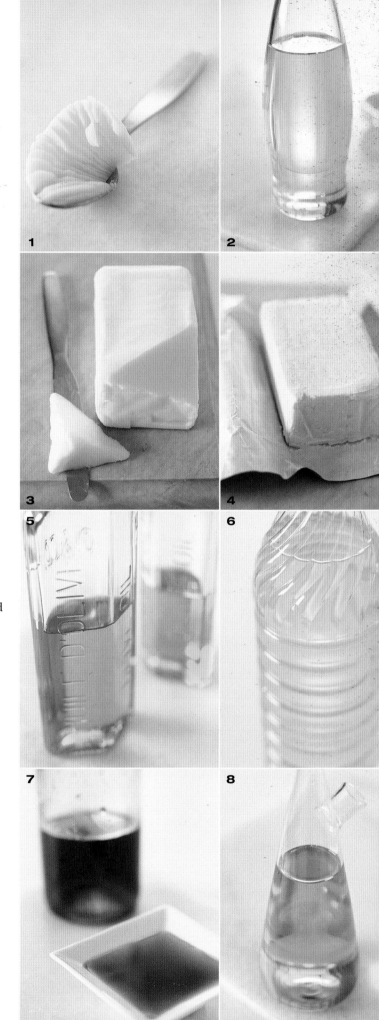

Lard (3)

Lard is made from rendered pork fat. It was once used widely in baking and for shallow and deep-frying, but for health reasons it is no longer popular.
Use a mixture of lard and butter in pastry-making, where it produces a light, crumbly texture.

Margarine (4)

All margarines are made from solidified vegetable oil, some with water added.
Use like butter, with the exception of frying. Soft margarine is not ideal for making pastry and low-fat spreads should not be used for cooking because they contain a high percentage of water.

Olive oil (5)

Olive oil is notable because of the sheer variety of types that are available, ranging from sweet and mellow to sharp tasting, and from golden to green in colour. The best and most expensive olive oils are extra virgin and virgin oils, which have a delicious fruity flavour and often a greenish colour. They are extracted from the first cold pressing of the olives. Ordinary olive oil is usually a blend of oils and is blander and paler than the virgin variety, since it has been refined. As oils go, olive oil is a healthier choice because it contains monounsaturated fats.
Use extra virgin and virgin oils to dress salads, pasta and grilled meats and fish, and choose a less expensive olive oil for frying and cooking, when the flavour of the oil is less important.

Rapeseed oil (6)

Also known as canola, rapeseed oil has a pale colour. It is particularly high in monounsaturated fats and low in saturated fats which makes it, like olive oil, a relatively healthy choice.
Use for frying and in salad dressings.

Safflower oil

Another light oil that can be used interchangeably with sunflower oil. It is made from the safflower plant, which is a type of thistle. Safflower oil is particularly low in polyunsaturated fats.
Use in low-cholesterol diets.

Sesame oil (7)

This oil, with a strong, nutty flavour and golden brown colour, is extracted from toasted sesame seeds.
Use in Chinese cooking, such as stir-fries, but for flavouring rather than cooking as it burns easily when heated to high temperatures.

Suet

Suet is the hard fat from around the kidneys of beef or mutton. Fresh suet used to be an important ingredient in dishes such as jam roly-poly and dumplings, but nowadays suet is usually bought ready-shredded in packets. Vegetarian suet is now produced for those who do not eat meat.
Use in suet pastry to make steak and kidney pudding or jam roly-poly. Also used to make mincemeat.

Sunflower oil

Sunflower oil is pale in colour, with a rather bland flavour. It is excellent as an all-purpose cooking oil, perfect for deep-frying.
Use in salad dressings and for frying. Combine with a stronger, more expensive olive oil to make a mild and creamy mayonnaise.

Vegetable oil

This is usually a mixture of the blander oils, such as safflower, sunflower, corn and groundnut oil. Vegetable oil is a good all-purpose oil because it can be heated to a high temperature.
Use for all types of cooking.

Walnut oil (8)

With a strong nutty flavour, this oil should be used sparingly and not for frying, since it cannot withstand high temperatures. Buy in small quantities and store in the refrigerator because it does not keep well.
Use as a flavouring; it is especially good in salads.

Flavoured oils

• Chilli oil is made by adding fresh or dried chillies to olive oil or vegetable oil and leaving them to infuse. Use in Oriental cooking or drizzle over pizzas and salads.
• Truffle oil is made by scenting good-quality olive oil with fresh truffles. It has the earthy, pungent aroma of truffles. It is extremely expensive, but is used very sparingly, so a bottle lasts a long time. Use to flavour pasta, risotto, salads and mushroom dishes.
• Herb oils are made by adding sprigs of fresh woody herbs, such as rosemary or thyme, to a bottle of olive oil. Leave to infuse for a week or so, then use in salad dressings, drizzle over risottos and pasta dishes, or freshly cooked vegetables.

Sweet flavourings and flours

The type of sugar and flour you use will greatly influence your baking, so choose wisely. The other sweet ingredients will add character to cakes, biscuits and delicious desserts.

Chocolate (1)

Plain, or dark, chocolate is widely available and is the best type to use for cooking. For the best flavour, choose one with at least 50 per cent cocoa solids. Milk chocolate is very rarely used in cooking as it contains a high proportion of sugar and low proportion of cocoa solids. When melting chocolate, melt it slowly because it scorches very easily if overheated.

Cocoa

Cocoa is produced by pulverizing the residue of the cocoa bean after most of the cocoa butter has been extracted. Cocoa powder may be used in baking and for making desserts, where it adds a rich chocolate flavour and can be used to replace a little of the flour. It can also be made into a hot drink with milk and sugar. To stop lumps forming in the drink, first mix the cocoa to a paste with a little milk.

Coffee (2)

The flavour of coffee depends on the type of bean and how it is roasted. To use coffee as a flavouring ingredient, mix together small and equal amounts of instant coffee and boiling water. Alternatively, brew some really strong fresh coffee.

Orange flower water

Distilled from orange blossom, this water is popular in Mediterranean countries and the Middle East. Used to flavour pastries, cream and preserves. Use quickly or the flavour will disappear.

Rosewater (3)

This perfumed water, distilled from rose petals, is used in sorbets, spicy chicken dishes, sweet pastries and sweets such as Turkish Delight. Store away from heat and light and use up quickly.

Vanilla (4)

Vanilla is available as whole pods, extract or essence. The pod has the best flavour and can be used, split in half, to flavour hot liquid such as milk for making sauces, custards, ice creams and other desserts. For an even stronger vanilla flavour, some of the small black seeds may be scraped out of the pod. The vanilla pod may be reused if rinsed and dried. Vanilla extract or essence can be used in much the same way.

Caster sugar

Finer than granulated sugar, this sugar dissolves easily. Use to make cakes, pastries, biscuits, puddings, custards and sweet mousses.

Demerara sugar

This sugar has a coarse texture with large golden crystals. It is made from partly refined sugar syrup and contains a small amount of treacle. Use in coffee or sweet yeast breads, or sprinkle on top of cakes before baking for a crunchy topping.

Granulated sugar (5)

This is a refined white sugar, coarser than caster sugar. Use to sweeten beverages, such as tea and coffee; for sweetening stewed fruit and for making boiled icings and frostings, fudges and toffees.

Palm sugar

Also known as jaggery, this sugar is made from palm sap. It is bought in hard brown cakes and has a flavour reminiscent of black treacle. It is used widely in Thai cooking in stews, curries and sweet puddings.

Soft brown sugar

This is simply white sugar that has been mixed with black treacle to provide colour, moistness and limited flavour. Dark soft brown sugar has had a higher percentage of black treacle added to it than has light soft brown sugar.

Honey (6)

Honey can vary enormously in texture, colour and flavour; some are set and opaque while others are clear and runny. The finest honeys are those named after their flower source, such as orange blossom, heather and lavender. Blended, mixed source honey tends to be cheaper and usually comes from a number of different countries. Clear runny clover honey is ideal for baking.

Golden syrup (7)
A rich gold in colour, this syrup is made from cane sugar juice. It will add flavour and moistness to cakes, puddings and biscuits. Also popular on its own as a topping for pancakes or porridge.

Maple syrup
Made from the sap of North American and Canadian maple trees, this syrup has a distinctive flavour. It has a thin consistency and can be used to drizzle over pancakes. It can be used in baking and ice-cream making instead of honey or treacle.

Treacle (8)
Treacle is obtained from sugar during refining. It is an extremely thick, dark syrup with a strong, slightly bitter flavour. Use in rich fruit cakes, gingerbread, bread and scones to add flavour and colour.

Cornflour
Cornflour is simply flour made from finely ground corn, or maize, kernels. It is used chiefly for thickening sauces and should be mixed to a paste with a little water before being added to hot liquids.

Plain flour
Plain flour is a basic ingredient in pastry, biscuits and many types of baking. It is produced from finely ground wheat grains which have had the bran removed to leave a fine white powder. It is also used for thickening sauces.

Self-raising flour
Self-raising flour is simply plain flour with a raising agent added to it. It is used mainly for cakes and desserts which need to rise in the oven to produce a light and airy texture.

Strong flour
Strong flour or bread flour has a high gluten content. It absorbs moisture and becomes springy and elastic when mixed to a dough. This gives great capacity for expansion and it is therefore used in making bread.

Wholemeal flour
Wholemeal flour is made from the whole wheat grain. It is high in fibre and has a distinctive flavour and nutty texture, but can give a rather heavy texture.

Savoury flavourings

It is often the little extra ingredients that make a big difference to a dish and provide the characteristic flavours. Use these savoury flavourings to enhance your cooking, but go easy until you know what effect you will achieve.

Anchovy paste

Made from mashed anchovy fillets, this paste imparts a salty flavour to fish dishes and tomato sauces. It is excellent spread very thinly on hot buttered toast.

Caper (1)

This is the pickled, unopened green flower bud of a Mediterranean plant. The smaller capers are prized for their subtle flavour. They are indispensable in tartare sauce and puttanesca sauce for pasta, and also go very well with fish dishes and shellfish salads.

Chilli sauce (2)

The heat of these thick, bright red sauces may vary greatly, so add them sparingly. They do not generally need refrigeration. Use in Chinese and South-east Asian food.

Coarse grain mustard (3)

This is a mild mustard with a grainy texture. Use it in dressings, sauces, casseroles and soups or serve as a condiment with meat or cheese.

Dijon mustard

This popular, smooth mustard has a slightly sweet flavour and is medium hot. It is the ideal mustard for making mayonnaise.

Fish sauce

Made from fermented fish or prawns, this sauce is indispensable in Thai cooking. It is used to offset the richness of coconut curries and soups, and also in fish stocks and fish dishes.

Horseradish (4)

Freshly grated, this root may be used in sauces to add an earthy piquancy. Horseradish sauce is available ready-made in jars. It is the classic accompaniment to roast beef and is excellent with smoked fish.

Hoisin sauce (5)

This pungent, sweet and spicy, reddish brown sauce is made from soya beans with spices, garlic and chillies. It is an essential condiment eaten with Peking duck.

Mirin

A Japanese sweetened rice wine which is used extensively in Japanese dishes.

Mustard powder

Made from mustard flour, wheat flour and spices, mustard powder is usually prepared by mixing with cold water. Use as a condiment with meat, especially ham and sausages, or use in powder form in cooking.

Oyster sauce

A thick, brown sauce used in Chinese cooking. Made from oysters, it imparts a rich, salty flavour to Chinese dishes. Once opened, keep refrigerated.

Salt (6)

The flavour of table salt is inferior to that of sea salt and rock salt, but it is good for baking and useful when you require a fine sprinkling. Sea salt is comprised of large crystals of pure salt and is made by evaporating sea water. It contains natural iodine and has the best flavour. Rock salt is hard and coarse and must be used in a salt mill or pounded with a pestle in a mortar.

Soy sauce

Used extensively in Chinese and Japanese cooking, soy sauce has a rich aroma and strong, salty flavour. It comes in light and dark forms. Use in marinades and barbecue sauces, stir-fries, soups and Asian curries.

Tomato purée

Made from highly concentrated tomatoes, a tablespoon or two can be added to pasta sauces, soups, stews and casseroles to give an intense tomato flavour. Sun-dried tomato purée is also readily available.

Balsamic vinegar (7)

This sweet, rich, dark brown vinegar comes from the Modena region of Italy. It is aged for many years in wooden barrels. Use sparingly in dressings or sprinkle over fish, meat, chicken or vegetables.

Cider vinegar

Made from crushed apples, this vinegar has a distinct taste of cider. Sharper than wine vinegar, it may be used in dressings and chutneys.

Malt vinegar

Brewed from malted barley, the brown colour of this vinegar is achieved by adding caramel to it. Excellent for pickling and with fish and chips.

Raspberry vinegar

This is a wine vinegar that has the natural flavour of raspberries added to it. Excellent with warm salads and in salad dressings.

Rice vinegar

This vinegar has a sweet, delicate flavour and is used in many Japanese and South-east Asian dishes. An important ingredient in sushi.

Sherry vinegar

Made from sweet sherry, this vinegar can be used instead of balsamic vinegar. Use in meat cookery, especially with kidneys and chicken livers.

Wine vinegar

Red and white wine vinegars are available. White wine vinegar is the best choice for making mayonnaise and Hollandaise sauce. Red wine vinegar can be used in dressings, marinades and pickles.

Wasabi (8)

Also known as Japanese horseradish, wasabi is bright green, and is usually served as an accompaniment to Japanese dishes such as sushi. Wasabi can be bought in a powder form, which is light brown, or as a paste in tubes.

Worcestershire sauce

Made from a long list of ingredients including mushrooms, vinegar, caramel and anchovies, this is a dark brown liquid sauce with a pungent flavour. Use in cooking and in the classic cocktail, Bloody Mary.

Did you know?
Soy sauces are made from fermented soya beans. There are many different varieties originating in many different countries, for example shoyu and tamari in Japan and kekap manis in Indonesia.

Tools of the trade

To cook successfully, you need to invest in a basic range of good-quality tools and utensils. This need not be extensive, but a collection of well-chosen items is essential to achieve the best results, as well as to save on unnecessary effort and time.

Knives

A good set of knives should come top of your list of things to buy for the kitchen. It is worth getting a well-made set of stainless steel or carbon steel knives, forged in one piece with a riveted wooden or plastic handle. They should be sharpened regularly and kept separately in a wooden block or on a magnetic rack, rather than in a drawer with other implements, to avoid dulling or damaging the blades. This will also prevent cut fingers when looking for an implement in the drawer.

Chopping knife

A heavy, wide-bladed knife is ideal for chopping vegetables, herbs and other ingredients. It is also useful for transferring chopped ingredients from the chopping board to the cooking pan. The side of the blade can also be used for crushing garlic.

Paring knife (1)

This small knife is ideal for trimming and peeling fruit and vegetables.

General kitchen knife (1)

A medium-sized, all-purpose knife, usually 15-25 cm (6–10 inches) long, which can be used for chopping, slicing and cutting all kinds of ingredients.

Bread knife (1)

A large knife with a serrated edge is useful for slicing bread, cakes and pastries, since it does not tear the food.

Other implements

There are a number of basic kitchen implements that are essential for cooking and worth investing in.

Balloon whisk (2)

A whisk made up of a number of curved wires to form a balloon shape, used to blend ingredients, such as butter and flour in sauces, for whisking egg whites and cream, and to incorporate air into batter mixtures.

Fish slice

A fish slice, or tirner, is indispensable for lifting and turning all kinds of food, such as rashers of bacon, fried eggs, pieces of meat or fillets of fish.

Garlic press (3)

This useful tool finely crushes garlic cloves by forcing the flesh through a series of tiny holes, so releasing the full flavour of the garlic into the dish. It also saves your hands from coming into contact with the garlic juices and avoids their pungent aroma lingering on the skin.

Grater (4)

Multi-purpose graters come in a box shape or a single flat sheet. They have different perforations for preparing various kinds of ingredients. The fine holes are used for grating whole spices, chocolate, Parmesan cheese and citrus rind; the medium and large holes are for grating fresh root ginger, other cheeses and vegetables. There is a special miniature grater for grating whole nutmeg, but either of the ordinary varieties of grater can be used instead.

Masher

A useful tool for mashing potatoes and other root vegetables, such as swede and parsnips.

Palette knife

Consisting of a long, flexible round-ended metal blade set in a handle, a palette knife is essential for spreading and smoothing the surface of cake mixtures and icings, and useful for scraping mixtures from around the inside of a bowl. It is also useful for lifting up and flipping over pancakes.

Pasta server

A long-handled stainless steel spoon designed to transfer pasta or noodles, such as spaghetti, from the cooking pan onto a serving dish. It has teeth that grasp the pasta and a hole that allows the cooking liquid to drain back into the saucepan.

Rolling pin

An essential item for rolling out pastry and also pasta and bread doughs. Rolling pins are available with or without handles and can be made out of wood, plastic, nylon or marble.

Sieve (5)

A fine-mesh stainless steel sieve or nylon sieve is essential for sifting and straining. It can also be used for puréeing, by rubbing cooked vegetables, fruit or beans and lentils through the mesh with the back of a ladle or wooden spoon.

Slotted spoon

A large spoon with perforations for lifting food from a pan, reserving the cooking oil or liquid.

Tongs (6)

Use these for picking up items of hot food or for turning them when grilling or barbecuing.

Two-pronged fork

This is a metal fork with long prongs that will hold meat or poultry firmly while it is lifted to or from a roasting pan or casserole.

Vegetable peeler (7)

In addition to its usual function of removing the skin from vegetables and fruit, a vegetable peeler can be used to pare carrot and courgette ribbons, or to make quick and easy chocolate curls. It is also excellent for Parmesan cheese curls for use in salads and to garnish other savoury dishes.

Wooden spatula

This has a wide, blunt blade and is useful for moving ingredients around in a pan or bowl. For instance, when cooking an omelette, it can be used to draw the egg mixture into the centre of the pan and to fold the omelette over.

Wooden spoon (8)

The wooden spoon is invaluable for beating, mixing and stirring; it will never burn your hand because wood is a bad conductor of heat; it will not scratch or wear away saucepans; and it is quiet and strong in use. The best are those made of a close-grained wood that is not likely to split. The design of wooden spoons has been honed by cooks over the centuries, and you will find shapes for all sorts of purposes, but especially useful are those whose bowl has a fairly thin edge that can get right to the bottom corner of steep-sided pans.

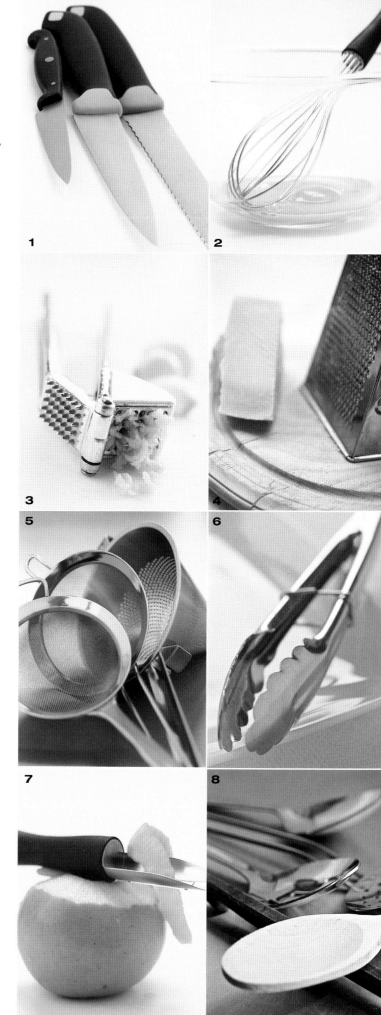

Pots and pans

Always buy the finest quality pots and pans that you can afford. Copper-based or other heavy-based ones are best, but it is useful to have some nonstick ones for cooking food that tends to stick, such as scrambled egg.

Saucepans (1)

Invest in good-quality, stainless steel saucepans that will last for years to come. They should be well-balanced and easy to hold, as well as having welded handles and lids that fit tightly. You will need three or four saucepans in the range of 1–7 litres (1¾–12 pints).

Frying pan

The best type of frying pan is made of heavy gauge, heat-conducting metal that allows heat to be transmitted rapidly and evenly. It should have a wide, flat base and shallow sides, sloping outwards to give space for lifting and turning food. A long handle makes it easier to lift.

Stove-top grill pan

Dry-frying, using a cast-iron grill pan, is a fast, direct and simple way to cook. The pan is heated until very hot and the seasoned food is cooked directly on the

TOP TIP

Use only wooden or plastic implements on non-stick pots and pans to avoid scratching the surface, and wash them with a soft cloth and warm soapy water.

Did you know?

Here's how to clean stained pans:

- Burned pans – cover burned matter with water, add 2 tablespoons of salt or vinegar, bring to the boil, remove from the heat and leave to stand overnight.
- Enamel pan stains – add 600 ml (1 pint) of water, add 1 teaspoon of bleach and leave for 2 hours. Wash and rinse thoroughly.
- Discoloured aluminium – boil a solution of rhubarb, tomatoes or lemon peel in it.
- Stainless steel – clean with a gentle bristle brush and warm soapy water, then polish the pan when dry.

---

ridged or flat surface, producing extra flavour where food comes into contact with intense heat. The food can be cooked without the addition of any fat, and can be marinated first for extra flavour.

Wok

Woks are large, round-bottomed pans used in Oriental cooking, especially stir-frying. They can be non-stick or steel. Choose one about 35 cm (14 inches) across, which is wide and deep enough for most purposes.

A new steel wok will have a protective film of grease. Remove the film by filling the wok with water and boiling for 30 minutes. Scrub the wok with an abrasive, rinse and dry over heat for 5 minutes. When cool, wipe both sides of the wok thoroughly with vegetable oil. Clean after each use; wash with water, using a mild detergent if necessary, and a clean cloth or soft brush. Dry off and rub with oil.

Colander

Choose a colander made from stainless steel with a long handle and a stable base, so that it can be held firmly while draining pasta or vegetables. It can also be used to steam food in place of a proper steamer.

Steamer (2)

This consists of a perforated container that holds foods to be steamed, placed inside a pan containing a small amount of boiling water. Make sure it has a tight-fitting lid. Steaming food is an excellent cooking method for maintaining the maximum texture and flavour of foods, while avoiding the use of cooking oils or fats.

Baking tins

Some baking tins have bright, shiny surfaces that deflect the heat away from the contents so that they do not scorch, while others have dark finishes that absorb and hold the heat. Tin plate is most widely used for bakeware. Aluminium, a good conductor of heat, is more expensive than tin. Non-stick surfaces, applied to either tin or aluminium, are hard-wearing but can easily be damaged by metal implements. Choose tins that are sturdy, smooth inside with no crevices for trapping food and with rolled edges which will make them easier and safer to handle.

Cake tins

The most useful of these is a 20-cm (8-inch) or 23-cm (9-inch) round tin and two 20-cm (8-inch) round sandwich tins.

Flan tins

These can be used for quiches or pies. Some have fluted edges and there is a choice between removable and fixed-base varieties. Flan tins are preferable to porcelain flan dishes, since they conduct heat effectively which prevents soggy pastry.

Patty tin

This is a sheet of cup-shaped hollows for baking tartlets, small cakes or individual Yorkshire puddings.

Pie dish

A classic pie dish for cooking sweet and savoury pies is oval-shaped with sloping sides and a wide, flat rim for holding the pastry lid; it should have a capacity of 1.2 litres (2 pints). A pie plate is shallower and round.

Other Equipment

The following basic equipment is useful for the preparation of food.

Chopping boards

It is best to have at least two chopping boards, one made from a hard wood, such as maple, which you can use for most tasks, and the other to be kept for the preparation of raw meat. This board should be made from a white, non-porous material which can be cleaned with hot water and a little bleach. Always remember to wash boards and knives between handling raw and cooked food.

Choose wooden boards at least 4 cm (1½ inches) thick. Ideally the grain on the main part of the board should run in the opposite direction to that on the reinforced ends. Melamine boards look attractive when new, but their hard surfaces soon blunt knife blades and may cause knives to slip.

Measuring jug (3)

This is a standardized measure with a pouring lip. It is usually marked in both metric and imperial. Available in a variety of materials, the most useful is made from heatproof glass that can withstand boiling liquids and you can see clearly how much is in the jug. Because it is a poor conductor of heat, the handle remains cool.

Mixing bowl (3)

Choose one made from heatproof glass or ceramic, which will be heavy enough to sit firmly on the work surface. It should also be large and wide enough to enable mixtures to be vigorously whisked or beaten without spilling over the rim. A couple of small bowls are also useful for beating eggs or holding small quantities of food.

Pestle and mortar (4)

A grinder and a bowl respectively, this is used for grinding herbs, for example for pesto, and whole spices. It can be made of marble, which does not absorb flavours, wood or ceramic.

Food processors

These versatile machines are only worth having if you have space to keep it on a worktop, with accessories readily to hand. Make a point of using your machine in a different way every couple of days to build up your understanding of how it works and just how time-saving and helpful it can be. You can buy a liquidizer as an attachment to a food processor, but it is useful to have a separate machine, because it is easier to deal with small quantities in one. Food for a baby, for instance, is more easily puréed in a goblet rather than in a bowl, which can leave a ring of ingredients round the edge.

mastering the basics

Dealing with meat

For many people, meat is the centrepiece of a meal. Knowing what to buy and how to prepare it is the secret to successful meats. There are many types of meat and different cuts, so it is satisfying to explore the enormous versatility of dishes you can create.

Choosing and buying meat

The amount of meat you need to buy for a meal depends on the type of meat you are serving and the way you plan to cook it. As a rough guide, allow 125–175 g (4–6 oz) of meat off the bone or 175–375 g (6–12 oz) of meat on the bone, per person.

Cuts for roasts

Beef – sirloin, topside, boned and rolled prime rib, wing rib, fore rib, rump or fillet
Pork – loin, leg, hand or shoulder
Lamb – leg, shoulder, loin, saddle, best end of neck, crown roast or guard of honour

Cuts for stews and casseroles

Beef – shin or leg, clod, chuck, blade, flank or skirt. Pot-roasting: silverside or brisket
Pork – blade, shoulder, leg steaks, loin or spare rib chops. Pot-roasting: leg, shoulder, belly, spare rib joint or hand and spring
Lamb – leg, shoulder, loin chops, boned and rolled breast and neck

Cuts for frying, grilling or barbecues

Beef – sirloin, rump, fillet, entrecôte or porterhouse steaks
Pork – tenderloin, spare rib or loin chops, loin or leg steaks, escalopes or belly slices
Lamb – neck fillet slices, loin, butterfly chops, leg steaks or cutlets

Right To make the job of carving lamb easier, separate the flesh from the bladebone with a sharp knife before roasting.

Storing meat

• Store meat in a film-covered plastic tray on a plate in the refrigerator.
• Any meat that is not pre-packed should be wrapped in foil or greaseproof paper and then refrigerated.
• Chops deteriorate faster than joints and should be used within 3 days.
• Use joints of beef, veal and lamb within 5 days.
• Use joints of pork within 4 days.
• Mince will last only a day or two in the refrigerator.
• All meat freezes well.
• Offal should be bought and consumed on the same day if possible.

Preparing meat

Some cuts of meat need more preparation than others. It is worth learning the basic rules of preparation so that you get the very best out of your cut of meat.

Lamb

Shoulder of lamb can be tricky to carve, but if you loosen the bladebone before cooking, the task becomes far easier. Feel along the cut edge of the shoulder to find the edge of the bladebone, then use a small sharp knife to separate it from the flesh on either side. Continue cutting into the joint, as close to the bone as possible, and make sure the bladebone is loosened right down to the joint on both sides. After roasting, grasp the bladebone with a cloth and twist it to break it free at the joint. Lift out the bone and the meat can be carved straight across.

Offal

Liver can be bought in a chunk or ready sliced. If it is sliced, simply rinse and dry it on kitchen paper. If you buy it in one piece, cut away the outer membrane and tubes, then cut it into thick slices. Rinse and dry.
Chicken livers should be thoroughly rinsed and dried, then check them over and remove any pieces of white membrane.
Kidneys are usually covered in a thin skin, so remove this and cut the kidneys in half horizontally through the core. Remove the core on each of the halves using a small sharp knife or kitchen scissors. Rinse and dry.

Tenderizing meat

Some cuts of meat can be tough, such as steaks, boneless chops and escalopes. There are several ways to tenderize meat. One way is to place the meat between sheets of clingfilm or greaseproof paper and beat it with a meat hammer or a wooden rolling pin. This helps to break down the connective tissue that makes meat tough.

Another way is to purée the flesh of a fresh papaya or kiwi fruit and spread this over the surface of the meat. Cover and chill for 2–3 hours before cooking. Alternatively, you could place the meat in a shallow dish and pour over just enough fresh pineapple juice to cover it. To tenderize liver, soak it in tomato juice, cover and place in the refrigerator for 2–3 hours.

Mincing meat

Use the chopping blade attachment of your food processor and pulse the power as you drop diced lean meat on to the blades of the food processor. Pulse the power until the meat is finely chopped. Take care not to overprocess the meat or it will become very soft and paste-like, losing its texture. For small meatballs the meat can be processed more finely.

TOP TIP

When cutting meat into slices, steaks or strips, cut across the grain, as this will give tender results and the pieces will keep their shape better during cooking. Always cut dice or strips of meat to the same size, so that they cook evenly in the same time. To slice meat very thinly for stir-fries, freeze the meat for about 30 minutes as this will make it firm and easier to slice.

Above Spreading puréed fruit, such as papaya, over the surface of meat can help to tenderize it.

Cooking meat

There are various ways to cook meat but one of the easiest ways is to roast it. This simple method of cooking is not only a delicious way to cook meat, but it also leaves you time to prepare the rest of the meal without having to worry about ruining the meat. The following guidelines will help you to prepare that perfect roast dinner for your family and friends.

Roasting basics

1 Preheat the oven to the correct temperature – this will ensure that the surface of the meat begins to seal immediately it goes into the hot oven, helping to retain both juices and flavour.
2 Place the joint of meat, uncovered, on a rack in a roasting tin with the largest cut surfaces exposed to the heat. Any surface covered in fat should be on top so that the joint is naturally basted as the fat melts during cooking. Baste the meat 2 or 3 times during roasting by spooning the cooking juices over it.
3 To test if meat is cooked, insert a skewer into the thickest part, near the bone if there is one, and look at the juices. For pork and veal, the juices should run clear, with no trace of pink. Beef and lamb juices may be red if you like your meat rare, pink if you like it medium, or clear and golden if you prefer it to be well-done.
4 Allow the cooked joint to stand in a warm place for 10–15 minutes to rest. This makes carving easier and the meat will be both flavoursome and tender.

Roasting times
Oven temperature 180°C (350°F), Gas Mark 4.

	Rare	Medium	Well done
Beef	20 mins per 500 g (1 lb) plus 20 mins	25 mins per 500 g (1 lb) plus 25 mins	30 mins per 500 g (1 lb) plus 30 mins
Lamb	–	25 mins per 500 g (1 lb) plus 25 mins	30 mins per 500 g (1 lb) plus 30 mins
Pork	–	30 mins per 500 g (1 lb) plus 30 mins	35 mins per 500 g (1 lb) plus 35 mins

Perfect pork crackling

Roast pork is not quite the same without really good crackling. Choose a joint that has thick, dry skin and a layer of fat. To ensure that your crackling is really crisp, make sure first of all that you dry the skin thoroughly with kitchen paper.

If your butcher has not already scored the rind of the pork, do this with a very sharp, rigid knife. The cuts should go all around the skin and they should be deep enough to penetrate the fat without going right through to the flesh. Rub the surface of the skin with a little sunflower oil, then sprinkle it generously with salt. Roast the joint with the skin uppermost and do not baste as this will prevent the skin from hardening.

Below To make perfect crackling on pork, dry the skin thoroughly, then score it all over with a sharp knife, right through the fat below.

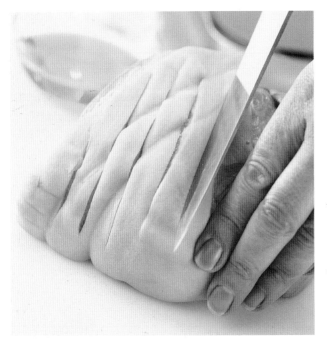

Simple flavourings for plain roasts

Mustard Rub mustard powder into the surface of fatty cuts of beef or pork before roasting.

Garlic and rosemary Stud a lamb or beef joint with garlic before roasting. Make deep, but narrow, cuts all over the joint with the tip of a knife and slip slivers of peeled garlic cloves and rosemary leaves into the slits.

Horseradish Mix equal quantities of creamed horseradish and dry white breadcrumbs. Spread the mixture over the surface of a beef joint for the final 20 minutes of roasting.

Pesto Mix a little pesto with fresh breadcrumbs, then spread the mixture over the surface of a roast for the final 20 minutes of roasting.

Using a meat thermometer

To take the guesswork out of checking whether meat is cooked, insert a meat thermometer into the thickest part of the joint, not touching the bone or fat. Check the temperature: for rare meat it should be 60°C (140°F); for medium it should read 70–75°C (158–167°F); and for well-done 80–85°C (176–185°F).

Carving

An essential tip is to always stand up to carve a joint as this will make it so much easier. Let the joint of meat rest for at least 10 minutes after you take it out of the oven before starting to carve it. This will allow the juices to settle back into the meat and make carving much easier.

Before you attempt to begin carving, remove any string or skewers that will be in the way then stand the joint on a flat, non-slip surface, such as a wooden board or a plate with spikes to hold it in position. A carving fork will help to hold it steady. Remove any outer bones from the joint before you start and then carve the meat into thin, even slices.

TOP TIP

Before cooking a steak or chop with a rim of fat around the edge, snip into the fat at regular intervals to prevent it from curling up as it shrinks during cooking.

Cooking the perfect steak

Steak may be grilled or fried: grilling is healthier as no extra fat is added. Whichever method you choose, preheat the grill or frying pan to very hot before adding the meat, to seal in the juices and flavour, then reduce the heat slightly.

Sirloin or rump, 2 cm (¾ inch) thick
Rare 2½ minutes in total
Medium 4 minutes in total
Well done 6 minutes in total

Fillet, 1.5–3 cm (¾–1¼ inch) thick
Rare 3–4 minutes in total
Medium 4–5 minutes in total
Well done 6–7 minutes in total

How to make perfect gravy

The best gravy is made in the roasting tin on the hob after the meat has been roasted. You can make it while the meat is resting. Remove the meat and use the tasty juices left in the pan for flavour. The amount of flour can be adjusted, depending on how thick you like your gravy and the type of meat you are serving it with. The flavour of the gravy can also be enhanced by adding herbs or red or white wine.

1 Carefully pour as much clear fat as possible from the roasting tin, leaving behind the cooking juices and any sediment.

2 Tip the roasting tin slightly so that the meat juices run to one side, then sprinkle 1–2 tablespoons of plain flour into the empty side of the tin and gradually blend it into the juices. It is important to do this bit by bit otherwise the gravy will end up with lumps of flour floating in it. Place the tin on the hob over a low heat and stir continuously for 1–2 minutes until it is bubbling.

3 Gradually stir in about 300 ml (½ pint) of stock or vegetable cooking water, then stir until the gravy boils. Cook for 2–3 minutes, still stirring, until the gravy is thickened and smooth. Taste and adjust the seasoning before serving.

Making stews and casseroles

1 Choose a heavy, flameproof casserole or a large pan with a tightly fitting lid. The pan can be covered closely, if necessary, by placing a double layer of foil over the top, under the lid.

2 It is important to brown the meat before adding liquid. This improves the flavour and colour, and helps to seal the juices into the meat. The oil or fat in the pan should be really hot before adding the meat. Brown the meat in small batches, removing it with a slotted spoon before adding another batch.

3 The liquid used depends on your recipe – well-flavoured stock, beer, cider or wine are ideal. Canned tomatoes or passata can also be used for moisture.

4 Once the stew is simmering, reduce the heat to low – the slightest bubble is all that is needed. This will slowly tenderize ingredients and bring out the flavour. Boiling meat fiercely toughens it and makes it shrink.

5 The flavour of most stews and casseroles improves if they are made a day in advance of being served. Cool the cooked casserole as quickly as possible, then place in the refrigerator and reheat thoroughly before serving.

Fillet Steak with Roquefort and Horseradish

These succulent steaks are topped with melted blue cheese and horseradish. Serve with a salad, steamed vegetables, or in a toasted ciabatta roll.

Preparation time 10 minutes **Cooking time** 5–10 minutes **Serves** 4

1 tbsp crushed black peppercorns

1 tsp crushed chilli flakes (optional)

4 rump steaks, at least 2.5 cm (1 inch) thick

3 tbsp vegetable oil

2 tbsp creamed horseradish

175 g (6 oz) Roquefort cheese, crumbled

½ tbsp chopped flat leaf parsley, plus extra to garnish

1 Mix together the crushed black peppercorns and the chilli flakes, if using, and place on a plate. Press one side of each steak into the mixture to create a light crust.

2 Heat the oil in a large frying pan until very hot, then add the steaks, crust downwards. Sear on both sides until golden brown. Turn the steaks peppercorn crust upwards.

3 Mix the creamed horseradish and crumbled Roquefort together with the chopped parsley and spoon on top of each steak.

4 Cook the steaks for 2 minutes more for medium; 4–5 minutes for well-done meat. Place briefly under a preheated hot grill to slightly brown the Roquefort crust. Serve immediately, garnished with extra flat leaf parsley.

Parmesan-breaded Lamb Chops

You need racks of lamb for this delicious recipe, preferably ones that have been French-trimmed. This means removing the meat and fat from the long bones so that it does not burn when the chops are cooking. Ask a butcher to do this for you, or simply trim them yourself.

Preparation time 20 minutes **Cooking time** 20 minutes **Serves** 4

75 g (3 oz) plain flour

1 tbsp sesame seeds

2 racks of lamb, about 625 g (1¼ lb) total weight

50 g (2 oz) Parmesan cheese, freshly grated

50 g (2 oz) fresh breadcrumbs

2 eggs, beaten

salt and pepper

lemon wedges, to serve

To garnish
flat leaf parsley sprigs

Parmesan shavings

1 Season the flour with salt and pepper and the sesame seeds. Dip the lamb into the seasoned flour, coating it evenly all over. Mix together the grated Parmesan and breadcrumbs and season with salt and pepper.

2 Dip the lamb first in the beaten egg and then in the Parmesan mixture and coat it all over, pressing the crumbs on to the lamb.

3 Roast the lamb in a preheated oven at 200°C (400°F), Gas Mark 6, for 20 minutes.

4 Cut the lamb into 4 pairs of cutlets and serve with lemon wedges. Garnish with flat leaf parsley and shavings of Parmesan. Baby new potatoes, carrot matchsticks and beans make good accompaniments.

Roast Pork with Bulgar and Celery Stuffing

A tender loin of pork is trimmed, stuffed and roasted to perfection. Serve with a selection of vegetables or a salad.

Preparation time 15 minutes **Cooking time** about 2½ hours **Serves** 6

1.75 kg (3½ lb) pork loin joint

50 g (2 oz) bulgar wheat

300 ml (½ pint) boiling water

1 small onion, finely chopped

2 celery sticks, finely chopped

50 g (2 oz) mushrooms, finely chopped

1 tbsp chopped sage

2 tbsp natural yogurt

salt and pepper

celery leaves, to garnish

1 Remove the skin and most of the fat from the pork, leaving only a thin layer, then score the surface into a diamond pattern. Turn the meat over and, using a sharp knife, remove the bones.

2 Place the bulgar wheat in a saucepan, pour over the measured water and bring back to the boil. Cover and simmer for 10-15 minutes, or until the liquid is absorbed. Stir in the onion, celery, mushrooms, sage and yogurt and season to taste with salt and pepper.

3 Spread the stuffing over the pork, roll it up and tie with fine cotton string. Place the pork on a rack in a roasting tin and sprinkle with pepper. Roast in a preheated oven, 160°C (325°F), Gas Mark 3, basting occasionally with the juices in the tin, for about 2 hours, until the juices run clear. Garnish with celery leaves. Skim the fat from the juices and serve as a gravy.

Griddled Liver and Bacon

The intense heat of a stove-top grill pan sears the meat, giving it a lovely char-grilled taste and seals in all the meat juices.

Preparation time 15 minutes **Cooking time** 35 minutes **Serves** 4

500 g (1 lb) waxy salad potatoes

4 tbsp olive oil

1 rosemary sprig, chopped

2 large onions, 1 finely sliced, 1 thickly sliced

2 tsp light muscovado sugar

450 ml (¾ pint) Vegetable Stock (see page 161)

1 tbsp cornflour, mixed to a smooth paste with a little water

8 rashers of streaky bacon

600 g (1¼ lb) lamb's liver, thickly sliced and seasoned

salt and pepper

1 Boil the potatoes for 6–8 minutes, until tender. Drain, refresh under cold water and cut in half. Mix with 3 tablespoons of olive oil and the rosemary. Season to taste.

2 Fry the finely sliced onion very gently in the remaining oil until golden brown. Add the sugar and stir until the onion has caramelized. Add the stock and bring to the boil. Reduce the heat, cover and simmer gently for 10 minutes. Stir in the cornflour paste and bring back to the boil, stirring until thickened. Season to taste.

3 Place the potatoes on a baking sheet and grill for 8-10 minutes until golden brown, turning frequently.

4 Heat a stove-top grill pan or large frying pan until hot. Add the bacon and thickly sliced onion and cook over a medium heat for 6 minutes, turning once. Remove and keep warm. Add the liver to the pan and cook for 3–4 minutes on each side. Serve the liver on a pile of grilled potatoes. Top with the onion and bacon and pour the hot onion gravy over and around.

Lamb Fillet with Beetroot and Mint Salad

You need best end of neck fillet or lamb loins for this dish. It is the eye fillet of the cutlets that makes up a rack, and it is quite an expensive cut, but really tender and flavoursome.

Preparation time 5 minutes **Cooking time** 20 minutes **Serves** 4

125 g (4 oz) Puy lentils

125 g (4 oz) fine green beans

4 tbsp extra virgin olive oil

2 lamb fillets (best end), about 300 g (10 oz) each

4 tbsp red wine

1 tbsp red wine vinegar

375 g (12 oz) cooked beetroot in natural juices, drained and diced

a small bunch mint, roughly chopped

salt and pepper

1 Put the lentils into a saucepan, cover with cold water and simmer for 20 minutes. Drain well and transfer to a bowl.

2 Meanwhile, blanch the green beans in lightly salted boiling water for 3 minutes. Drain and pat dry on kitchen paper.

3 Heat 1 tablespoon of the oil in a frying pan and fry the lamb fillets for 7 minutes for rare lamb. Transfer to a low oven at 150°C (300°F), Gas Mark 2, to rest for 5 minutes, reserving the juices in the pan.

4 Add the wine to the pan juices and boil until 1 tablespoon remains. Remove from the heat and whisk in the vinegar, remaining oil and salt and pepper, to taste.

5 Combine the lentils, beans, beetroot and mint leaves in a bowl, add the dressing and toss to coat. Serve with the lamb.

Poultry and game

Most of us are familiar with dealing with poultry, in particular chicken and turkey, but it's always useful to have the basics in preparation and cooking. Game, however, isn't as familiar to us so here are a few tips on the basics.

Storing poultry

• Raw poultry can be stored in a refrigerator for up to four days, but if you buy it from a supermarket check the best before date. For longer storage, freeze on purchase.

• Freezer burn on a frozen chicken will make it dry and tasteless, so wrap it well.

• Thaw frozen birds or poultry joints thoroughly before cooking. There should be no ice crystals on the inside or undue coldness before cooking begins.

• Thaw slowly in the refrigerator, at room temperature, or in a bath of cold water. Never use warm water to speed up the defrosting process, as this will spoil the texture of the meat.

• As soon as possible, remove the giblet bag so that air can get to the cavity.

Jointing

Jointing a whole bird is not as difficult as you may think. You will need a strong cook's knife or poultry shears for the best results.

1 Place the bird breast side up on a board and cut off the wing tips at the last joint. These have no meat on them so discard them unless you are planning to make stock or a soup.

2 To remove the leg and thigh in one portion, pull the leg away from the body and slice through the skin and flesh where the thigh joins the body. Cut through the ball and socket joint at the base of the thigh. Repeat to remove the other leg.

3 If necessary, divide each leg portion into two smaller pieces by cutting through the joint between the drumstick and the thigh.

4 Hold the chicken upright with the neck end downwards. Cut down firmly widthways through the body, separating the top, breast side (and wings) from the underside of the body. When you have cut through the ribs, pull the top and underside of the carcass apart. The bony underside of the carcass can be used for making stock or soup, or can be discarded if you don't need it.

5 Place the breast half of the carcass skin upwards. Cut in half along the backbone, cutting close to the bone from the ridge of the breast and down through one side. Repeat on the second side, giving two portions each with breast and wing.

6 Cut each breast portion in half again, if required. Cut across the middle just behind the wing to separate the breast from the wing. If you want the wing portion to be meatier, include some of the breast with it.

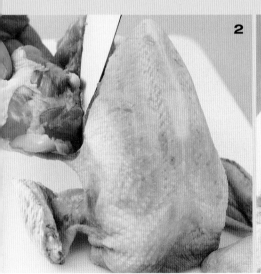
2

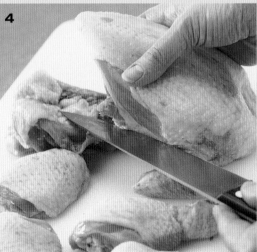
4

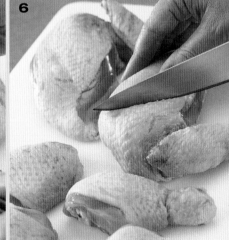
6

Preparing poultry

Preparing poultry first can improve the flavour, reduce the fat content as well as aid the cooking process. Choose a bird with plump breasts, a dry skin and no sign of deterioration or bruising. The legs should be flexible. Generally, the more you pay for a bird, the better the flavour – the more expensive birds tend to be organic and/or free range, having been fed on a better diet and allowed to roam around, hence the more flavoursome meat.

Skinning portions

Much of the fat in poultry is in and directly under the skin, so if you remove the skin, the fat level (and the saturated fat level) will be considerably reduced. To remove the skin from joints, use the point of a knife to loosen the skin from the flesh. Using a firm grip, grasp the skin with a piece of kitchen paper and pull it away.

Flattening breast fillets

To prepare breast fillets for cooking, place a boneless, skinless fillet between two large sheets of non-stick baking paper or clingfilm then use a rolling pin or meat hammer to beat the breast all over the surface, flattening it evenly, then remove the paper or film. The beaten-out poultry breast is ready for stuffing and rolling or for coating with egg and breadcrumbs before shallow-frying.

Spatchcocking

This is used for small and medium birds, such as poussin, small chickens, pheasant, quail or guinea fowl so that they lie flat and can be grilled, barbecued or roasted quickly and evenly. Spatchcocked birds can be marinated or flavoured with herbs and spices before cooking.

1 With the bird breast side down, use a strong knife or poultry shears to cut through the flesh and ribs to one side of the backbone.

2 Cut down the other side of the backbone, then remove and discard it. Remove the small wishbone at the neck end.

3 Turn the bird over, breast side up. To open out and flatten the bird, press firmly on the breastbone with the heel of your hand.

4 To keep the bird flat and easy to turn during cooking, thread two wooden or metal skewers diagonally across through the bird. Push the first through a wing on one side and out through the thickest part of the thigh on the other side. Push the second skewer through parallel to the first towards the other end of the bird.

Above Poultry breast meat can be beaten flat to help it cook quickly or to allow it to be rolled around a delicious stuffing.

Kitchen hygiene

- Wash your hands and utensils thoroughly before and after handling raw poultry as it can be contaminated with salmonella, a common cause of food poisoning.
- Prepare raw poultry on non-porous boards that can be washed in hot water and bleach.
- Avoid any contact between cooked and raw foods, during both storage and preparation.
- Cool poultry that you have cooked for eating later as quickly as possible. When cool, cover or wrap in clingfilm and refrigerate as soon as possible. It can be stored in the refrigerator for up to two days.
- If you want to reheat cooked poultry, do it thoroughly. It is better to reheat the meat in a sauce or gravy to prevent it drying out. Make sure the liquid is boiling for at least 5 minutes and that the meat is piping hot before serving.

Marinating

Marinating moistens and flavours foods, particularly poultry and game, prior to grilling or roasting. The marinade can be a simple mixture of olive oil and lemon juice, but it is also an opportunity to add a delicious sauce, coating or glaze.

Arrange the joints or portions in a large dish, preferably in a single layer. Mix the marinade ingredients thoroughly and pour over the meat. Turn the pieces to coat them evenly, then cover with clingfilm and leave in the refrigerator to marinate for at least 30 minutes. Depending on the ingredients and the result required, marinating can take from minutes to hours, or even days. Drain off the excess marinade before cooking, reserving it to baste the meat or to make a sauce. Any of the following marinades can be used for grilled or barbecued poultry.

Herb and lemon marinade

Mix together:

4 tbsp dry white wine

4 tbsp olive oil

finely grated rind and juice ½ lemon

2 tbsp finely chopped fresh herbs, such as parsley, thyme and chives

freshly ground pepper

Honey and soy sauce

Mix together:

3 tbsp sunflower oil

2 tbsp clear honey

1 tbsp soy sauce

3 tbsp orange juice

1 tsp prepared English mustard

Spiced yogurt

Mix together:

50 ml (¼ pint) natural yogurt

1 small onion, minced

1 garlic clove, crushed

1 tsp grated fresh root ginger

1 tsp ground coriander

1 tsp ground turmeric

Orange marinade

Mix together:

juice and finely grated zest of 1 orange

1 cm (½-inch) piece fresh root ginger, peeled and finely chopped

3 tbsp honey

1 tbsp dark soy sauce

sea salt and black pepper

Stuffing a bird

It is best to stuff large whole birds only at the neck end. Stuffing the body cavity creates a dense area of food that slows down the heat penetration and can prevent thorough cooking. Cook any spare stuffing in a separate dish or roll it into balls and cook in the oven alongside the bird.

Before stuffing, make sure that the bird and stuffing are both at room temperature. Lift the neck flap of skin, loosening it gently from the meat with your fingers. Use a small, sharp knife to cut out the V-shaped wishbone just below the surface of the flesh. Spoon the stuffing into the neck cavity of the bird. Do not overfill the cavity since the stuffing will expand, and if it is packed in too tightly it may burst out in the oven. Smooth the skin back over the stuffing and tuck it underneath the bird to hold the stuffing in place.

Always weigh the bird after stuffing it to calculate the roasting time. Cook the bird promptly once stuffed or refrigerate it immediately until ready to cook.

Stuffings can consist of all sorts of different flavouring ingredients, but usually contain a starchy base such as breadcrumbs or cooked rice. A beaten egg helps to hold the stuffing together.

Below To keep the bird upright when spooning in the stuffing, place the bird neck-end up in a bowl.

Apricot stuffing
Mix together:

125 g (4 oz) ready-to-eat dried apricots

1 onion, chopped and fried in a little butter until soft

2 tbsp chopped parsley

finely grated rind ½ lemon

pinch mixed spice

75 g (3 oz) fresh breadcrumbs

1 egg, beaten

salt and pepper

Pecan stuffing
Mix together:

40 g (1½ oz) cooked rice

1 onion, chopped and fried in a little butter until soft

1 tbsp chopped parsley

1 tsp chopped thyme

40 g (1½ oz) chopped pecans

¼ tsp ground coriander

1 egg, beaten

salt and pepper

Stuffing a chicken breast

1 Place the breast skin- (or skinned-) side uppermost on a board. Use a sharp knife to cut a slit horizontally into the side of the breast. Slice into the flesh, cutting parallel with the board, to make a deep pocket in the flesh. Take care not to cut all the way through.

2 Use a small spoon to fill the pocket with stuffing – ricotta cheese flavoured with pesto makes a delicious change from traditional stuffings. Alternatively, tuck in sprigs of herbs, ready-soaked dried apricots, prunes or diced mozzarella cheese. Take care not to overfill the pocket or the stuffing will ooze out during cooking.

3 Secure the opening with a wooden cocktail stick or wrap a rasher of streaky bacon or a slice of Parma ham around the breast to keep the stuffing in place.

Scoring duck skin

When preparing duck breasts for grilling or frying with the skin on, use a sharp knife to score the skin deeply with lines or a diagonal pattern to allow the fat to run out evenly. When cooking fatty duck breasts, start under a high heat and cook until the skin is golden brown, then turn over and reduce the heat to finish cooking. Drain well on kitchen paper.

Cooking poultry

Like any meat, poultry needs careful cooking so that it stays moist and does not become dry and tough. You also need to ensure that chicken is cooked right through to avoid the risk of food poisoning.

Above Score the skin of duck breasts all over in a criss-cross pattern to allow the fat to run out freely and the skin to crisp.

Frying

Coating poultry portions helps to seal in flavour and juices when frying, and prevents low-fat cuts becoming dry. It can also be a good way of adding extra flavour.

Fresh fine white or brown breadcrumbs make a good coating, but they do not have to be plain. Try stirring in curry spices, chopped herbs, finely chopped nuts or sesame seeds. For a different texture, use freshly grated coconut, desiccated coconut or rolled oats. Dip the portions into flour and then into beaten egg before turning them in the mixture to coat them evenly.

Dry spice mixes can also be used to flavour poultry before frying or grilling. Brush the poultry with melted butter or oil and turn the pieces in a mixture of dry spices until evenly coated. To do this easily with the minimum of mess, put the spices in a large polythene bag, add the poultry pieces and hold the bag closed while tossing the poultry in the spices.

Hot cajun spice mix
Mix together:

2 tsp garlic salt

2 tsp black pepper

1½ tsp paprika

1½ tsp ground cumin

1 tsp cayenne pepper

Roasting

To roast poultry, especially chicken and turkey, successfully, do not truss the bird too tightly, since this can prevent even cooking. Usually, it is enough to tie the ends of the drumsticks together to hold the bird in shape. This keeps the cavity open and allows hot air to get inside and cook the bird right through. The centre of the bird is thus cooked before the outside has dried out too much.

To prevent poultry from drying out too much, turkey in particular, you can cover the top of the breast with streaky bacon. This will keep it moist during cooking as well as giving the bird extra flavour. Alternatively, it can be smeared with butter and covered loosely with foil or basted regularly during cooking. For large birds that require lengthy cooking, such as turkey, the breast should be covered with foil once it has browned to prevent it from overcooking and drying out. Remove the foil for the final 15–30 minutes of cooking time to crisp up the skin.

To allow fat to drain away easily from fatty poultry, such as duck or goose, prick the skin with a fork or skewer, penetrating through to the flesh. This allows the fat directly under the skin to run out as it melts during roasting. Always roast fatty birds on a rack in a deep roasting tin to raise the bird above the fat, which collects during cooking. If you don't have a rack, use scrunched-up foil instead. Pour off the fat occasionally, especially when roasting goose.

Is it cooked?

Poultry must be cooked thoroughly to avoid any risk of contamination and food poisoning. Use a fork or metal skewer to pierce the meat deeply through the thickest part of the flesh – usually the thigh area of a whole bird. When you pull out the fork, press gently and the juices that run out should be clear, not pink. If there is any trace of pink, the meat is not cooked.

Duck and goose can be served a little pink inside, which helps to keep the meat moist, but all other types of poultry should be cooked through.

Turkey roasting times
Oven temperature 190°C (375°F), Gas Mark 5.

	Time
1.5–2.3 kg (3–5 lb)	1½ -1¾ hours
2.7–3.2 kg (6–7 lb)	1¾-2 hours
3.6–4 kg (8–9 lb)	2-2½ hours
4.5–5 kg (10–11 lb)	2¼-2¾ hours
5.4–5.9 kg (12–13 lb)	2¾-3 hours
6.3–6.8 kg (14–17 lb)	3¼-3½ hours
8.2–10 kg (18–22 lb)	3½-3¾ hours

Roasting times
Oven temperature and roasting times vary depending on the type of bird.

	Time	Temperature
Chicken	20 mins per 500 g (1 lb), plus 20 mins	190°C (375°F), Gas Mark 5
Duckling	15 mins per 500 g (1 lb), plus 15 mins	200°C (400°F), Gas Mark 6
Goose	15 mins per 500 g (1 lb), plus 15 mins	200°C (400°F), Gas Mark 6
Guinea fowl	20 mins per 500 g (1 lb), plus 20 mins	190°C (375°F), Gas Mark 5
Poussin	45–60 minutes (depending on size)	190°C (375°F), Gas Mark 5
Pheasant	about 50 minutes	200°C (400°F), Gas Mark 6
Partridge	about 40 minutes	200°C (400°F), Gas Mark 6
Grouse	30–45 minutes (depending on size)	200°C (400°F), Gas Mark 6
Pigeon	about 30 minutes	200°C (400°F), Gas Mark 6
Quail	20 minutes	200°C (400°F), Gas Mark 6

Above Start carving by removing the legs using a sharp knife to allow easier access to the breast.

Above Carve the breast meat into even slices. Start on one side of the breast, then repeat on the other side.

Carving

Chicken and turkey The only essential tools are a sharp knife and a carving fork to hold the bird safely in position. Once the bird is roasted, remove it from the oven and leave it in a warm place for 15 minutes. This allows the meat time to become firmer and easier to carve. Next place the bird, breast uppermost, on a board and remove any trussing string or skewers.

Lift one end of a drumstick and use it to pull the whole leg away from the body, then cut through the joint between the thigh and the body. Cut the leg in half at the joint to separate the thigh and drumstick. If it is large, carve off the meat in slices. Now cut down through the corner of the breast where the wing joins the body, cutting off the wing with some of the adjoining breast meat. Continue cutting the meat down into slices on one side of the breast, working back from the wing end. Repeat the process on the other side of the bird.

Duck and goose As before, place the bird breast-side up on a board. Lift one end of a drumstick and use it to pull the whole leg away from the body, then cut through the joint between the thigh and the body. Serve the leg portions whole.

Next cut down through the corner of the breast next to the wing, cutting through the joint to separate the wing from the body. Cut off the meat down the length of one side of the body, carving it vertically in long, narrow slices. Repeat the process on the other side of the bird.

Choosing game

Game is always hung for a number of days before it is plucked or skinned to tenderize the meat and develop the flavour. The length of time required for hanging depends on the type of game, the weather conditions and the degree of ripeness preferred. Always check with your butcher how long the game has been hung and therefore how strong the flavour will be. Also check on the age of the animal. Young animals can be simply roasted or grilled, whereas older ones, which are tougher with more flavour, are better for casseroles and pies.

Some types of game – venison, quails and rabbits, for example – are now farmed, so they are available all year and the quality is more consistent. Farmed venison is wonderfully tender as only the young animals are used.

Cooking game

All these meats can be a little dry as they contain little fat. Young rabbits and hares can be simply roasted if they are draped in streaky bacon or brushed with oil, but older animals will need to be cooked more slowly in pies, casseroles, game terrines and pâtés for best results.

Most venison that is available now is farmed, which means it comes from young, tender animals. Larger joints are good for roasting, but be sure to brush with oil and baste well to keep the meat moist. Whole joints can also be pot-roasted or braised in a little liquid to prevent them from drying out. Vension chops can be grilled, pan-fried or roasted, but do not overcook. Use cubed venison for rich pies, stews and casseroles.

Chicken with Mozzarella and Sun-dried Tomatoes

These tasty stuffed chicken breasts are delicious served with roasted vine tomatoes and rocket leaves, drizzled with a little olive oil.

Preparation time 20 minutes **Cooking time** 25 minutes **Serves** 4

4 boneless, skinless chicken breasts

125 g (4 oz) mozzarella cheese, cut into 4 thick slices

4 large pieces of sun-dried tomato in oil, drained

2 tbsp olive oil

8 slices of Parma ham

salt and pepper

lemon wedges, to serve (optional)

1 Cut a long horizontal slit through the thickest part of each chicken breast without cutting right through. Stuff each chicken breast with a thick slice of mozzarella and a large piece of sun-dried tomato. Season with salt and pepper.

2 Heat the oil in a shallow flameproof casserole, add the stuffed chicken breasts and sauté for 4 minutes on each side. Transfer the casserole to a preheated oven at 200°C (400°F), Gas Mark 6, and cook for 15 minutes. While the chicken is cooking, pan-fry the Parma ham for 1 minute only, just to make it crispy.

3 Place the cooked chicken breasts on serving plates, and top each with 2 slices of the Parma ham. Serve each with a wedge of lemon, if liked.

Tandoori Chicken

Spicy tandoori chicken is very popular, and it couldn't be easier to make. The chicken quarters are simply baked in the oven after marinating.

4 large chicken quarters, skinned

200 ml (7 fl oz) natural yogurt

1 tsp grated fresh root ginger

2 garlic cloves, crushed

1 tsp garam masala

2 tsp ground coriander

¼ tsp ground turmeric

1 tbsp tandoori masala

4 tbsp lemon juice

1 tbsp vegetable oil

sea salt

lime or lemon wedges, to garnish

Preparation time 10 minutes, plus marinating **Cooking time** 20 minutes **Serves** 4

1 Put the chicken into a non-metallic, shallow, ovenproof dish and make 3 deep slashes in each piece, to allow the flavours to penetrate. Set aside.

2 In a bowl, mix together the yogurt, ginger, garlic, garam masala, ground coriander, turmeric, tandoori masala, lemon juice and oil. Season with salt and spread the mixture over the chicken pieces to cover. Cover and marinate overnight in the refrigerator, if time allows.

3 Bake the chicken in a preheated oven at 240°C (475°F), Gas Mark 9, for 20 minutes or until cooked through. Remove from the oven and serve hot, garnished with lime or lemon wedges.

Roast Turkey with Chestnut and Apple Stuffing

The tartness of the apple counterbalances the richness of the meat in this classic festive dish.

Preparation time about 30 minutes **Cooking time** 2¾–3¼ hours **Serves** 8

4.5–5.4 kg (10–12 lb) oven ready turkey

1 small onion, peeled and halved

40 g (1½ oz) butter, softened

2 tbsp vegetable oil

salt and pepper

freshly cooked vegetables, to serve

Stuffing

500 g (1 lb) canned chestnuts, drained

4 shallots, finely chopped

1 tbsp chopped parsley

1 small egg, beaten

500 g (1 lb) dessert apples, peeled, cored and chopped

250 g (8 oz) belly pork, finely chopped

1 To make the stuffing, chop the chestnuts and mix with the shallots, parsley and egg, and season with salt and pepper to taste. Mix the apples into the stuffing, with the pork. Pack the stuffing loosely into the neck cavity of the bird. Smooth the skin back over and tuck underneath the bird to hold in place. Place the onion in the body cavity and season to taste with salt and pepper. Weigh the stuffed turkey and calculate the roasting time (see page 74).

2 Place the turkey in a large roasting tin and rub all over with butter. Add the oil to the tin and season the outside of the turkey with salt and pepper.

3 Roast in a preheated oven at 190°C (375°F), Gas mark 5, basting from time to time, for 2¾–3¼ hours, or until the juices run clear. Cover with greaseproof paper or foil when the bird is sufficiently browned.

4 Transfer the turkey to a large dish. Pour off the fat from the tin and use the juices to make the gravy (see page 65). Arrange the turkey on a warmed serving platter and serve with the gravy and an assortment of vegetables.

4 duck quarters

2 tsp Chinese five spice powder

2 lemon grass stalks, bruised

5 garlic cloves, crushed

4 shallots, chopped

125 g (4 oz) dried shiitake mushrooms, soaked in boiling water for 30 minutes

5-cm (2-inch) piece of fresh root ginger, peeled and cut into matchsticks

600 ml (1 pint) Chicken Stock (see page 161)

25 g (1 oz) dried cranberries

15 g (½ oz) dried black fungus (optional), broken into pieces

1 tbsp fish sauce

2 tsp cornflour

4 spring onions, each cut into four

salt and pepper

coriander sprigs, to serve

Aromatic Braised Duck

In this fragrant Vietnamese dish, the duck is first fried to brown the skin, then slowly braised in stock until meltingly soft. Stir-fried pak choi and plain boiled rice are good accompaniments to this dish.

Preparation time 15 minutes **Cooking time** 2¼ hours **Serves** 4

1 Season the duck portions with the five spice powder. Place the duck skin-side down in a very hot frying pan or casserole to brown the skin. Add the lemon grass, garlic, shallots, mushrooms and ginger to the pan then cover the duck with the chicken stock. Cover the pan with a lid and simmer very gently for 1½ hours.

2 Remove the duck from the pan and add the cranberries, black fungus (if using), fish sauce and season with salt and pepper to taste. Mix the cornflour to a smooth paste with a little water and add to the pan. Stirring constantly, bring the sauce to the boil and cook until thickened. Return the duck to the pan and simmer gently for about 30 minutes.

3 Add the spring onions to the sauce and serve the duck with coriander sprigs.

Venison Steaks with Red Fruit Sauce

Tender venison steaks are quickly seared in a hot dry pan and served with a fruit sauce. Venison steak from the loin or fillet is not always available, so ask your butcher if he can recommend another cut.

Preparation time 10 minutes, plus marinating **Cooking time** 20 minutes **Serves** 4

1 tsp crushed juniper berries

4 x 175 g (6 oz) venison steaks, from the fillet or loin

salt and pepper

shredded orange rind, to garnish

Sauce
125 g (4 oz) redcurrant jelly

125 g (4 oz) cranberries

grated rind and juice of 1 orange

2 tablespoons red wine

1 Mix the crushed juniper berries with some pepper and spread over both sides of the venison steaks. Set aside to allow the flavours to mingle for at least 1 hour, but preferably overnight.

2 To make the sauce, place the ingredients in a small saucepan and simmer gently for 10 minutes, stirring constantly.

3 Heat a stove-top grill pan or frying pan until hot. Add the venison steaks and cook for 3 minutes on each side for rare, or 5 minutes for well done. Serve immediately with the red fruit sauce poured over the top and garnished with the shredded orange rind.

Seafood for beginners

Many cooks are nervous of dealing with fresh fish and seafood, but it is really quite simple. If you don't fancy filleting or boning the fish yourself, get your fishmonger to do it – most are very happy to help out.

Choosing and buying fish

Always buy fish from a reputable fishmonger to ensure it is perfectly fresh. A good fishmonger will trim, scale, skin, gut and fillet for you in a matter of seconds. Seafood perishes more quickly than meat and poultry, so take great care, when you come to buy it, that it is fresh. Look for all the following signs:
• Your supplier's shop should be clean, have plenty of ice and display the fish well.
• Freshness is easily seen in a whole fish. It should be stiff and firm, not limp.
• Eyes should be full, shiny and bright, and never sunken or opaque.
• The skin should be shiny, not dry and gritty.
• The gills should be rosy pink, not brownish or dry.
• Fillets should be translucent, not milky white, firm with no sign of discoloration, and spring to the touch.
• The flesh should be intact.
• Smoked fish should have a bright, glossy surface, a firm texture and a pleasant smoky smell.
• Commercially frozen fish which has been thawed out badly will be unpleasantly watery and woolly.
Fish should be eaten as fresh as possible, at least within 24 hours of purchase. Otherwise it should be cleaned, gutted and frozen. Fish fillets and steaks can be prepared up to 12 hours in advance, loosely covered in foil and refrigerated. To keep fish overnight, wrap it in several layers of newspaper and put it in the coldest part of the refrigerator.

Fresh mackerel, herrings and sardines are best eaten on the day of purchase.

Right Filleting a flat fish, such as sole or plaice, results in four small fillets. The flesh is eased off the bones rather than cut.

Preparing fish

If you are not cooking your fish whole, follow the guidelines below for different ways to prepare fish.

Boning whole round fish

1 Cut off the head, tail and fins. Slit the fish along the belly side, where it has been cleaned, and place it skin-side uppermost on a board.
2 Using your thumbs, press down firmly along the backbone, to release the bone from the flesh.
3 Turn the fish over and lift out the bone, easing it out with a knife if necessary. Any fine bones that are left may be removed with tweezers.

Filleting round fish

1 Holding the fish firmly, cut through behind the gills on one side to separate the fillet from the head.
2 Cut along and into the backbone, from tail to head, then slide the knife between the flesh of the top fillet and bones. Lift the fillet gently away from the bones as you release it from the backbone.
3 Turn the fish over and remove the fillet on the other side in the same way.

Filleting flat fish

1 Lay the fish on a board. Cut a line down the back along the centre of the fish, from the head to the tail.
2 Starting at the head end, insert the knife under the flesh, between it and the bones. Using long strokes, slide the knife between the flesh and bones. Keep the blade flat against the bones and work towards the outer edge, turning back the loosened fillet as you go.
3 Remove the fillet on the other side of the fish, then turn the fish over to remove the fillets on the underside.

Skinning fish fillets

1 Place the fillet skin-side down on a board with the tail end towards you. Dip your fingers in salt to give a good grip, and hold the tail end of the fillet.

2 Use the tip of a knife to separate the flesh from the skin at the tail end. Grasp the skin firmly, then hold the knife at a slight angle so that it is almost parallel to the fish skin, and slide it between the skin and flesh.

3 Use a sawing action to cut the flesh off the skin and fold the fillet back as you go.

Coating fish fillets with flour

When shallow-frying fish fillets, a simple flour coating will keep the juices in and prevent the flesh of the fish from breaking up during the cooking process.

1 Sprinkle a shallow layer of plain or wholemeal flour on a large plate and season it with salt and pepper.

2 Pour a shallow covering of milk into a wide dish. Wash the fish and dry it on kitchen paper. Dip the fillets into the milk, turning to moisten both sides evenly, then drain off the excess.

3 Dip the fish into the flour. Press and turn to coat the other side.

Oily fish fillets, such as mackerel, herring or trout, are excellent coated in oatmeal or rolled oats instead of flour before frying.

Cooking fish

Since fish has such a small amount of connective tissue, it requires very little cooking. If it is overcooked, the flakes fall apart and the fibres become tough, dry and tasteless so pay attention to the cooking time. There are several ways of cooking fish, but the process should, in general, be short and gentle. Although fillets are popular, most cooks agree that fish on the bone – as with meat – has more flavour.

TOP TIPS

- Cook only very fresh fish – if possible, buy the fish on the day you plan to cook it.
- Most fish cooks quickly and dries out if cooked for too long.
- To test whether fish is cooked, insert the point of a knife into the thickest part of the flesh: it should flake apart and lift away from the bone easily. Cooked fish should be opaque right through.
- Serve fish as soon as it is cooked – if it is kept hot it will dry out and lose its flavour.

Above To skin a fillet of fish, lay it on a board skin-side down. Hold the skin tightly and draw a sharp knife between it and the flesh.

Frying

Fish can be shallow- or deep-fried. Coat the flesh with egg and breadcrumbs, batter, flour or oatmeal to protect the delicate flesh. Use vegetable oil for deep-frying, and a combination of butter and oil for shallow-frying.

Grilling

This method is used for whole fish, steaks, fillets and cutlets, particularly oily fish. The flesh is usually scored with a knife (if the fish is on the bone) to ensure even and thorough cooking. Dot the fish with butter to prevent it drying out. Set the grill at a moderate heat rather than high, so that the fish does not dry out. The smaller the fish, the higher the grill.

Baking

Fish can be baked whole, brushed with butter or oil, and stuffed; they may be open or lightly covered with buttered foil for protection. They can also be cooked in a liquid (milk, sauce, wine, stock).

Poaching

This method ensures that the fish remains moist. It is cooked in a liquid, such as fish stock, wine, water or milk, which can be flavoured with herbs, a little onion or lemon juice. Cook the fish on top of the stove in a pan or fish kettle, or in the oven. The liquor is usually used as a basis for the accompanying sauce.

Steaming

This is a moist and gentle way to cook fish. Place the fish in a heatproof dish and add flavouring ingredients, such as herbs, spices, wine or soy sauce. Place the dish in a steamer and cook over a saucepan of gently simmering water until the fish is opaque.

Shellfish

The following tips cover the preparation and cooking of the most common types of shellfish.

Lobster

If the lobster is live, place it in the freezer for 20 minutes to make it drowsy. Bring a large pan of salted water to the boil and add the lobster. Cover with a lid and simmer for 15–20 minutes until the shell turns bright red. Leave to cool in the cooking liquor. Next twist off the lobster's claws. Using shellfish crackers, a hammer or a heavy knife, crack the claws and pull out the white meat. Turn the lobster on its back and use a sharp, heavy knife to cut it in half lengthways down the middle. Remove the thin grey vein of intestine running along its back.

Remove the lobster tail meat from the two shells. You can also remove and eat the liver – the grey-green flesh near the head – which is delicious. Using a lobster pick or skewer, pick out any white flesh in the head. If it is a female lobster it may also have tasty red coral (roe).

Prawns

To peel either raw or cooked prawns, grip the head between finger and thumb, and pinch it firmly to pull it away from the body. Grip the legs and pull them away. Peel off the shell. You can leave the tip of the tail in place if you like.

The dark intestinal vein in large prawns, such as tiger prawns, has a bitter flavour, so remove it before cooking. Make a shallow cut along the curved back of the prawn, then use the tip of the knife to scrape out the black vein.

To butterfly large prawns, peel them when raw leaving the tail on. Use a sharp knife to cut a deep slit down the underside, from head to tail, cutting almost through to the other side, but leaving the two halves attached. Place the prawns, cut-side down, on a board and press flat to open them out into a butterfly shape. Dip into lightly whisked egg white, then into cornflour, shaking off any excess. Deep-fry in hot oil until golden, then serve hot with a dip or soy sauce.

Crab

1 If the crab is live, put it into a large saucepan, cover with cold water and add a tablespoon of salt. Cover with a lid, slowly bring to the boil and simmer gently for 10–12 minutes per 500 g (1 lb). Leave to cool in the cooking liquor.
2 When it is cold, rinse the crab under cold water. Place it shell down on a large board, with the legs uppermost. Twist off the legs and claws at the joints with the body.
3 With the tail flap facing you, hold the crab firmly with both hands, and using the thumbs push and prise the body section or 'apron' upwards so that the whole body section is released from the hard back shell.

4 Pull away and discard the greyish white stomach sac (just behind the mouth) and the long, white, pointed 'dead men's fingers' which are very obvious.
5 Using a small spoon, scoop out all the brown meat from the back shell. Next use a crab pick or skewer to pick out the white meat from all the little crevices in the crab body section, dismantling the shell as you go. Be careful to remove all pieces of shell.
6 Crack the claws, using a hammer or shellfish crackers, and remove the white meat. Break the legs at the joints and extract the meat.
7 Now, either pile the brown and white meat back into the large shell and serve with bread and mayonnaise, or use the crab meat in a recipe.

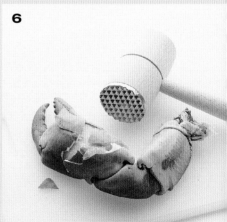

Above Remove the dark intestinal vein along the back of each prawn before cooking, using a small sharp knife.

Oysters

An oyster knife is the ideal tool for this, but any short, strong, thick-bladed knife will do the job. Hold the oyster in a clean tea towel to protect your hand, with the rounded side underneath and the flatter shell on top. Holding firmly, carefully push the knife point through the hinge between the two sides of the shell. Slide the knife blade to and fro, twisting it slightly to break the hinge. Lift off the top part of the shell, taking care not to spill the juices which are retained in the lower shell.

Scallops

If the scallops are in their shells, slide a knife between the top and bottom shells and twist apart, cutting the muscle that attaches the scallop to the shell. Discard the flat shell. Pull off the grey frill and black intestinal thread that runs from the central white muscle to the base of the coral tongue. If the scallops are large, separate the coral from the white muscle and slice the white part into rounds.

Scallops need very little cooking as they will shrink, become tough and lose their flavour if overcooked. Simply sear in a hot pan, stir-fry or grill or steam in their shells until they turn opaque. They should be only just cooked inside.

Squid

Wash the squid well in cold water. Holding the body in one hand, pull off the head and tentacles. Feel inside the body pouch and pull out the pen or quill (a long piece of cartilage that looks like a semi-transparent stick) and the ink sac, if not already removed with the head parts. Unless the ink is needed for the recipe, both of these can be discarded. Rub off and pull away the mottled membrane covering the body pouch. Remove and discard the mouth from the centre of the cluster of tentacles. Small squid may be left whole, or larger ones sliced into rings or strips. Cut up the tentacles into smaller pieces if necessary.

Squid needs to be cooked either hot and quick, or long and slow, or it will be tough. It lends itself to fast stir-frying, deep-frying, barbecuing or poaching, or long slow cooking in a paella or seafood stew.

Mussels

To clean mussels, place them in a bowl of cold water, then scrub them under running water with a stiff brush to remove any dirt. Scrape off any barnacles with a knife and pull off the hairy 'beard' protruding from the edge of the shell by holding the mussel under the water and pulling at the same time (the mussel will open a fraction if in water which allows the beard to come away freely). Rinse well. Discard any damaged mussels or any open mussels that do not close when tapped.

To cook the mussels, heat about 150 ml (¼ pint) of dry white wine, fish or vegetable stock, or water in a large saucepan with a few parsley sprigs and slices of onion for flavour. When the liquid boils, tip in the mussels and cover the pan with a tight-fitting lid. Cook for 3–4 minutes, shaking the pan occasionally, until the mussels open. Use a slotted spoon to remove the mussels from the pan and discard any shells that have not opened during cooking.

Below Once you get the knack, opening oysters is fairly simple. Make sure you have the deep shell underneath.

Paella

Paella is a Spanish dish of rice and seafood. It also contains meat such as chicken or rabbit, but this can be omitted if you prefer. Saffron gives the dish a wonderful colour and flavour.

Preparation time 15 minutes **Cooking time** 40–45 minutes **Serves** 4

4 skinless, boneless chicken thighs

2 garlic cloves, crushed

1 onion, chopped

½ red pepper, deseeded and chopped

1 tablespoon olive oil

250 g (8 oz) risotto rice

125 g (4 oz) squid, cleaned and sliced into rings (see page 83)

pinch of saffron strands

600 ml (1 pint) Fish Stock (see page 161)

1 bay leaf

250 g (8 oz) fresh mussels in their shells, scrubbed (see page 83)

50 g (2 oz) unpeeled raw prawns

50 g (2 oz) frozen petit pois

salt and pepper

chopped parsley, to garnish

1 Place the chicken, garlic, onion and red pepper in a heavy-based frying pan, together with the oil. Fry over a medium heat for about 10 minutes, turning the chicken so that it is golden all over.

2 Add the rice and squid and continue cooking for 5 minutes, until the rice starts to turn opaque. Stir in the saffron and pour over the stock. Add the bay leaf.

3 Add the shellfish to the rice mixture and lower the heat to a gently simmer. Cook, without stirring, for 20–25 minutes, until the rice is tender and the stock absorbed. About 5 minutes from the end of the cooking time, add the peas. Stir occasionally. Season to taste with salt and pepper, sprinkle with chopped parsley and serve immediately.

Lobsters with Garlic Sauce

Roasting lobsters in a really hot oven is a good way to cook them. Unfortunately, for the best results, the lobster must be cut in half while alive – your fishmonger can do this for you.

Preparation time 15 minutes **Cooking time** 15 minutes **Serves** 4

4 whole lobsters, each about 500 g (1 lb), cut in half

8 large rosemary sprigs, about 15 cm (6 in) long

salt and pepper

Garlic sauce
200 ml (7 fl oz) extra virgin olive oil

4 red chillies, deseeded and finely chopped

4 garlic cloves, crushed

2 tablespoons snipped rosemary

juice of 1 lemon

salt and pepper

1 First prepare the garlic sauce. Mix together all the ingredients in a bowl and season with salt and pepper to taste.

2 Using a mallet or rolling pin, crack the claws of each lobster to allow the meat to cook more evenly and ease eating.

3 Using half of the sprigs, make a bed of rosemary in a shallow roasting dish and place the lobsters, shell-side down, on top. Spoon over a little of the sauce, season with salt and pepper and cover with the remaining rosemary. Roast in a preheated oven, 240°C (475°F), Gas Mark 9, for 15 minutes.

4 Allow the lobster to rest for a few minutes, then serve with the remaining garlic sauce drizzled over the flesh.

Roast Cod with Beetroot Mash and Butter Beans

Beetroot is fabulously sweet and utterly delicious when it is simply roasted, wrapped in foil. The beets can be served whole or they can be roughly mashed to a purée.

Preparation time 25 minutes **Cooking time** 2 hours **Serves** 4

4 x 175 g (6 oz) thick cod steaks

4 tbsp olive oil, plus extra for drizzling

2 garlic cloves

400 g (14 oz) butter beans

1 tbsp chopped flat leaf parsley

salt and pepper

Beetroot mash
1 kg (2 lb) raw beetroot

1–2 tbsp freshly grated horseradish or creamed horseradish

1 Wrap each beetroot in foil and bake in a preheated oven, 200°C (400°F), Gas Mark 6, for 1–2 hours, depending on the size of the beets. They are cooked when the tip of a knife or skewer can be inserted easily into the flesh. Remove the beets from the oven, remove the foil wrapping, allow to cool slightly, and peel away the skins. Allow to cool completely.

2 Meanwhile, season the cod steaks with a little salt and pepper, place them in a roasting tin and drizzle with a little olive oil. Roast in the centre of the oven for 15–20 minutes or until the flesh is just cooked through.

3 To make the mash, roughly chop the beetroot and place it in a food processor or blender with the horseradish and salt and pepper and blend to a coarse purée.

4 Heat the olive oil in a saucepan, add the garlic and fry gently for 30–60 seconds. Do not allow the garlic to burn. Add the butter beans and chopped parsley and toss in the hot oil for 1–2 minutes, then remove from the heat.

5 Serve the cod hot from the oven on a large spoonful, or two, of beetroot mash and accompanied by the garlic butter beans.

Salmon Fish Cakes with Spinach and Poached Egg

Salmon fish cakes are quick to make and cook and are delicious served with homemade chips and a green salad.

Preparation time 20 minutes, plus chilling **Cooking time** 20 minutes **Serves** 4

250 g (8 oz) King Edward potatoes, quartered

300 g (10 oz) salmon fillet, skinned and bones removed

1–2 tbsp plain flour

6–8 tbsp sunflower or groundnut oil

500 g (1 lb) spinach leaves

4 eggs

salt and pepper

1 Put the potatoes into a saucepan of boiling water and boil until they are just cooked – test by piercing with a sharp knife. Drain well and leave to cool.

2 Either roughly chop the salmon or process it briefly in a food processor to make a coarse mince. Using a fork or the back or a wooden spoon, roughly mash the potatoes with salt and pepper. Add the minced salmon and mix together.

3 With floured hands, divide the mixture into 4 pieces and press firmly into 4 plump fish cakes. Coat each fish cake in flour and chill in the refrigerator for about 1 hour.

4 Put the oil in a large frying pan and heat until hot. Add the fish cakes to the hot oil and cook for 3–4 minutes on each side.

5 Shake the washed spinach leaves dry, pack them into a saucepan and cover with a lid. Heat gently for 2–3 minutes or until the spinach just begins to wilt. Drain the spinach thoroughly and season with a little salt and pepper.

6 Poach the eggs (see page 126) until just cooked. Remove the fish cakes from the oil and set them on individual plates, on a bed of spinach. Top each one with some of the spinach and finish with a hot poached egg.

Mussels with Cream and Saffron

This makes an impressive starter for four or a simple and satisfying supper for two. Serve in large bowls with plenty of crusty bread. You probably won't need to add any salt as the mussels will be a little salty.

Preparation time 25 minutes **Cooking time** 15 minutes **Serves** 2–4

2 kg (4 lb) mussels

150 ml (¼ pint) double cream

¼ tsp saffron threads

15 g (½ oz) butter

1 shallot, chopped

3 parsley stalks

6 large celery leaves

300 ml (½ pint) dry white wine

2 tbsp chopped flat leaf parsley, to garnish

1 Prepare the mussels according to the instructions on page 83.

2 Warm the cream in a small saucepan, add the saffron and heat almost to boiling point. Remove from the heat and cover the pan.

3 Melt the butter in a very large saucepan, then add the shallot, parsley stalks and celery leaves and cook gently for 4 minutes. Tip the mussels into the pot, add the wine and bring to the boil quickly. Cover the pan and cook for 3–4 minutes, until the mussel shells have opened. Lift out the mussels with a slotted spoon and place in a warm tureen or soup bowls. Discard any that have not opened.

4 Strain the cooking liquid into a clean pan and reheat, then add the cream. Boil together for a moment, then pour over the mussels and serve sprinkled with parsley.

Fresh Crab and Mango Salad

This bright, colourful salad contains a range of contrasting flavours – rich crab, hot chilli, sweet mango and tangy coriander, vinegar and mustard. Serve it as a light lunch dish or as a simple but elegant starter.

Preparation time 25 minutes **Cooking time** 3 minutes **Serves** 4

1 small egg yolk

1 tsp Dijon mustard

1 tbsp fresh lemon juice

8 tbsp extra virgin olive oil

250 g (8 oz) fresh crab meat

1 red chilli, deseeded and chopped

125 g (4 oz) fine green beans

1 small mango

1 head chicory

2 tbsp chopped coriander

salt and pepper

1 Whisk the egg yolk, mustard and lemon juice until frothy and then slowly whisk in 5 tablespoons of the oil. Season to taste with salt and pepper.

2 Carefully pick through the crab to remove any small pieces of shell or cartilage. Stir the chilli into the crab meat with the dressing.

3 Blanch the beans in lightly salted boiling water for 3 minutes. Drain and refresh under cold running water, then pat dry with kitchen paper. Peel the mango and then thinly slice the flesh from the stone. Separate the chicory into spears. Arrange the chicory, mango, beans and crab on serving plates.

4 In a food processor or blender, process the remaining oil with the coriander leaves and a little salt to make a fresh green tangy dressing. Pour the dressing around the salad and serve.

Vegetables and herbs

As well as being highly nutritional, vegetables and herbs can also be incredibly versatile.

Preparing vegetables

Most vegetables are straightforward to deal with, but there are ways to make preparation a little easier.

Slicing and chopping onions

When slicing an onion, cut it in half through the root, using a sharp knife. Peel both halves, but leave the root intact as this helps to reduce the eye-stinging effect and also gives you something to hold when cutting. Place one onion half cut-side down on a board and, using your knuckles as a guide, slice down with a forward action.

To chop an onion, peel and halve it as above, then place one half cut-side down on a board. Holding the root end, make a series of parallel vertical cuts from the root end, keeping all the pieces in place. Finally, slice across and the onion will fall apart into small pieces.

Shredding cabbage

Separate the leaves and cut away any thick stalk ends. Roll up several leaves firmly together. Holding the rolled leaves securely, use a sharp knife to slice across the roll – the cabbage will fall away in fine shreds.

Peeling tomatoes

There are two simple ways to peel tomatoes. The first is to drop them whole into a bowl of boiling water and leave for 1 minute. Then lift them out with a slotted spoon and drop them into a bowl of cold water. Slit the skins and peel. Alternatively, spear a tomato firmly on a fork then hold it in the flame of a gas hob. Turn the tomato evenly until the skin blisters and splits and peel.

Peeling peppers

The easiest way to remove the skins from peppers is to grill them until blistered and charred. This also tenderizes the flesh and improves its flavour. Preheat the grill on the hottest setting, cut the peppers in half and remove the seeds and core. Then place the peppers cut-side down on a foil-lined grill pan and place under the hot grill. Cook until the skins are blackened and split then remove from the heat and place the peppers in a plastic bag. Leave them until cool enough to handle, when the skins will peel easily.

Preparing asparagus

Slice or break off the woody ends of the larger spears of asparagus. Use a vegetable peeler to shave off any tough outer skin at the base. Trim the stalks to the same length for easier cooking.

TOP TIP

To crush garlic with a knife, place the unpeeled clove on a board and hit with the flat blade of a heavy knife. Peel off the skin, sprinkle with salt and chop. Press with the flat of the knife to mash the garlic to a paste.

Cutting julienne strips, or matchsticks

Trim the vegetables (carrots, courgettes, parsnips, swede) or peel them thinly, then cut them into 6-cm (2½-inch) lengths. Slice the lengths into 3-mm (⅛-inch) thick slices. Stack the slices, hold them together firmly, then slice them lengthways, as finely as possible, to make thin matchstick strips.

Vegetables prepared in this way are ideal for stir-fries as they cook quickly and evenly. They also look attractive served as an accompaniment to meat or fish.

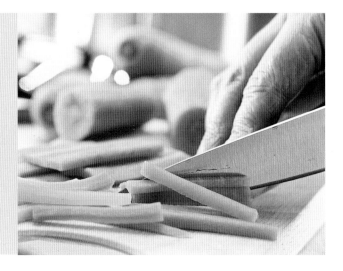

Preparing chillies

When preparing chillies, it is a good idea to wear rubber gloves as the juices from both the seeds and flesh can irritate the eyes and skin. Alternatively, wash your hands thoroughly after preparing the chillies and avoid touching your eyes until your hands are thoroughly clean.

The seeds are the hottest part of the chilli, so for a slightly milder flavour, you may prefer to remove the seeds before use. Discard the stalk from the chilli and cut it in half lengthways. Use the tip of a sharp knife to scrape out the seeds and pith from the centre. Slice or chop the flesh of the chilli.

Chopping herbs

Before chopping herbs, wash and dry them on a clean tea towel or on kitchen paper. Hold the leaves together firmly in a bunch and, using your knuckles as a guide, slice through the leaves with a straight-bladed, sharp knife to chop the herbs into coarse pieces. Hold the knife handle with one hand and the tip down firmly with the other hand, then use a rocking action to chop the herbs finely. Alternatively, use scissors to snip herbs, such as chives, directly on to food.

Preparing lettuce

Treat salad leaves gently because they bruise easily and can turn brown if overhandled. To prepare lettuce for a salad, first remove any damaged or coarse outer leaves from the lettuce head and break the remaining leaves off from the stem. Wash the leaves thoroughly in plenty of cold water to remove any dirt or pesticide residues, then drain the leaves and pat them dry very gently with a clean tea towel. Alternatively, put them in a salad spinner and spin to dry.

Most leaves should be torn into smaller pieces rather than being cut with a knife. This ensures the cells are left as undamaged as possible and the lettuce retains as many vitamins as possible. Use a very sharp knife if you want to shred the lettuce.

Salting aubergines

To remove the bitter juices from aubergines, and to help them absorb less oil during cooking, salt them before use. Slice or dice the aubergine, depending on your recipe, then place it in a colander, sprinkling liberally with salt between layers. Leave to drain for about 30 minutes, then rinse under cold running water and dry on kitchen paper. If you plan to cook the aubergines in halves, score the cut surface of the flesh deeply in a diamond pattern with a sharp knife and sprinkle with salt, then drain and rinse.

Above Wear gloves when preparing chillies to avoid the juice getting on your hands. Remove the seeds for a milder flavour.

Preparing avocado

Prepare avocado just before serving as the flesh will discolour when exposed to air. Alternatively, brush the cut surfaces with lemon juice or vinegar to prevent them going brown.

Cut the avocado in half lengthways all the way around and into the stone. Hold one half in each hand, then twist the halves in opposite directions and pull apart. To remove the stone, tap the blade of a sharp knife into it and twist it out.

If you want to serve the avocado in slices, peel off the skin with a sharp knife or scoop out the flesh in one piece using a large spoon and keeping as close to the skin as possible. Slice the avocado halves lengthways or crossways, as you like. Cut the slices across to make dice if necessary.

Brush or toss the flesh with lemon juice, lime juice or a little vinegar to prevent discolouring.

Did you know?

The easiest, quickest way to prepare root ginger is to grate it. There is no need to peel it: just trim off any tough areas or dried parts and grate the root on a fine food grater. Most of the skin will be left behind, and the juicy flesh is ready to use. If you want chopped or sliced ginger, peel the root with a sharp knife and cut it across the grain into thin slices. Chop the slices finely if the recipe requires it.

Cooking vegetables

Most vegetables take little time to cook and are best served while they still have a little bite, rather than soft right the way through. This is true of all green vegetables. On the other hand, potatoes and other root vegetables such as beetroot and parsnips need to be cooked until tender.

Perfect roast potatoes

It is important to choose the correct potatoes for really crisp, golden roasties – the most suitable varieties are Nadine, Wilja, Desirée, Maris Piper, Romano or King Edward. This method can also be used for roasting parsnips.

1 Cut the potatoes into even-sized chunks, about 3.5 cm (1½ inches) in diameter.

2 Par-boil the potatoes in lightly salted, boiling water for 5 minutes. Drain well, then return the potatoes to the pan and cover with a lid. Shake the pan to slightly roughen up the surface of the potatoes.

3 Pour vegetable oil into a large roasting tin to a depth of 1 cm (½ inch) and place it in a preheated oven at 220°C (425°F) Gas Mark 7, for a few minutes until very hot.

4 Tip the potatoes into the hot oil and turn them to coat them lightly in the oil. Roast the potatoes for 45–50 minutes, turning them twice, until they are golden and crunchy. Drain on kitchen paper before serving, lightly sprinkled with salt.

Roasting vegetables

Most vegetables respond well to this method of cooking and it is a very easy way to cook a variety of vegetables together, especially if you are roasting a joint of meat or baking a main dish at the same time. Choose a selection of root vegetables, such as carrots, turnips, parsnips, swede and beetroot, or a Mediterranean-style mixture of vegetables, such as aubergine, courgettes, peppers, fennel, red onions and plum tomatoes. Toss the vegetables in olive oil and add herbs to flavour. Alternatively, marinate for 30 minutes in olive oil, honey and balsamic vinegar.

1 Prepare the vegetables according to type and cut them into large, even-sized pieces or keep baby vegetables whole. Arrange them in a single layer in a large roasting tin and drizzle with olive oil. Toss the vegetables to coat them in the oil.

2 Tuck cloves of garlic and thyme or rosemary sprigs between the vegetables, then sprinkle them with salt and pepper. Roast in a preheated oven at 220°C (425°F), Gas Mark 7, for 30–40 minutes, or until tender and golden, turning occasionally.

Roasting garlic

Roasting transforms pungent garlic, giving it a subtle, caramel-like flavour. Add the tender pulp from the roasted cloves to soups, stews or salsas; smear it over grilled meats; tuck it into baked jacket potatoes; or simply spread it on grilled slices of ciabatta bread to make a savoury snack or accompaniment for cheese or main dishes.

1 Place the whole garlic head on a square of foil on a baking sheet and drizzle with olive oil.

2 Wrap the foil around the garlic to enclose it completely and roast in a preheated oven at 200°C (400°F), Gas Mark 6, for 20–25 minutes, turning occasionally, until soft and lightly browned.

3 Snip the top from each clove and squeeze out the soft fragrant pulp.

TOP TIP

The freshest garlic can be bought in summer through to autumn. When choosing, look for compact bulbs with little dry skin. Garlic can be stored for about 2–3 months.

Below Roasting is an easy and delicious way to cook vegetables. Try adding rosemary to Mediterranean-style vegetables.

TOP TIP

Jacket potatoes are delicious if you moisten the skins with water or drizzle them with a little oil, then sprinkle on some coarsely ground salt before cooking. If you are cooking more than one potato at a time, choose even sizes so they all cook at the same rate.

Perfect mash

This method is suitable for potatoes or other roots, such as parsnips, turnips, sweet potato and swede. For potato mash, choose a floury variety of potato, such as Pentland Squire, Romano or King Edward.

1 Cut the potatoes into even-sized chunks and add them to a saucepan of boiling, lightly salted water. Cover and simmer for 20 minutes or until tender. Drain the potatoes and return them to the pan.

2 Meanwhile, heat the milk until almost boiling, then pour it over the potatoes. Add the butter or oil and mash the potatoes until smooth. Do not use a food processor, since this is too harsh and will make the potatoes glue-like in texture.

3 Adjust the seasoning to taste and serve immediately. Alternatively, if the mash must be kept hot, cover the pan with a clean tea towel instead of a lid, to keep it fluffy.

Flavoured mash

Apple and Bacon Mash Peel, core and roughly chop 1 Bramley cooking apple and cook it gently in 3 tablespoons of water and 1 tablespoon of lemon juice until soft. Mash with the potato, then stir in 25 g (1 oz) finely diced, crisply fried bacon.

Garlic and Herb Mash Add the pulp from 2–3 cloves of roasted garlic to the potato before mashing, then stir in a handful of finely chopped thyme or rosemary.

Lemon-mustard Mash Stir 1 tablespoon of wholegrain mustard and the finely grated rind of 1 small lemon into the mash.

Minted Mash Stir 2 tablespoons chopped fresh mint and 2 tablespoons crème fraîche into the mash.

Parmesan, Olive Oil and Pine Nut Mash Using an electric whisk, whisk the olive oil and Parmesan into the mash, season with salt and pepper and scatter over a handful of pine nuts.

Right It is better to make mash by hand since a food processor will turn it into a sticky gloop.

Cooking Asparagus

You can cook asparagus in one of two ways:

1 Arrange the asparagus in a single layer on a baking sheet or in an ovenproof dish. Drizzle with olive oil and lemon juice, and sprinkle with salt and pepper. Cover with foil and cook in a preheated oven at 190°C (375°F), Gas Mark 5, for 20–25 minutes or until tender.

2 Tie the trimmed asparagus stems together in bundles. Wedge the bundles upright in a large, deep saucepan of boiling water: the water should come about half-way up the spears. If possible, cover with a lid, or if the tips stand above the top of the pan, make a foil cover. Simmer for 8–12 minutes, depending on thickness and age, until tender. The tips will cook gently in the steam, so they will not overcook.

Stir-frying spinach

If you do not like soggy spinach, try stir-frying it instead of the usual steaming. Wash the spinach leaves and drain, then pat dry with kitchen paper. Heat a little oil in a wok or large saucepan and add the spinach. Stir lightly over a high heat until just wilted. The moisture in the spinach will evaporate and it will be perfectly cooked in a matter of minutes, with no liquid to drain off. Be careful not to cook the spinach for too long or it will start to become mushy. A little grated nutmeg enhances the flavour of spinach.

TOP TIP

Add a pinch of sugar to all cooked tomato dishes, whether you are using fresh or canned tomatoes. This will greatly improve the flavour of the dish and enriches soups, sauces and casseroles.

Cooking cabbage

If you find plain cooked cabbage dull, try these simple ways to add flavour and variety.

Braised cabbage Finely shred the cabbage and simmer it with a small amount of well-flavoured stock and a knob of butter. Cook, covered, for 4–5 minutes.

Steamed wedges Trim a whole cabbage and cut it into slim wedges leaving the core intact to keep the leaves in shape. Arrange the cabbage in a steamer and cook over boiling water for 6–8 minutes, or until just tender.

Stir-frying Heat a small amount of oil in a wok and add 1 teaspoon each of finely chopped fresh root ginger and garlic. Stir-fry for 30 seconds, then add finely shredded green cabbage and stir-fry for 4–5 minutes or until just tender.

Vegetable purées

This is a trendy way to serve vegetables. Almost any vegetable can be served as a purée, but carrots, parsnips, broad beans, spinach, pumpkin, sweet potato or celeriac are particularly successful.

To purée vegetables, first steam or boil them until tender, then drain thoroughly. Process the vegetables in a food processor, use a hand blender, or press them through a fine sieve or mouli until just smooth. Do not overprocess the vegetables or their texture will be spoiled. Finally, stir in a little cream or butter and season to taste with salt and pepper.

Flavouring vegetable purées

Carrots Ginger is a wonderful accompaniment to carrots. Try mixing a little, grated, along with a knob of butter and some chopped chives.

Celeriac Stir through some apple purée with a pinch of cloves and some fresh, chopped parsley.

Parsnips Chopped fresh sage with a little walnut or hazelnut oil is delicious stirred through parsnip purée.

Pumpkin Garlic and sour cream work well with pumpkin.

Spinach Purée spinach along with crème fraîche and a little grated nutmeg.

Sweet potato Try adding grated Parmesan cheese along with some fresh chopped thyme.

TOP TIP

The best cooking method for spaghetti squash is to bake it in the oven. Its spaghetti-like strands can then be scooped out and tossed with butter and grated Parmesan cheese.

Above Scoop out the flesh of a baked butternut squash and mash or dice it with a little butter to make a delicious side dish.

Cooking squashes

All varieties of squash can be eaten as a vegetable accompaniment to meats, or served as a vegetarian main course. The following are basic cooking methods for squash.

Baking Halve the squash and discard the seeds, but leave the skin on. Brush the cut surface with oil and place it cut-side down on a baking sheet. Cover with foil and bake in a preheated oven at 190°C (375°F), Gas Mark 5, until the flesh is tender. When cooked, scoop out the flesh and dice or mash to serve.

Roasting Peel and deseed the squash, then cut it into 3.5 cm (1½ inch) chunks. Toss lightly in oil, season with salt and pepper, and, if you like, add a few fresh thyme or rosemary sprigs. Turn into a roasting tin and cook in a preheated oven at 220°C (425°F) Gas Mark 7, until tender and golden brown.

Braising Peel and deseed the squash, then cut it into 2.5 cm (1 inch) dice. Small squash, such as patty pans, can be halved. Heat 25 g (1 oz) butter and 2–3 tablespoons of stock per 500 g (1 lb) squash in a saucepan. Add the squash, season well, cover and simmer, shaking the pan occasionally, for 10–12 minutes, or until tender.

Herb-flavoured oils and vinegars

Commercial herb-flavoured oils and vinegars are expensive, but they are easy to make at home. You can use any fresh herbs you like and add the sprigs to a bottle of good-quality olive oil or to wine vinegar, sherry vinegar or cider vinegar.

Fresh, clean rosemary or thyme sprigs, bay leaves, lengths of chives or sprigs of oregano are particularly successful. If you want additional flavour, add a whole chilli, a twist of lemon or orange rind and a few peppercorns. A whole peeled garlic clove is also a good addition. Cover tightly and allow to stand for at least 2 weeks before using. Use in salad dressings or drizzle over cooked meat and vegetables.

Flavouring oil with basil is an excellent way to make a fragrant cooking oil, but it is also a very successful way to preserve basil for winter months. Pack a handful of basil leaves into a screw-top bottle or jar and pour in olive oil to cover them. Leave undisturbed for 1–2 weeks. The oil can be used to make salad dressings or drizzle a little into soups or simple savoury dishes before serving.

Above Use fresh herbs from your garden to make a flavoursome oil for cooking or as part of a salad dressing.

Making herb butters

Herb butters are excellent for melting over grilled meats and fish, hot potatoes and steamed vegetables. Alternatively, serve with salad and fresh bread.

1 Prepare 2 tablespoons of finely chopped fresh herbs, such as parsley, mint, chives, or chervil. Add 125 g (4 oz) unsalted butter at room temperature and a squeeze of lemon or lime juice.

2 Beat well with a wooden spoon or electric mixer to combine evenly.

3 Turn the butter out on to a piece of clingfilm or non-stick baking paper.

4 Fold the wrapping over the butter and shape it into a roll 5 cm (2 inches) in diameter. Wrap tightly and chill until firm. Unwrap and slice with a knife.

Alternatively, turn the butter out onto clingfilm or non-stick baking paper and spread it out evenly. Place another sheet on top and press lightly with a rolling pin to an even thickness of about 5-mm (¼-inch) thick. Chill until firm, then use small cutters to stamp out shapes.

Tomato and Aubergine Parmigiana

With rich, creamy fried aubergines and the fresh flavour of ripe tomatoes, this quick and simple bake makes an appealing supper dish. Serve with a crisp green salad and crusty bread.

Preparation time 10 minutes **Cooking time** 30–40 minutes **Serves** 4

olive oil, for frying

1 large aubergine, cut into thin slices

500 g (1 lb) ripe plum tomatoes, cut into wedges

50 g (2 oz) Parmesan cheese, freshly grated

salt and pepper

flat leaf parsley sprigs, to garnish

1 Heat a little olive oil in a frying pan and fry the aubergine slices in batches until golden brown on both sides and tender. Drain on kitchen paper.

2 Arrange the tomato wedges and the fried aubergine slices in alternate layers in a shallow ovenproof dish, with a sprinkling of grated Parmesan and a little salt and pepper between each layer.

3 Bake in a preheated oven at 190°C (375°F), Gas Mark 5, for 15–20 minutes, until browned and bubbling. To serve, either allow to cool slightly and serve warm, or leave to cool completely and serve at room temperature. Garnish with parsley before serving.

Chilli Chips

These spicy oven-roasted potato wedges are an easy and healthy alternative to chips. Use as little or as much chilli powder as you like to coat them.

Preparation time 5 minutes **Cooking time** about 1 hour **Serves** 4–6

4 large baking potatoes

4–6 tbsp olive oil

½ tsp salt

1–2 tsp chilli powder, to taste

salad leaves, to garnish

soured cream or mayonnaise, to serve

1 Cut each potato into 8 wedges and place them in a large bowl. Add the oil, salt and chilli powder and toss until evenly coated.

2 Transfer the potatoes to a baking sheet and roast in a preheated oven at 220°C (425°F), Gas Mark 7, for 15 minutes. Turn them and cook for a further 15 minutes. Turn once more and cook for a final 15 minutes until crisp and golden.

3 Cool the potatoes slightly and serve them with soured cream or mayonnaise for dipping, garnished with salad leaves.

Charred Leek Salad with Hazelnuts

This elegant salad is bursting with different flavours and shows sweet baby leeks at their best and most succulent.

Preparation time 10 minutes **Cooking time** 14 minutes **Serves** 4

1 Brush the leeks with a little hazelnut oil and cook them in a stove-top grill pan, or under a hot grill, turning frequently, for 6–8 minutes, until evenly browned and cooked through. Toss with a dash of lemon juice and season to taste with salt and pepper. Set aside to cool.

2 Meanwhile, dry-fry the hazelnuts until browned, cool slightly and then roughly chop them. Separate the lettuce leaves and pull the mint leaves from their stalks.

3 Arrange the leeks in bowls or on plates and top with the lettuce leaves, mint and nuts. Whisk the dressing ingredients together and pour over the salad. Shave the Pecorino over the salad and serve garnished with the olives.

500 g (1 lb) baby leeks

1–2 tbsp hazelnut oil

dash of lemon juice

40 g (1½ oz) blanched hazelnuts

2 Little Gem or Cos lettuce hearts

few mint sprigs

15 g (½ oz) Pecorino cheese

20 black olives, to garnish

Dressing
4 tbsp hazelnut oil

2 tbsp extra virgin olive oil

2 tsp sherry vinegar

salt and pepper

1 tsp saffron threads

500 g (1 lb) ready-cooked polenta

1 tbsp plain flour

2 tsp chilli powder

oil, for shallow-frying

25 g (1 oz) butter

1 onion, chopped

2 garlic cloves, crushed

400 g (13 oz) mixed wild and cultivated mushrooms, halved if large

250 g (8 oz) mascarpone cheese

2 tbsp chopped tarragon

finely grated rind and juice of ½ lemon

salt and pepper

Saffron Mushrooms

A rich dish of mixed mushrooms cooked in a creamy saffron sauce. Serve as a main course or starter with polenta chips. Ready-cooked polenta is available in blocks in supermarkets.

Preparation time 10 minutes **Cooking time** 25 minutes **Serves** 4

1 Place the saffron in a bowl with 1 tablespoon of boiling water and leave to stand.

2 Cut the polenta into 1 cm (½ inch) slices, then cut the slices into neat 1 cm (½ inch) chips. Mix together the flour, chilli powder and salt and pepper and use the mixture to coat the polenta pieces.

3 Heat 1 cm (½ inch) depth of oil in a frying pan and fry the polenta chips, half at a time, for about 10 minutes until golden all over. Once they are cooked, drain them on kitchen paper and keep warm.

4 Meanwhile, melt the butter in a separate frying pan, add the onion and garlic and fry gently for 5 minutes until soft. Stir in the mushrooms and fry for 5 minutes. Add the mascarpone, tarragon, lemon rind and juice, saffron and soaking liquid, and season with salt and pepper. Stir until the mascarpone has melted to make a sauce. Serve with the polenta chips.

Panzanella

This is a flavoursome Italian salad of roasted peppers and ripe tomatoes. Serve as a starter, a main course or an accompaniment to grilled fish or meat.

Preparation time 15 minutes **Cooking time** 10 minutes **Serves** 4

3 red peppers, cored, deseeded and quartered

375 g (12 oz) ripe plum tomatoes, skinned

6 tbsp extra virgin olive oil

3 tbsp wine vinegar

2 garlic cloves, crushed

125 g (4 oz) stale ciabatta bread

50 g (2 oz) pitted black olives

small handful of basil leaves, shredded

salt and pepper

1 Place the peppers, skin-side up, on a foil-lined grill rack and grill under a preheated moderate grill for 10 minutes, or until the skins are blackened.

2 Meanwhile, quarter the tomatoes and scoop out the pulp, placing it in a sieve over a bowl to catch the juices. Set the tomato quarters aside. Press the pulp with the back of a spoon to extract as much juice as possible.

3 Beat the oil, vinegar, garlic, salt and pepper into the tomato juice.

4 When cool enough to handle, peel the skins from the peppers and discard. Roughly slice the peppers and place them in a bowl with the tomato quarters. Break the bread into small chunks and add to the bowl with the olives and basil.

5 Add the dressing and toss the ingredients together before serving.

Celeriac and Potato Remoulade with Asparagus

To make this summery lunch or supper dish a bit more substantial, lightly poach some eggs and arrange them on top of the asparagus spears.

Preparation time 10 minutes **Cooking time** 7 minutes **Serves** 4

500 g (1 lb) celeriac, peeled

375 g (12 oz) potatoes, peeled

1 tbsp extra virgin olive oil, plus extra for drizzling (optional)

500 g (1 lb) asparagus, trimmed

Sauce
150 ml (¼ pint) mayonnaise

150 ml (¼ pint) Greek yogurt

1 tsp Dijon mustard

6 cocktail gherkins, finely chopped

2 tbsp capers, chopped

2 tbsp chopped tarragon

salt and pepper

1 Cut the celeriac and potato into matchstick-sized pieces, but keep the two vegetables separate. Cook the celeriac in lightly salted boiling water for 2 minutes until softened. Add the potatoes and cook for a further 2 minutes until just tender. Drain the vegetables and refresh under running water.

2 Meanwhile, mix together the ingredients for the sauce and set aside.

3 Heat the oil in a frying pan or griddle pan. Add the asparagus and fry for 2–3 minutes until just beginning to colour.

4 Mix the celeriac and potato with the sauce and spoon the mixture on to 4 serving plates. Top with the asparagus spears. Serve immediately, drizzled with a little extra olive oil, if liked.

Cooking with fruit

Fruits make a fresh, tangy addition to both sweet and savoury dishes alike, adding their own distinctive flavours and textures. Be sure to use ripe but firm fruits for the best results.

Preparing fruit

There are many interesting ways to prepare fruit other than just peeling and cutting. Try the following methods for garnishes or presenting fruit as a dessert.

Citrus rind

Citrus rind, particularly from lemons, is used in all kinds of savoury and sweet dishes. Choose unwaxed fruit if you want to use the rind, or scrub the fruit first under warm water. Use the fine side of a box grater to remove the coloured rind from the fruit, avoiding the white pith underneath, which will be bitter. Use a small stiff brush to remove the grated rind from the grater.

A zester or canelle knife is the best tool for creating fine strips of citrus rind. If the strips are not to be used immediately, blanch them in boiling water for a few seconds, then refresh them in cold water. Drain and cover to prevent the shreds from shrivelling.

Peeling and segmenting an orange

Cut a thin slice off the top and bottom of the fruit with a sharp knife then stand the fruit on a board and cut off all the peel and white pith, slicing downwards in sections. Hold the fruit over a bowl to catch any juice. Keeping the knife blade away from you, cut between the membranes and the flesh of each segment, easing out the segments as you work around the fruit.

Dealing with a fresh pineapple

Pineapple has a tough skin, spines and a fibrous core that need to be removed. To do this, trim off the base and the top of the pineapple, removing the leaves, then stand the pineapple on a board and cut off the peel in long slices down the length of the fruit. To remove the sharp, brown eyes or spines from the flesh, use a small sharp knife to cut long, spiralling grooves around the fruit, following the natural lines of the eyes.

Cut the pineapple across into slices and remove the core from each slice by stamping it out using a small round cutter. To cut wedges or dice the flesh, cut the fruit lengthways into quarters then cut away the tough line of core down the length of each wedge.

How to prepare a mango

Hold the mango with the narrow side down and cut a thick slice from each side of the fruit, as close to the stone as possible, then cut off any flesh remaining around the stone. Peel each large slice before dicing or slicing the flesh. If you want to present the mango in a more elaborate way, use the tip of a knife to score deep lines in a diamond pattern into the flesh of each slice. Gently push up each slice from the skin side, so that the cut flesh pops up in a squared pattern.

Below, left to right Zesting an orange, segmenting an orange, preparing pineapple and preparing mango.

Marinating fruit

Any ripe, tender fruits, particularly soft fruits such as strawberries or raspberries, are enhanced by gentle marinating to bring out their flavour to the full. Sweetly-scented muscat wines, such as Beaumes de Venise, or fruit liqueurs, such as cassis, are the perfect choice. If you use stronger spirits, such as rum, brandy or kirsch, add only a small amount to moisten the fruit, and balance the flavour with a light sprinkling of caster sugar.

Hull the fruit and place it in a bowl. Sprinkle liberally with the chosen wine or liqueur. Go easier if you are using spirits. Cover the bowl and chill for 2–3 hours, turning once. Scatter with fresh mint sprigs or borage to serve.

Cooking fruit

Fruit can be used in both sweet and savoury dishes, from crumbles and flans to curries and salads. Baking and poaching are common methods of cooking fruit for desserts. Try the following recipes for a delicious dinner-party dessert.

Baked apples

Baked apples make a wonderful hot winter pudding. Bramleys are the best choice – choose fruits that are even in size and not too large for a single portion.

1 Wash and dry the apples and remove the cores with a corer or small knife.

2 Run a sharp knife around the middle of the apple to slit the skin. This will prevent the apple from bursting during cooking.

3 Place the apples in a shallow ovenproof dish and spoon the chosen filling (see below) into the central hole left by the core. If you do not want to add a filling, just sprinkle in caster sugar and cinnamon and dot with butter.

4 Sprinkle with lemon juice and bake in a preheated oven at 180°C (350°F), Gas Mark 4, for 45–60 minutes or until tender.

Fillings for baked apples

- Mincemeat or jam
- Chopped walnuts and dates
- Chopped ready-to-eat dried apricots and almond paste
- Crumbled ratafia biscuits or ginger nuts and flaked almonds
- Cranberries and maple syrup

Above Cinnamon sticks add an aromatic flavour to wine-poached pears. Star-anise, cloves or ginger can also be used.

Poached pears

To poach whole pears in wine, choose firm fruit, such as Williams or Conference, which will endure long, slow simmering without breaking up so that the flavours can develop.

1 Peel the pears thinly, leaving the stalks on. Trim a thin slice from the base of each so that it stands upright. Place them in a large saucepan.

2 Sprinkle with sugar and pour in wine to come about half way up the pears. Add extra flavourings, such as cinnamon sticks, star anise or ground ginger, if using.

3 Bring to a gentle simmer, then cover the pan and cook very gently for about 1 hour. Gently turn the pears in the syrup, then poach for 45–60 minutes more or until very tender, turning occasionally.

4 Carefully lift the pears from the syrup and discard the flavourings. Mix some arrowroot with a little cold water to make a paste, then stir it into the hot syrup.

5 Bring to the boil, stirring, then stir for 1 minute and remove from the heat. Do not cook the syrup any longer, since the arrowroot thins slightly with long simmering. Pour the syrup over the pears. Serve the pears warm or cold.

Orange and Avocado Salad

The creamy avocado in this salad is well complemented by the tangy sweetness of fresh oranges. The oranges can be segmented in advance, but prepare the avocados at the last minute to prevent browning.

Preparation time 15 minutes **Serves** 4

4 large juicy oranges

2 small ripe avocados, peeled and stoned

2 teaspoons cardamom pods

3 tablespoons light olive oil

1 tablespoon honey

dash of ground allspice

2 teaspoons lemon juice

salt and pepper

watercress sprigs, to garnish

1 Cut the skin and the white membrane off the oranges. Working over a bowl to catch the juice, cut between the membranes to remove the segments. Slice the avocados and toss gently with the orange segments. Pile on to 4 serving plates.

2 Reserve a few whole cardamom pods for garnishing. Crush the remainder using a mortar and pestle to extract the seeds, or place in a small bowl and crush with the end of a rolling pin. Pick out and discard the pods.

3 Mix the seeds with the oil, honey, allspice, lemon juice, salt and pepper to taste, and reserved orange juice. Garnish each salad with the watercress sprigs and reserved cardamom pods, and serve with the dressing spooned over the top.

16 large raw tiger prawns, peeled and deveined

1 tbsp sunflower oil

4 tbsp lemon juice

2 garlic cloves, crushed

1 tsp grated fresh root ginger

½ tsp chilli powder

1 tbsp clear honey

1 tsp sea salt

1 large mango, peeled, stoned and cut into 8 bite-sized pieces

dressed salad, to serve

Prawn and Mango Kebabs

Chunks of sweet, luscious mango make a fine contrast to these spicy prawns. Serve as a starter or as a nibble with drinks. Soak the wooden skewers in water for 20 minutes before use to prevent them burning.

Preparation time 10 minutes, plus marinating **Cooking time** 4–5 minutes **Serves** 4

1 Put the prawns into a large bowl and add the oil, lemon juice, garlic, ginger, chilli powder, honey and salt. Mix well and marinate for about 10 minutes.

2 Remove the prawns from the marinade and thread 2 prawns alternately between 2 pieces of mango on each of 8 presoaked wooden skewers.

3 Place the skewers under a preheated hot grill, brush with the remaining marinade and grill for 2 minutes on each side, or until the prawns turn pink and are cooked through. Serve 2 skewers on each plate with some dressed salad.

25 g (1 oz) fresh breadcrumbs, toasted

1 tbsp chopped parsley

1 tsp chopped thyme

1 tbsp dried cranberries, finely chopped

4 x 50 g (2 oz) pieces of Brie

1 egg, beaten

Relish
250 g (8 oz) cranberries, defrosted if frozen

3 tbsp grated orange rind

5 tbsp orange juice

1 cm (½ inch) piece of fresh root ginger, grated

125 g (4 oz) sugar

To serve
rocket or assorted lettuce leaves

4 thick slices of French bread, toasted

1 garlic clove, halved lengthways

snipped chives

Baked Brie with Cranberries

Wedges of creamy brie are baked in a crust of herbs and dried cranberries, and served with ruby-red cranberry relish.

Preparation time 25 minutes **Cooking time** 8 minutes **Serves** 4

1 To make the relish, place the cranberries, grated orange rind and juice, ginger and sugar in a blender or food processor and work to a coarse purée. Leave to stand for 1 hour before serving.

2 To make the Brie, mix the breadcrumbs with the parsley, thyme and cranberries. Dip each piece of Brie into the beaten egg, then coat with the breadcrumbs.

3 Place the pieces of coated Brie on a greased baking sheet and bake on the middle shelf of a preheated oven at 220°C (425°F), Gas Mark 7, for 8 minutes. Remove the Brie from the oven and leave to cool briefly.

4 Arrange the rocket or lettuce leaves on 4 plates. Spoon some cranberry relish on each plate and place each piece of warm Brie on a slice of toasted French bread, which has been rubbed with a garlic half and topped with extra cranberry relish. Garnish with chives and serve.

Honeyed Ricotta with Summer Fruits

This makes a simple summery dessert which can be prepared well in advance and assembled at the last minute. It also makes a very elegant breakfast dish and looks fantastic.

Preparation time 10 minutes **Serves** 4

1 Rub the raspberries through a fine sieve to make a purée, then mix them with the rosewater. Alternatively, process together in a food processor or blender and then sieve to remove the pips. Toast the pumpkin seeds.

2 Slice the ricotta into wedges and arrange on plates with the berries. Drizzle the honey and raspberry purée over the ricotta, adding a little honeycomb, and serve scattered with the pumpkin seeds and a sprinkling of cinnamon.

125 g (4 oz) raspberries

2 tsp rosewater

2 tbsp pumpkin seeds

250 g (8 oz) ricotta cheese

250 g (8 oz) mixed summer berries

2 tbsp clear honey with honeycomb

pinch of ground cinnamon

Bananas with Palm Sugar Toffee Sauce

Pan-fried bananas make a fantastic and simple dessert. Top with ice cream and this sticky toffee sauce.

Preparation time 2 minutes **Cooking time** 4 minutes **Serves** 4

4 bananas

125 g (4 oz) unsalted butter

125 g (4 oz) palm sugar

125 ml (4 fl oz) double cream

dash of lime juice

vanilla ice cream, to serve

ground cinnamon or grated nutmeg, to decorate (optional)

1 Peel the bananas and cut them into quarters or in half lengthways. Melt the butter in a frying pan and fry the banana pieces for about 30 seconds on each side, until lightly golden. Transfer to a warm dish with a slotted spoon.

2 Stir the sugar and cream into the pan and heat gently to dissolve the sugar. Simmer gently for 2–3 minutes, until thickened. Add lime juice to taste.

3 Serve the bananas drizzled with the toffee sauce and with a scoop of ice cream. Sprinkle with cinnamon or nutmeg to decorate, if liked.

125 g (4 oz) caster sugar

300 ml (½ pint) water

2 strips lemon rind

2 cardamom pods

1 vanilla pod

12 apricots, halved and pitted

1 tbsp lemon juice

1 tbsp rosewater

25 g (1 oz) shelled pistachio nuts, finely chopped

vanilla ice cream or Greek yogurt, to serve (optional)

Poached Apricots with Rosewater and Pistachios

Simply poached apricots are elegance itself. This dish is perfect for a dinner party as it can be prepared well in advance.

Preparation time 10 minutes **Cooking time** 5 minutes, plus cooling **Serves** 4

1 Place a large bowl in the freezer to chill. Put the sugar and water into a wide saucepan and heat gently to dissolve the sugar. Meanwhile, cut the lemon rind into thin strips, crush the cardamom pods and split the vanilla pod in half. Add the lemon rind, cardamom and vanilla pod to the pan.

2 Add the apricots and simmer gently for about 5 minutes, until softened. Remove from the heat, add the lemon juice and rosewater and transfer to the chilled bowl. Leave to cool until required.

3 Spoon the apricots and a little of the syrup into serving bowls, scatter with the pistachio nuts and serve with vanilla ice cream or yogurt, if liked.

How to cook pulses

Pulses are available in canned or dried form. Many people believe dried pulses have a better texture in the finished dish but their canned equivalents are very convenient and still delicious. Pulses have a high energy value and low water content which means they can be stored for long periods.

Preparing pulses

Many dried pulses need to be soaked in water for several hours or overnight to rehydrate before cooking. Follow the packet or recipe instructions for best results. Dried beans labelled 'quick-cooking' have been presoaked and redried before packaging; they require no presoaking and so take less time to prepare. However, their texture will not be as firm as that of ordinary dried beans.

Soaking pulses

Lentils, green and yellow split peas, black-eyed beans and mung beans are ready to be cooked once rinsed; other dried pulses require soaking first. Soaking times can be 4–12 hours, depending on the type and age of the pulse – soya beans and chickpeas are the hardest pulses and need soaking the longest. During the soaking process, change the water two or three times to help counteract flatulence.

There are two ways to soak pulses:

1 Put the pulses in a large bowl, cover with four times their volume of cold water and leave to soak overnight – the longer they are allowed to soak, the softer they become and the quicker they cook.

2 Put the pulses in a saucepan with four times their volume of cold, unsalted water. Bring to the boil, then boil the pulses vigorously for 5 minutes. Cover the pan, remove from the heat and allow the pulses to stand in the hot water for 1 hour.

Once the pulses have been soaked, drain them (always discard the soaking water) and rinse them in fresh water. They are now ready to cook.

Did you know?

- Dried pulses are rich in protein, carbohydrate and dietary fibre, and low in fat, which is mostly unsaturated. They also supply useful amounts of minerals and vitamins: calcium, iron, phosphorous, magnesium and some B vitamins.

- Dried pulses have a long shelf life and will keep well for up to a year if kept in a dry, airtight container at room temperature and away from the light. However, it is best to eat them as fresh as possible since they do toughen with age and older ones will take longer to cook.

- A serving of baked beans will provide nearly half the recommended daily fibre intake and more protein than an egg or cup of milk. So beans are an essential ingredient for a healthy diet, particularly if you are a vegetarian.

Above Most dried pulses should be soaked overnight in cold water to rehydrate them before cooking.

Canned pulses

Canned pulses are already cooked and are a quick and convenient alternative to dried. Many different types of pulses are available in cans, including chickpeas, kidney beans, haricot beans, butter beans and mixed beans. Simply drain and rinse well to remove the canning liquid. To substitute canned beans for dried, remember that the weight of dried beans roughly doubles during soaking and cooking so a recipe that calls for 125 g (4 oz) of dried beans would require about 250 g (8 oz) of drained canned beans.

Cooking pulses

Pulses are an extremely versatile ingredient and very easy to cook. If you don't have the time to pre-soak them then simply opening a can of beans, lentils or other legumes provides you with one of the most versatile vehicles for a quick and easy meal. Using highly flavoured additions such as garlic, spices, herbs and aromatics can transform them into a culinary delight.

Dried beans

Place them in a saucepan and cover with fresh water until the water level is 2.5–5 cm (1–2 inches) above the pulses. Bring the pulses to the boil, then reduce the heat and simmer gently. The exception to this is red kidney beans, which must be boiled vigorously for 10 minutes before simmering to ensure that any toxins on the outside skins of the beans are completely destroyed. Continue simmering the beans gently until soft, frequently removing the scum that forms on the surface. Adding a little oil to the cooking liquid can help prevent the scum forming.

The beans are cooked when soft to the bite and evenly coloured all the way through. The length of cooking time varies according to the type of pulse, the quantity of pulses being cooked and their age – old pulses can take twice as long to cook. If the beans are required cold, leave them to cool in the cooking liquid to prevent them drying out and their skins splitting.

Toxins in dried beans

Dried beans must be prepared properly as they contain lectin, a toxin that is rendered harmless only during the soaking and cooking processes. In particular, it is not safe to eat raw or undercooked kidney and soya beans. Canned beans are precooked and safe to use as they are.

Above Cook rehydrated dried pulses in a large saucepan of water until they are tender. Do not add salt or the skins will toughen.

Lentils

Green and brown lentils retain their shape, becoming tender rather than mushy. To cook them, simply bring them to the boil in plenty of water (or stock or wine) and cook until just soft. Green and brown lentils are popular for casseroles, particularly for pork, bacon and spicy sausages, and also for salads.

To cook split lentils, or red lentils, for a purée or pâté, measure the water exactly according to the recipe, or the end result may be too sloppy. Red lentils are also popular for soups and dahl.

Making purées

Cooked or canned beans and lentils make delicious purées which can be served as dips or accompaniments.
1 Drain the beans or lentils and purée them in a blender or food processor, adding a little single cream or stock to moisten them to a soft consistency. Process until fairly smooth, but still retaining a little texture. Alternatively, rub the pulses through a coarse sieve with the back of a wooden spoon. For a coarse purée, mash the beans or lentils with a fork, adding a little butter or cream to hot beans to soften the texture.
2 Stir some flavouring ingredients into the purée. A little crushed garlic, chopped fresh herbs or a little grated nutmeg all work well. Season with salt and pepper to taste. Serve warm as a side dish or cold as a dip with pitta breads and crudités.

Chilli con Carne

You can make this dish as hot or mild as you like by adjusting the amount of chilli powder. For a really fiery meal, serve with bottled or smoked chillies.

Preparation time 5 minutes **Cooking time** 45 minutes **Serves** 4

2 tbsp vegetable oil

1 large red onion, sliced

1–2 garlic cloves, crushed

750 g (1½ lb) minced beef

1 tsp hot chilli powder

½ tsp ground cumin

425 g (14 oz) can tomatoes

150 ml (¼ pint) Beef Stock (see page 161)

1 tsp caster sugar

2 tbsp tomato purée

425 g (14 oz) can red kidney beans, drained

salt and pepper

long-grain rice, to serve

1 Heat the oil in a flameproof casserole. Add the onion and garlic and fry over a medium heat, stirring occasionally, for 7 minutes, until golden. Add the minced beef, chilli powder and cumin and fry, stirring constantly, until the beef is browned.

2 Stir in the tomatoes with their juice, the stock, sugar and tomato purée, and season with salt and pepper to taste. Bring to the boil, then lower the heat, cover and simmer gently for 30 minutes.

3 Add the kidney beans 5 minutes before the end of cooking time. Adjust the seasoning to taste and serve immediately on long-grain rice.

Broad Beans with Chorizo

Tapas bars all over Spain serve versions of this dish. Chorizo is a type of Spanish sausage, made with pork and flavoured with paprika, black pepper and garlic.

Preparation time 15 minutes **Cooking time** 10 minutes **Serves** 4

250 g (8 oz) shelled young broad beans

1 tbsp extra virgin olive oil

2 garlic cloves, roughly chopped

125 g (4 oz) spicy chorizo, cut into slices about 5 mm (¼ inch) thick

1 tbsp chopped dill

1 tbsp chopped mint

2 tbsp lemon juice

salt and pepper

crusty bread, to serve

1 Blanch the broad beans in a saucepan of lightly salted boiling water for 1 minute. Drain, rinse immediately under cold running water and drain again. Dry well.

2 Heat the oil in a frying pan, add the garlic and fry gently for 2–3 minutes until softened, then discard. Increase the heat, add the sliced chorizo and stir-fry for 2–3 minutes, until it is golden and has released some of its oil.

3 Stir in the blanched beans and cook for a further 2–3 minutes, then add the herbs and lemon juice and season to taste with salt and pepper. Mix well. Serve warm with crusty bread.

500 g (1 lb) dried red or white kidney beans, soaked overnight, drained and rinsed

2 celery sticks, halved

2 bay leaves

4 parsley sprigs

4 tbsp extra virgin olive oil

500 g (1 lb) onions, chopped

5 garlic cloves, crushed

2 red chillies, deseeded and chopped

4 red peppers, cored, deseeded and chopped

1 tbsp paprika

large handful of mixed chopped mint, parsley and coriander

salt and pepper

mint leaves, to garnish

Tomato sauce
1 kg (2 lb) canned chopped tomatoes

2 tbsp extra virgin olive oil

4 parsley sprigs

1 tbsp sugar

Bean Tagine

Tagine is the name for a North African cooking pot and the thick stew of meat or vegetables cooked slowly within it.

Preparation time 15 minutes, plus soaking **Cooking time** 2¾ hours **Serves** 8

1 Boil the beans in a large saucepan of unsalted water for 10 minutes then drain. Tie the celery, bay leaves and parsley together with string. Cover the beans with fresh unsalted water, add the celery and herbs and simmer for 1 hour until the beans are tender. Drain, reserving the liquid, and discard the celery and herbs.

2 Meanwhile, make the sauce. Empty the tomatoes and juice into a saucepan, add the oil, parsley and sugar and bring to the boil. Simmer, uncovered, for 20 minutes.

3 Heat the oil in a heavy-bottomed flameproof casserole. Add the onions, garlic, chillies, red peppers and paprika and cook gently for 5 minutes. Stir in the beans, the tomato sauce and enough of the reserved cooking liquid to just cover the beans. Season with salt and pepper, cover and cook in a preheated oven at 150°C (300°F), Gas Mark 2, for 1½ hours, stirring occasionally.

4 Just before serving, stir in the mint, parsley and coriander. Garnish with the mint leaves and serve with a bowl of harissa (spiced paste).

75 g (3 oz) French beans, trimmed and roughly chopped

2 tbsp groundnut or vegetable oil

1 red pepper, cored, deseeded and diced

4 garlic cloves, crushed

2 tsp mild chilli powder

425 g (14 oz) can red kidney beans, drained and rinsed

75 g (3 oz) fresh white breadcrumbs

1 egg yolk

oil, for shallow-frying

salt and pepper

Lemon mayonnaise
4 tbsp mayonnaise

finely grated rind of 1 lemon

1 tsp lemon juice

salt and pepper

Red Pepper and Bean Cakes with Lemon Mayonnaise

Pack these crisp bean cakes into warm pitta bread and serve with salad for a fairly substantial lunch or supper dish.

Preparation time 15 minutes **Cooking time** 15 minutes **Serves** 4

1 Blanch the French beans in a saucepan of lightly salted boiling water for 1–2 minutes until softened. Drain. Heat the oil in a frying pan and sauté the pepper, garlic and chilli powder for 2 minutes.

2 Transfer the mixture to a blender or food processor and add the red kidney beans, breadcrumbs and egg yolk. Process very briefly until the ingredients are coarsely chopped. Add the drained beans, season to taste with salt and pepper and process until the ingredients are just combined.

3 Turn the mixture into a bowl and divide into 8 portions. Using lightly floured hands, shape the portions into little 'cakes'.

4 Mix the mayonnaise with the lemon rind and juice, and season to taste with salt and pepper.

5 Heat the oil for frying in a large frying pan and pan-fry the cakes for about 3 minutes on each side until crisp and golden. Serve with the lemon mayonnaise.

Mushroom and Chickpea Curry

This spicy curry makes a good after-work supper dish as it is quick and easy to prepare. This is where canned pulses come into their own, making a dish like this achievable in a short time and with no advance planning.

Preparation time 10 minutes **Cooking time** 25 minutes **Serves** 4

1 Melt the butter in a frying pan and fry the onion, garlic, ginger and mushrooms for 5 minutes.

2 Add the curry powder, ground coriander, cinnamon, turmeric and potatoes, stir, then add the chickpeas. Season to taste with salt and pepper and add just enough water to cover. Bring to the boil, cover and simmer gently for 15 minutes.

3 Stir the cashew nuts into the curry, if using, along with the yogurt and chopped fresh coriander. Heat through without boiling and serve with rice.

50 g (2 oz) butter

1 onion, chopped

2 garlic cloves, crushed

2.5-cm (1-inch) piece of fresh root ginger, peeled and grated

250 g (8 oz) button mushrooms

2 tbsp hot curry powder

1 tsp ground coriander

1 tsp ground cinnamon

½ tsp turmeric

375 g (12 oz) potatoes, diced

425 g (14 oz) can chickpeas, drained and rinsed

50 g (2 oz) cashew nuts, toasted and chopped (optional)

125 ml (4 fl oz) Greek yogurt

chopped fresh coriander

salt and pepper

basmati rice, to serve

Hummus

The quantities for this delicious chickpea and sesame dip are imprecise because people's tastes vary, but the flavour of sesame (tahini) should not overpower that of the chickpeas. Tahini is a thick oily paste made from ground toasted sesame seeds.

Preparation time 20 minutes, plus soaking and cooling **Cooking time** 1–1½ hours
Serves 6

250 g (8 oz) dried chickpeas, soaked overnight, drained and rinsed

2–3 garlic cloves, crushed with a little salt

about 250 ml (8 fl oz) lemon juice

about 5 tbsp tahini

salt

warm pitta bread, to serve

To garnish
extra virgin olive oil

paprika

olives

1 Cook the chickpeas in a large saucepan of boiling water until soft, about 1–1½ hours depending on their quality and age. Drain and reserve the cooking liquid. Purée the chickpeas in a blender or food processor with a little of the cooking liquid, then press the purée through a sieve to remove the skins.

2 Beat the garlic into the chickpea purée. Stir in the lemon juice and tahini alternately, tasting before it has all been added to get the right balance of flavours. Add a little more salt, if necessary, and more of the cooking liquid to make a soft, creamy consistency. Spoon the purée into a shallow dish, cover and leave in the refrigerator for several hours.

3 Return to room temperature before serving. Create swirls in the surface with the back of a spoon then trickle olive oil into the swirls and sprinkle lightly with paprika. Garnish with olives and serve with warm pitta bread.

Gammon Steaks
with Creamy Lentils

Lentils make a good starchy accompaniment to meat, game and fish. They can be cooked with a whole host of flavourings to match the style of the dish they are accompanying.

Preparation time 10 minutes **Cooking time** 25 minutes **Serves** 4

125 g (4 oz) Puy lentils, rinsed

50 g (2 oz) butter

2 shallots

1 garlic clove, chopped

2 thyme sprigs, crushed

1 tsp cumin seeds

4 tsp Dijon mustard

2 tsp clear honey

4 gammon steaks

125 ml (4 fl oz) dry cider

75 ml (3 fl oz) single cream

salt and pepper

thyme leaves, to garnish

1 Place the lentils in a saucepan and cover with cold water. Bring to the boil and cook for 20 minutes.

2 Meanwhile, melt the butter in a frying pan and fry the shallots, garlic, thyme and cumin seeds, stirring frequently, for 10 minutes, until the shallots are soft and golden. Take care not to let them brown too much.

3 Blend the mustard and honey together and season to taste with salt and pepper. Brush the mixture over the gammon steaks and grill them for 3 minutes on each side, until golden and cooked through. Keep warm.

4 Drain the lentils and add them to the shallot mixture. Pour in the cider, bring to the boil and cook until reduced to about 4 tablespoons. Stir in the cream, heat through and season to taste with salt and pepper. Serve the lentils with the gammon steaks, garnished with thyme leaves.

Pasta, rice and grains

Pasta, noodles, rice and other grains make up an important part of many people's diets. These versatile staples can be flavoured with a whole host of different ingredients which set the character of a dish.

Making your own pasta

Making pasta is a very simple and rewarding process. You do not need a special pasta-making machine because the dough can be rolled and cut by hand. If you plan to make pasta often, a pasta machine may prove to be a useful investment.

Basic pasta dough

300 g (10 oz) pasta flour or strong plain flour
pinch of salt
3 eggs

1 Sift the flour and salt into a mound on a work surface and make a well in the centre.
2 Break the eggs into the well and use your fingertips or a fork to work the ingredients together, gradually working the flour into the eggs and mixing to form a soft paste. If the pasta is too sticky, work in a little extra flour. Draw the dough together into a ball.
3 Wash your hands and wash and dry the work surface, then dust it lightly with flour. Knead the dough for about 10 minutes, or until it is smooth and elastic.
4 Wrap the dough in clingfilm and leave it to rest for 20–30 minutes before use. Do not put in the refrigerator.

Variations

Tomato Pasta Add 2 tablespoons of concentrated tomato purée with the eggs.
Spinach Pasta Thaw 150 g (5 oz) of frozen chopped spinach and press out as much moisture as possible in a fine sieve. Add the spinach with the eggs.
Garlic and Herb Pasta Add 1 garlic clove, finely crushed, and 1 tablespoon finely chopped fresh herbs with the eggs.

TOP TIP
If you are allergic to wheat, there is a good range of dried pastas made from corn (maize) and other non-wheat flours, available in supermarkets or health-food shops.

Rolling and cutting pasta

The pasta dough should be used or cooked immediately for filled pasta, such as ravioli, or for lasagne sheets, but cut shapes should be allowed to dry for 5–10 minutes before cooking. Do not allow the pasta to dry for too long, or it will become brittle and break easily.

Noodles and Tagliatelle Cut the rolled pasta sheets into 25–30 cm (10–12 inch) lengths, then roll up the pieces fairly loosely, like a Swiss roll, and slice them with a sharp knife. The thickness of the slices determines the width of the noodles. Shake out the cut slices to separate the strips of pasta.
Lasagne or Cannelloni Cut the rolled pasta sheets into 10 x 15 cm (4 x 6 inch) rectangles. When making cannelloni, the cooked pieces of pasta are rolled around the filling.

Below If you plan to make pasta on a regular basis, it is worth investing in a pasta machine.

Making ravioli

1 Roll out the dough to 2 thin sheets of the same size. Cover 1 sheet with clingfilm while putting filling on the other sheet.
2 Working quickly to prevent the pasta drying out, place teaspoonfuls of filling in rows over the pasta. Keep the mounds of filling and rows evenly spaced at 3.5 cm (1½ inch) intervals.
3 Brush a little egg white or water between the piles of filling. Carefully lay the second sheet of dough over the top; be careful not to stretch it. Use your fingers to press firmly between the mounds of stuffing to seal them between the sheets of stuffing.
4 Using a knife or pasta cutting wheel, cut between the stuffing to make ravioli squares. Leave to dry for 20–30 minutes before cooking.

Making gnocchi

Gnocchi are classed as pasta even though they are in fact miniature dumplings. They can be made from potatoes, semolina or soft cheese. Potato gnocchi are very simple to make. For the best texture, choose a floury variety of potatoes, such as Maris Piper.

Potato Gnocchi

1 kg (2 lb) potatoes, peeled
1 egg, beaten
1 tablespoon olive oil
250 g (8 oz) plain flour
salt and pepper

1 Cook the potatoes in lightly salted boiling water for about 20 minutes or until tender. Drain and leave to cool.
2 Mash the potatoes thoroughly in a bowl, then make a well in the centre and add the seasoning, egg, oil and half the flour. Mix the ingredients until the flour is incorporated, then gradually knead in the remaining flour until you have a soft, smooth dough. Cover and leave the dough to rest for about 15 minutes.
3 Cut the dough in half and roll 2 long sausages, about 2.5 cm (1 inch) in diameter. Cut the rolls into 1.5 cm (¾ inch) lengths. Press each piece into a neat oval over the prongs of a fork.
4 Heat a large saucepan of salted water and cook the gnocchi in batches for 3–4 minutes, until they float to the surface. Drain and serve with butter and grated Parmesan cheese, or with a pasta sauce.

Cooking pasta

There are just a few simple rules for cooking perfect pasta and they apply to both fresh and dried types. Use a large saucepan, allowing 2 litres (3½ pints) of water to each 200 g (7 oz) of pasta. If you do not have a large enough pan, use the largest you have and make sure there is plenty of water to allow the pasta to move while it cooks.

Bring the water to a fast, rolling boil before adding the pasta and add the salt at the same time as you add the pasta – about 2 teaspoons to each 2 litres (3½ pints) of water. Add the pasta quickly, stirring once to prevent it from sticking together, then bring the water quickly back to the boil.

To cook long pasta, such as spaghetti, gather the pasta in a bunch and hold one end in the boiling water, gradually lowering it as it softens.

Cooking times vary according to the type and shape of pasta. Fresh pasta takes 2–3 minutes; dried pasta 8–12 minutes. The best way to check if pasta is cooked is to taste a piece – it should be tender, but still slightly firm to the bite. This is known as 'al dente'.

Drain the pasta as soon as it is cooked, turning it out into a colander. When draining filled pasta, such as ravioli, use a slotted spoon to remove the pieces as soon as they are cooked. This will help to prevent them from splitting open.

Toss the pasta in a little butter or oil to prevent the pieces from sticking together and serve on its own with a little black pepper or toss with a sauce.

Cooking rice

It is not necessary to rinse regular rice before cooking, but basmati, glutinous and jasmine rice are best rinsed thoroughly to remove excess starch from the surface of the grains. Place the rice in a sieve and rinse under cold running water until the water runs clear. There are two main methods of cooking rice.

Absorption method Put 250 g (9 oz) of rice in a saucepan. Add the measured amount of cold water (see chart right) and bring to the boil. Stir once, then cover the pan and reduce the heat to a gentle simmer. Avoid removing the lid and allowing the steam to escape. Cook for the recommended time, until the rice is tender and the water has all been absorbed. Leave to stand for 5 minutes, covered.

Free simmer method Bring 1.5 litres (2½ pints) of water to the boil in a large saucepan. Add 250 g (9 oz) of rice, bring back to the boil and reduce the heat. Simmer, uncovered, for the recommended time, until the rice is tender. Drain well.

Cooking rice – 250 g (9 oz)
suitable for both cooking methods

	water quantity	cooking time
long-grain	500 ml/17 fl oz	12 minutes
easy-cook long-grain	550 ml/18 fl oz	15 minutes
basmati (white)	450 ml/¾ pint	10 minutes
brown long-grain	625 ml/21 fl oz	35 minutes
easy-cook brown long-grain	650 ml/23 fl oz	30 minutes

Basic risotto

Risotto should be prepared immediately before serving so it is fresh and creamy. The following recipe is for a basic risotto with Parmesan cheese, which illustrates the general technique for all risottos.

1–1.2 litres (1¾–2 pints) stock
50 g (2 oz) butter, preferably unsalted
2 shallots, finely chopped
300 g (10 oz) risotto rice
5 tbsp dry white wine
40 g (1½ oz) Parmesan cheese, freshly grated
salt

1 Bring the stock to simmering point in a large pan and keep hot.

2 Melt half the butter in a second large, heavy-based pan over a low heat. Add the shallots and sauté gently over a low heat, stirring occasionally. Cook for about 5 minutes until they are softened and translucent.

3 Add the rice to the pan and stir constantly with a wooden spoon over a low heat for 1–2 minutes, until all the grains are coated with butter and translucent. They will begin to stick to the base of the pan.

4 Pour in the white wine and bring the mixture to the boil over a medium heat, stirring constantly. Cook the rice, continually stirring, until almost all the liquid has evaporated.

5 Add a ladleful of the simmering stock and cook over a medium heat, still stirring, until it has been absorbed by the rice. Continue adding the stock, a ladleful at a time, and continue cooking and stirring. Make sure that each addition of stock has been completely absorbed before adding more. The liquid should be at a fairly vigorous simmer, so adjust the heat if necessary. It will take about 20 minutes for the rice to cook. The grains should be plump and tender, but still firm, and the texture should be creamy.

6 Remove the pan from the heat and stir in the remaining butter and the Parmesan. Cover the pan and leave the risotto to rest for 2–3 minutes. Remove the lid and stir vigorously to increase the creaminess and serve immediately.

Oven-baked polenta

15–25 g (½–1 oz) butter
1.8 litres (3 pints) water
2 teaspoons salt
375 g (12 oz) polenta flour (not instant)

To serve:
garlic butter
rosemary sprigs
grated Parmesan cheese

1 Butter a large ovenproof dish.
2 Pour the water into a large saucepan, add the salt and bring to the boil. Remove the pan from the heat and sprinkle the polenta into the water in a continuous shower, stirring or whisking to prevent lumps forming. Return the pan to the heat, bring to the boil then simmer for 5 minutes, stirring constantly.
3 Spoon the polenta into the prepared dish, levelling the top. Cover with buttered or oiled kitchen foil and cook in a preheated oven, 190°C (375°F), Gas Mark 5, for 1 hour. Remove the dish from the oven, loosen the polenta and turn it out on to a board. Slice with a sharp knife and serve topped with garlic butter, rosemary sprigs and Parmesan.

Cooking grains

Some varieties of bulgar wheat, buckwheat, couscous and millet are already partially cooked and simply require soaking in boiling water to plump them up. Others require cooking: place the grain in a saucepan and cover with about double its volume of boiling water. Bring to the boil, reduce the heat and cover the pan. Simmer gently for 10–15 minutes or until the grains are tender and all the water is absorbed.

Couscous

Put the couscous into a large heatproof bowl and pour in enough boiling water to cover it. Allow about 400 ml (14 fl oz) to 250 g (9 oz) of couscous. Cover and leave to soak for 20 minutes. Don't cook the couscous again once it has soaked or it will become very stodgy.

Polenta

Allow 1.5 litres (2½ pints) of water and 2 teaspoons of salt to 300 g (10 oz) of instant polenta. Bring the water to the boil in a large saucepan. Add the salt and sprinkle in the polenta, stirring continuously to prevent lumps from forming. Bring to the boil, then simmer gently, stirring constantly, for 10–12 minutes, until the polenta begins to come away from the sides of the pan.

Polenta can be served in this moist form, often with the addition of herbs or cheese to flavour it. It can also be allowed to set, cut into slices and fried.

To do this, grease a shallow tin and spread the polenta into it to a thickness of about 1.5 cm (¾ inch). Leave to set. To serve, cut into slices, brush with olive oil and grill or fry until golden.

TOP TIP

Polenta can be frozen quite successfully for up to 3 months. Follow the instructions for making polenta and either freeze it in moist form in a tub or in slabs in a shallow freezer-proof dish. Be sure to let it defrost thoroughly before cooking.

Chicken and Artichoke Cannelloni

You can use cannelloni tubes or lasagne sheets. If using lasagne, soak it in boiling water until soft, then roll it around the filling.

Preparation time 20 minutes **Cooking time** 1½ hours **Serves** 4

1 To make the tomato sauce, heat the oil in a pan. Add the onion and garlic and cook gently until soft, but not brown. Add the remaining ingredients. Bring to the boil, stirring occasionally. Lower the heat, cover and simmer for 40 minutes.

2 To make the filling, heat the oil in a frying pan. Add the onion and fry over a moderate heat until soft, but not brown. Add the minced chicken and cook for a few minutes, until just cooked. Remove from the heat. Stir in the artichoke hearts, soft cheese and basil, with salt and pepper to taste. Mix well and use to fill the cannelloni tubes.

3 Place the filled cannelloni in a lightly greased ovenproof dish. Pour over the prepared tomato sauce and sprinkle with the grated Parmesan. Bake on the middle shelf of a preheated oven at 190°C (375°F), Gas Mark 5, for 40 minutes. Serve immediately, garnished with extra basil leaves.

2 tbsp oil

1 small onion, finely chopped

175 g (6 oz) boneless, skinless chicken, minced

200 g (7 oz) artichoke hearts in olive oil, drained and chopped

65 g (2½ oz) full-fat soft cheese

handful of basil leaves, plus extra to garnish

8 ready-to-cook cannelloni tubes or fresh lasagne sheets

3 tbsp grated Parmesan cheese

salt and pepper

Tomato sauce
1 tbsp olive oil

1 large onion, finely chopped

2 garlic cloves, crushed

400 g (13 oz) can chopped tomatoes

2 tsp sugar

150 ml (¼ pint) water or Chicken Stock (see page 161)

1 tsp dried mixed herbs

300 g (10 oz) firm goats'
cheese

1 lemon

75 g (3 oz) butter

2 tbs olive oil

3 shallots, finely chopped

2 garlic cloves, crushed

25 g (1 oz) mixed
chopped herbs, such as
tarragon, chervil,
parsley, dill

3 tbsp capers

300 g (10 oz) fresh linguini
or 250 g (8 oz) dried
linguini

salt and pepper

Goats' Cheese Linguini with Garlic and Herb Butter

If you cannot get fresh pasta for this dish, use dried, and cook it while you make the sauce. Always lightly drain pasta so that it retains plenty of moisture and does not dry out the sauce.

Preparation time 5 minutes **Cooking time** 7 minutes **Serves** 4

1 Thickly slice the goats' cheese and arrange on a lightly oiled, foil-lined grill rack. Grill under a preheated hot grill for about 2 minutes until golden. Keep warm.

2 Using a zester, pare strips of rind from the lemon, then squeeze the juice.

3 Melt the butter in a frying pan or sauté pan with the oil. Add the shallots and garlic and fry gently for 3 minutes. Stir in the herbs, capers and lemon juice, and season to taste with salt and pepper.

4 Cook the pasta in plenty of lightly salted boiling water for about 2 minutes or until just tender. Drain lightly and return to the saucepan. Add the goats' cheese and herb butter and toss the ingredients together gently. Serve scattered with the strips of lemon rind.

Tabbouleh with Fruit and Nuts

An abundance of herbs gives this salad its wonderful flavour.
Substitute apricots or sultanas for the prunes if you prefer.

150 g (5 oz) bulgar wheat

75 g (3 oz) unsalted, shelled pistachio nuts

1 small red onion, finely chopped

3 garlic cloves, crushed

25 g (1 oz) flat leaf parsley, chopped

15 g (½ oz) mint, chopped

finely grated rind and juice of 1 lemon or lime

150 g (5 oz) ready-to-eat prunes, sliced

4 tbsp olive oil

salt and pepper

Preparation time 10 minutes, plus soaking **Serves** 4

1 Place the bulgar wheat in a bowl, cover with plenty of boiling water and leave to soak for 15 minutes.

2 Meanwhile, place the pistachio nuts in a separate bowl and cover with boiling water. Leave to stand for 1 minute, then drain. Rub the nuts between several thicknesses of kitchen paper to remove most of the skin, then peel away any remaining skin with the fingers. Mix the nuts with the onion, garlic, parsley, mint, lemon or lime rind and juice and prunes in a large bowl.

3 Drain the bulgar wheat thoroughly in a sieve, pressing out as much moisture as possible with the back of a spoon. Add to the other ingredients with the oil and toss together. Season to taste with salt and pepper and chill until ready to serve.

Saffron and Cardamom Rice

Flavoured with aromatic cardamom and saffron, this fragrant rice dish makes a delicious centrepiece for any Indian meal.

Preparation time 5 minutes, plus soaking and standing **Cooking time** 15 minutes **Serves** 4

15 g (½ oz) unsalted butter

1 tbsp vegetable oil

1 onion, finely chopped

2 dried red chillies

6 cardamom pods, lightly crushed

1 cinnamon stick

1 tsp cumin seeds

2 bay leaves

225 g (7½) oz basmati rice, washed and soaked in cold water for 15 minutes

1 tsp saffron threads, soaked in 1 tbsp hot milk

475 ml (16 fl oz) boiling water

sea salt and pepper

crispy fried onions, to garnish

1 Heat the butter and oil in a large, heavy-based saucepan and add the onion. Stir and cook over a medium heat for 2–3 minutes. Add the chillies, cardamom, cinnamon, cumin and bay leaves.

2 Drain the rice, add to the pan and stir-fry for 2–3 minutes. Add the saffron mixture and boiling water, season with salt and pepper and bring back to the boil. Cover tightly, reduce the heat to low and simmer gently for 10 minutes. Do not lift the lid, as the steam is required for the cooking process.

3 Remove the pan from the heat and leave the rice to stand, covered and undisturbed, for 8–10 minutes. Fluff up the grains with a fork and serve garnished with crispy fried onions.

Chocolate Risotto

When you are adding the chocolate to this sumptuous, creamy dessert, try not to over-mix it. The brown and white marbled effect makes it look even better.

Preparation time 5–10 minutes **Cooking time** 25–35 minutes **Serves** 4

600 ml (1 pint) milk

25 g (1 oz) sugar

50 g (2 oz) butter

125 g (4 oz) risotto rice

50 g (2 oz) hazelnuts, toasted and chopped

50 g (2 oz) sultanas

125 g (4 oz) good-quality dark chocolate, grated

splash of brandy (optional)

grated chocolate, to decorate

1 Put the milk and sugar into a saucepan and heat until almost boiling.

2 Melt the butter in a heavy-based saucepan, add the rice and stir well to coat the grains with the butter.

3 Add the hot milk, a large ladleful at a time, stirring until each addition is absorbed into the rice. Continue adding milk in this way, cooking until the rice is creamy but the grains are still firm. This should take about 25–35 minutes.

4 Finally, add the hazelnuts, sultanas, grated chocolate and a splash of brandy, if using, and mix quickly. Serve decorated with grated chocolate.

Easy ways with eggs

The egg is a great starting place when you are learning to cook. Eggs are found all over the world, eaten at all times of day – breakfast, lunch, tea, dinner and supper, as well as at picnics and in packed meals – and at every sort of social gathering.

Choosing and storing eggs

Eggs are sold by size, graded into very large, large, medium and small. As a general rule, choose large eggs when using them in recipes. Very large and large are a good choice for boiling, frying, poaching, scrambling and omelettes, and small are useful for binding ingredients or glazing when only a small amount is required.

Fresh eggs will keep for about 2 weeks. Cool storage is essential to keep eggs at their best, but remember to remove them from the refrigerator 20–30 minutes before you use them.

Below Eggs are incredibly versatile and can be cooked in a multitude of different ways.

Are they fresh?

Very fresh eggs are best for poaching and whisking, and they are also easier to separate. Egg shells are porous, allowing moisture to evaporate from the white and air to enter the shell, forming a pocket between the shell and the lining membrane. The older eggs are, the larger the air pocket at the rounded end of the shell. This air pocket will act as a float, so this quick and simple test can be used to indicate the freshness of an egg.

Dissolve 1 tablespoon of salt in a bowl containing 600 ml (1 pint) of water and lower the egg into it. A very fresh egg will sink and lie on its side. If it lies at a slight angle it is about a week old and if it tilts straight upwards or floats it is stale.

Cooking eggs

There are so many different ways to cook eggs, from poaching, boiling, frying, baking and scrambling to whisking the egg whites and turning them into meringues. The choice is endless.

Poached eggs

A perfect poached egg is lightly set and compact in shape. You will need very fresh eggs to achieve this. Make sure you do not overcook the eggs or the yolks will set hard.

1 Pour about 4 cm (1½ inches) of water into a frying pan or shallow saucepan and add a little salt. Put the pan over a low heat and bring the water just to simmering point – too many bubbles will cause the egg white to break up before it sets.

2 Break the egg into a cup or small dish and slide it into the water. If necessary, gently stir the water around the egg to draw the white into shape. Leave to poach over a very low heat for 2–3 minutes, until the white is just set, but the yolk is still soft.

TOP TIPS

To prevent eggs from cracking when boiling them, carefully prick the rounded end with a pin before placing them in the saucepan.

To prevent hard-boiled eggs overcooking and avoid the formation of a black ring around the yolk, drain them immediately at the end of cooking. Tap on a hard surface to crack the shell, then leave the eggs in cold water to cool.

Making a classic omelette

1 For each omelette, break 2–3 eggs into a bowl and beat lightly with a fork, just enough to break up the white and yolk. Add salt and pepper to taste and 1 tablespoon of water.

2 Heat a small knob of butter in an omelette pan or small frying pan until it is foaming, but not browned.

3 Pour in the eggs and leave for a few seconds until they begin to set around the edge. Use a spatula or fork to draw the sides of the egg towards the centre, so that the liquid egg flows to the edge.

4 When most of the egg is set, fold the omelette in half and serve. If you want a filled omelette, sprinkle over grated cheese, chopped ham, fried mushrooms or crème fraîche mixed with herbs before you fold the omelette in half.

Boiled eggs

Using cold water Place the eggs in a saucepan and pour in enough cold water to cover them completely. Place the pan over a high heat. As soon as the water reaches boiling point, reduce the heat so that the water simmers and start the timer for cooking. Cooking times for eggs (large):
• Soft boiled eggs – 3–4 minutes
• Firm white, runny yolk – 4 minutes
• Hard-boiled eggs – 10 minutes

Using hot water Lower the eggs into a saucepan of simmering water. Make sure there is enough water in the pan to cover the eggs completely. Don't use eggs straight from the refrigerator or they will crack. Bring back to simmering point and start the timer for cooking. Cooking times for eggs (large):
• Soft boiled eggs – 3–4 minutes
• Firm white, runny yolk – 7 minutes
• Hard-boiled eggs – 12 minutes

Fried eggs

1 Heat about 2 tablespoons of oil or melted bacon fat in a heavy or nonstick frying pan until it is really hot. Break an egg into a cup and quickly tip it into the pan – the white should begin to set immediately on contact with the hot pan.

2 Reduce the heat to medium and spoon the fat over the egg to cook the top. Cook for about 1 minute or until the white is set. Use a fish slice to lift the egg from the pan and drain on absorbent kitchen paper.

Scrambled eggs

1 Beat the eggs with a fork, adding salt and pepper to taste. Add 1 tablespoon of milk for every 2 eggs if you like a creamy mixture.

2 Melt 15 g (½ oz) of butter in a heavy or nonstick saucepan and add the eggs, then stir gently over a medium heat until they are beginning to set.

3 Grated cheese, smoked salmon strips, diced cooked bacon or snipped chives can be added to the mixture.

Baked eggs

1 Grease several ramekin dishes with butter, then place them in a roasting tin with 2½ cm (1 inch) warm water. Break 1 egg into each dish, sprinkle it with salt and pepper and dot the surface with a little butter or one or two tablespoons of cream.

2 Cook the eggs in a preheated oven, 180°C (350°F), Gas Mark 4, for 8–10 minutes until the eggs are just set.

3 Remove the ramekins from the roasting tin straight away or they will continue cooking. Serve immediately.

Did you know?
Eggs are a valuable source of protein and rich in calcium, iron, zinc, the B group vitamins and vitamins A, D, E and K. They are a concentrated source of nutrients and help promote good bones and joints. They also boost the immune system.

Above To separate an egg, tap it against the rim of a bowl, then carefully divide the two halves of shell, allowing the white to run out.

How to separate an egg

Many recipes require only the yolk of an egg, or only the white. There is a knack to separating eggs, but it is soon mastered.

1 Tap the egg against the rim of a bowl to crack it around the middle.

2 Holding the egg over the bowl, carefully open the shell with your thumbs, holding the two halves together to let some of the white run out. If pieces of the shell fall into the bowl, scoop them out using a clean spoon.

3 Gently tip the yolk from one half of the shell to the other, letting the white run into the bowl and taking care not to break the yolk. Use the sharp edges of the shell to cut through any white threads.

If you are separating more than 1 egg, use a second bowl and tip the whites into the main bowl when separated. If a yolk then breaks, it won't spoil the whole batch of whites. It is important to separate eggs cleanly as even a trace of the yolk can prevent the egg white becoming stiff when it is whisked. If, however, some of the yolk does get into the bowl, use the egg shell to remove it.

Whisking egg whites

Whisked egg whites are used in recipes such as soufflés and meringues since, when cooked, they expand and increase the volume of whatever they are mixed with. In savoury dishes, a small pinch of salt added to egg whites at the beginning of whisking will help to stiffen them. For sweet dishes, add a little sugar, although this should be added after the whites have begun to stiffen. The use of egg whites in sorbets has a stabilizing effect, minimizing the formation of ice crystals.

A large balloon whisk is the best tool for whisking egg white, since it incorporates as much air as possible into the whites. An electric hand mixer will also give good results and save you quite a bit of time and effort. Choose a large, wide bowl for whisking to allow plenty of air to be whisked in. Copper or metal bowls are preferable as the egg white tends to detach from the sides of glass or ceramic bowls and then separate.

Before you start, make absolutely sure that the bowl and whisk are completely clean and grease-free, since any trace of grease will give the whisked whites a poor volume, and you may find that you will not be able to whisk them stiffly at all.

Continue to whisk hard and fast until the egg whites begin to hold their shape. Try lifting the whisk from the mixture – at first the whites will hold soft peaks, bending over slightly at the peak. The longer you whisk, the stiffer the foam will become and as you lift the whisk the peaks will form stiff points that stay firm and upright.

Whisk the whites to soft or stiff peaks, depending on the recipe, but take care not to overwhisk. Overwhisked whites become dry and powdery, and it is difficult to fold them into mixtures. Use the whisked whites straight away: if they are left to stand, the foam will begin to collapse and it cannot be re-whisked.

Using egg yolks

Egg yolks are very versatile ingredients and have an important part to play in many dishes. They can be used as emulsifiers, holding oil or butter in suspension and keeping the two from separating; the classic examples of this are mayonnaise and Hollandaise sauce. Egg yolks also act as a binding agent in stuffings, fish cakes and burgers, holding the surrounding ingredients together.

Folding in egg whites

Some recipes, including soufflés, require whisked egg whites to be folded into another mixture. It is important that the mixture into which you are folding whisked egg whites is neither too hot nor too cold, as either can cause much of the volume to be lost. First lighten the mixture by stirring in 1–2 tablespoons of the whisked whites. This makes it easier to fold in the rest without knocking out too much air.

Use a large metal spoon to fold in the egg whites lightly, with a cutting and folding action, until the mixture is evenly mixed and there are no clumps of white foam visible. Avoid using a wooden spoon as this will squash the mixture and avoid using a stirring action otherwise you will knock out some of the air.

Cheese soufflé

Being able to make a successful soufflé is one feat that every amateur cook would be proud to claim. The secret is to make sure that the base sauce is of the right consistency, the egg whites are beaten stiffly and that the two are folded together very gently so that enough air is retained to make the soufflé rise perfectly. It's not as hard as it sounds and it's well worth the effort.

50 g (2 oz) butter
50 g (2 oz) plain flour
250 ml (8 fl oz) milk
2 tablespoons single cream
4 egg yolks
150 g (5 oz) Gruyère cheese, grated
¼ teaspoon freshly grated nutmeg
5 egg whites
salt and pepper

1 Make a white sauce by melting the butter in a saucepan and stirring in the flour. Cook for 1–2 minutes over a low heat, then gradually add the milk, stirring well after each addition until the sauce is thick and smooth. Cook gently for 15 minutes, stirring constantly. Remove from the heat and stir in the cream.
2 Stir in the egg yolks, a little at a time. Add the Gruyère, salt, pepper and nutmeg to taste. Beat well until the cheese melts and the mixture is smooth.
3 Whisk the egg whites in a clean bowl until stiff, then fold them gently into the cheese sauce mixture.
4 Transfer the mixture to a greased 1.2 litre (2 pint) soufflé dish. Bake in a preheated oven at 190°C (375°F), Gas Mark 5, for 15 minutes. Increase the temperature to 200°C (400°F), Gas Mark 6, and cook for a further 15 minutes until the soufflé is well risen and golden. Serve immediately.

Above When whisking egg whites, be careful not to overwhisk as this will cause them to separate and become grainy.

Perfect meringues

A classic meringue is white and crisp, light and sweet. To achieve this you need very stiffly whisked egg whites and a low heat to dry the mixture out slowly, without browning the meringues. Aim to retain a little chewiness in the centre of the meringues, with a light crisp exterior.

3 large egg whites
175 g (6 oz) caster sugar
whipped cream or créme fraîche

1 Line a baking sheet with non-stick baking paper.
2 Whisk the egg whites in a large bowl until they form stiff peaks. Gradually whisk in about half the sugar, a tablespoonful at a time, whisking hard between each addition, until the meringue is very stiff. Fold in the rest of the sugar lightly and evenly, using a large metal spoon. The mixture should be thick enough that you can turn the bowl upside down without it falling out.
3 Spoon or pipe the mixture into about 12–14 rounds or ovals on the baking sheet, then place in a preheated oven at 110°C (225°F), Gas Mark ¼, for 2–3 hours, until the meringues are crisp and dry but have not begun to brown.
4 Carefully lift the meringues from the paper and cool on a wire rack. Sandwich the meringues together with whipped cream or crème fraîche, and serve with summer fruits or chocolate sauce.

Eggs Florentine

Perfect as a first course or light lunch, this is a divine mixture of lightly cooked egg and meltingly tender spinach, finished with a topping of crème fraîche, Cheddar and Parmesan.

Preparation time 15 minutes **Cooking time** 15–20 minutes **Serves** 6

40 g (1½ oz) butter

1 kg (2 lb) fresh spinach, washed

2 large tomatoes, diced

freshly grated nutmeg

6 large eggs

150 ml (¼ pint) crème fraîche

50 ml (2 fl oz) double cream

40 g (1½ oz) Cheddar cheese, grated

40 g (1½ oz) Parmesan cheese, freshly grated

salt and pepper

1 Melt half the butter in a large saucepan. Add the fresh spinach with just the water that clings to the rinsed leaves. Cover tightly and sweat until the leaves have wilted, the spinach is tender and any liquid has evaporated. Transfer to a large sieve or colander and squeeze out any liquid that remains. Return to the pan, add the tomatoes and season with nutmeg, salt and pepper.

2 Grease 6 x 175 ml (6 fl oz) gratin dishes with the remaining butter. Divide the spinach among the dishes, making a well in the centre of each for an egg and leaving a 1 cm (½ inch) space between the spinach and the rim of the dish.

3 Break an egg into the centre of each gratin dish and dust with salt and pepper. Mix together the crème fraîche and cream. Spoon evenly over the eggs and sprinkle with the Cheddar and Parmesan.

4 Set the gratin dishes on a heavy baking sheet and bake in a preheated oven at 220°C (425°F), Gas Mark 7, for 10-12 minutes, until the whites are set but the yolks are still runny.

5 Remove the dishes from the oven and place under a preheated hot grill until the topping is bubbling and the cheese golden brown. Serve immediately.

250 g (8 oz) shortcrust pastry (see page 146)

2 tbsp extra virgin olive oil

1 small onion, finely sliced

2 courgettes, finely sliced

50 g (2 oz) drained sun-dried tomatoes in oil, sliced

250 g (8 oz) ricotta or curd cheese

2 tbsp milk

2 eggs, beaten

4 tbsp chopped fresh herbs (basil, rosemary, sage, thyme)

12 black olives, pitted and halved

salt and pepper

Courgette, Sun-dried Tomato and Ricotta Flan

Many quiches and flans are made from eggs. The beaten eggs are poured into the pastry case with other ingredients, and they set in the oven to form a firm filling.

Preparation time 30 minutes, plus chilling **Cooking time** about 1 hour **Serves** 4

1 On a lightly floured surface, roll out the pastry and use it to line a greased 23-cm (9-inch) flan tin. Prick the base with a fork and chill for 20 minutes. Line the pastry case with foil and baking beans and cook in a preheated oven at 200°C (400°F), Gas Mark 6, for 10 minutes. Remove the foil and beans and bake for a further 10–12 minutes until the pastry is crisp and golden.

2 Heat the oil in a frying pan, add the onion and courgettes and fry gently for 5–6 minutes until lightly golden. Scatter over the base of the pastry case and top with the sun-dried tomatoes.

3 Beat together the ricotta, milk, eggs, herbs and salt and pepper and spread over the courgette mixture. Scatter the olives over the top, and bake the flan for 30–35 minutes until firm and golden.

Fresh Pea and Tomato Frittata

2 tbsp extra virgin olive oil

1 bunch spring onions, sliced

1 garlic clove, crushed

125 g (4 oz) cherry tomatoes, halved

125 g (4 oz) frozen peas

6 eggs

2 tbsp chopped mint

a handful pea shoots (optional)

salt and pepper

To serve
rocket leaves

Parmesan cheese shavings (optional)

Frittata is a traditional Italian dish, rather like a thick omelette. Serve cut into wedges for a light supper or lunch dish.

Preparation time 8 minutes **Cooking time** 12 minutes **Serves** 4

1 Heat the oil in a nonstick frying pan and fry the spring onions and garlic for 2 minutes, then add the tomatoes and peas.

2 Beat the eggs, add the mint, and season with salt and pepper. Swirl the egg mixture into the pan, scatter over the pea shoots, if using, and cook over a moderate heat for 3–4 minutes, or until almost set.

3 Transfer the pan to a preheated grill and cook for 2–3 minutes longer, or until lightly browned and cooked through. Allow to cool slightly then serve in wedges with the rocket and Parmesan shavings, if liked.

Spaghetti Carbonara

400 g (13 oz) dried spaghetti or other long thin pasta

2 tbsp olive oil

1 onion, finely chopped

200 g (7 oz) pancetta or streaky bacon rashers, diced

2 garlic cloves, finely chopped

3 eggs

4 tbsp grated Parmesan cheese

3 tbsp chopped flat leaf parsley

3 tbsp single cream

salt and pepper

This rich spaghetti sauce is made using beaten eggs and cream. The eggs are poured on to the hot spaghetti which lightly cooks the mixture and makes it thicken.

Preparation time 10 minutes **Cooking time** 10 minutes **Serves** 4

1 Cook the pasta in a large saucepan of boiling salted water for 8–10 minutes, or according to the packet instructions, until al dente – tender but with bite.

2 Meanwhile, heat the oil in a large nonstick frying pan. Add the onion and fry until it is soft but not browned. Add the pancetta or bacon and the garlic, and cook gently for 4–5 minutes.

3 Beat the eggs with the Parmesan, parsley and cream. Season with salt and pepper to taste and set aside.

4 Drain the pasta and add it to the onion and pancetta. Stir over a gentle heat until combined, then pour in the egg mixture. Stir and remove the pan from the heat. Continue mixing well for a few seconds, until the eggs are lightly cooked and creamy, then serve immediately.

Tiramisu with Raspberry Surprise

This dessert is best made the night before so that it can set completely. The egg yolks are beaten with creamy mascarpone cheese to make a rich mixture, then the whites are whisked and folded in to make it light and foamy.

Preparation time 20 minutes **Serves** 4

4 tbsp very strong espresso coffee

2 tbsp grappa or brandy

10 sponge fingers

125 g (4 oz) raspberries

175 g (6 oz) mascarpone cheese

2 eggs, separated

50 g (2 oz) icing sugar

25 g (1 oz) plain chocolate

mint sprigs, to decorate

1 Combine the coffee and grappa or brandy. Dip the sponge fingers into the liquid to coat them evenly, then arrange them in a small shallow dish or a serving platter, pouring any excess liquid over them. Sprinkle the raspberries evenly over the soaked sponge fingers.

2 In a bowl, whisk together the mascarpone, egg yolks and icing sugar until smooth and well blended.

3 In another bowl, whisk the egg whites until stiff and glossy, then fold them into the mascarpone mixture until well blended.

4 Spoon the mixture over the sponge fingers and smooth the surface. Finely grate the chocolate straight on to the mixture. Cover and chill until the mixture is set. Decorate with mint leaves and serve.

Lime Meringue Pie

This classic dessert of creamy, egg-set filling topped with crispy meringue is flavoured with lime rather than lemon.

Preparation time 15 minutes, plus chilling   **Cooking time** 35 minutes   **Serves** 6–8

300 g (10 oz) ready-made sweet shortcrust pastry

grated rind and juice of 3 limes

175 g (6 oz) caster sugar

3 eggs, beaten

250 g (8 oz) butter

Meringue
3 egg whites

75 g (3 oz) caster sugar

1 Roll out the pastry and use it to line a 23-cm (9-inch) flan tin. Prick the pastry base with a fork and chill for 20 minutes.

2 Line the pastry case with nonstick baking paper and baking beans and place in a preheated oven at 220°C (425°F), Gas Mark 7, for 10 minutes. Remove the paper and beans and bake for a further 10–12 minutes until the pastry is crisp and golden. Remove from the oven and reduce the temperature to 190°C (375°F), Gas Mark 5.

3 Meanwhile, make the pie filling. Put the grated lime rind and juice in a heavy-based saucepan with the caster sugar and eggs. Place over a very low heat and stir well. Cut the butter into small dice and add to the lime mixture in the pan, one cube at a time. Continue stirring all the time over a low heat, until all the butter has been incorporated and the mixture is hot.

4 Pour the lime mixture into the pastry case and return it to the oven for about 10 minutes, or until the filling is just set. Remove from the oven and allow to cool. Keep the oven at the same temperature while you make the meringue topping.

5 Beat the egg whites until they stand in stiff peaks. Gradually beat in the caster sugar, a little at a time. Pile the meringue on top of the lime filling and bake in the oven for 12–15 minutes, until the meringue is delicately browned. Serve hot or cold.

butter, for greasing

25 g (1 oz) caster sugar, plus extra for dusting

200 g (7 oz) no-soak prunes, halved

½ teaspoon cornflour

6 tablespoons brandy

150 g (5 oz) plain chocolate, broken up

3 tablespoons double cream

6 eggs, separated

cocoa powder, for dusting

Hot Chocolate Soufflé

These intensely chocolaty soufflés can be prepared several hours in advance, leaving you free to enjoy your meal. Serve with a jug of pouring cream.

Preparation time 15 minutes **Cooking time** 15 minutes **Serves** 8

1 Butter eight 150 ml (¼ pint) ramekin dishes or small ovenproof serving dishes and dust lightly with caster sugar. Put the prunes in a small pan with 125 ml (4 fl oz) water and simmer gently for 1 minute. Blend the cornflour with 1 tablespoon water and add to the pan. Cook, stirring over a gentle heat, for 1 minute or until the sauce has thickened. Stir in the brandy and divide the mixture among the dishes.

2 Melt the chocolate with the cream in a small bowl. Whisk the egg yolks with the sugar until thickened and pale. Stir in the chocolate cream.

3 Whisk the egg whites in a clean bowl until stiff. Use a large metal spoon to fold about one-quarter of the whites into the chocolate mixture, then fold in the rest.

4 Spoon the mixture into the dishes and put them on a baking sheet. (If you are making them in advance put them on a baking sheet and chill until ready to cook.) Bake in a preheated oven, 200°C (400°F), Gas Mark 6, for about 15 minutes until well risen and slightly springy. Dust with cocoa powder and serve immediately.

simple techniques

Cooking methods

Cooking is a rewarding art, but intensely disappointing when things go wrong. Success is more easily achieved if you understand how and why things happen. Mastering these basic techniques will ensure your successes are more frequent.

Boiling

Boiling is cooking food in a liquid at a temperature of 100°C (212°F). The liquid used can be stock, salted water or a mixture containing wine, herbs or spices.

• Salt added to the water raises the boiling point and makes food cook more quickly. Add salt at the start of cooking when you are boiling vegetables, but close to the end for stocks and stews as the long cooking may result in some of the liquid evaporating and the dish becoming too salty.

• Fast boiling – a rolling boil – is used for cooking pasta, reducing liquid and jam making.

• Simmering takes place at a lower temperature than boiling. A liquid is simmering when small bubbles break just below the liquid's surface. This is a gentler form of cooking than boiling.

• Poaching is gentler still and is used for cooking delicate foods, such as fish fillets, in liquid.

• Vegetables such as peas and greens are cooked in an open pan in fast-boiling, well-salted water.

• Root vegetables are simmered in a covered pan.

• Blanching is cooking foods very briefly in boiling water to loosen skins or, for freezing, to prevent deterioration in colour and flavour. Food is put into the boiling water for a set time, then plunged into ice-cold water to stop the cooking process.

• Reducing is when the liquid is boiled uncovered over a high heat in a pan with a large surface area. This is used for stocks, soups and casseroles when less liquid and a more intense flavour is required.

Steaming

Cooking food in hot steam over a pan of boiling water is a delicate cooking method that retains plenty of flavour in the food, as well as most of the nutrients, which can be destroyed by boiling. You can use a tiered steamer, a flowered trivet or colander inside a saucepan, or a pressure cooker. The food can be placed directly in the steamer or on a plate inside the steamer.

Steaming is a good way to cook vegetables such as broccoli, asparagus and leeks because they stay intact and do not absorb a lot of moisture as they do when boiled. Steaming is a popular method in Oriental cuisines, and is used for cooking dumplings and seafood dishes particularly.

Braising

This is a method of cooking meat, fish or vegetables slowly on a bed of finely chopped vegetables. The pan is placed over a gentle heat with a tight-fitting lid. A small amount of liquid, such as stock, water or wine, is used.

Casseroling

Casseroling cooks a selection of meat and vegetables in more liquid than is used for braising. Tight-lidded pots prevent the liquid evaporating and keep the food moist. To stop any steam escaping, cover the pot first with foil and then the lid.

Frying

This is a method of quickly cooking or browning food in hot fat or oil. It is suitable for tender pieces of meat, fish and certain vegetables. Always pay attention when frying because deep fat will catch fire if it is allowed to become too hot.

Above Bring the water to a rolling boil when cooking pasta. Adding a little salt will raise the boiling point to reduce cooking time.

Above Stir-frying is one of the healthiest ways of cooking food as very little oil is needed and it is easy to avoid overcooking.

• Shallow frying is carried out over medium heat using equal amounts of sizzling oil and butter, or just oil.
• Sautéeing uses very little fat, and the food is moved constantly throughout the process to prevent sticking and burning.
• Dry-frying uses a thick-based pan and is used for toasting nuts, pine nuts and spices.
• Stir-frying uses very little oil and takes place in a wok or stir-fry pan over a high heat. The cooked foods are pushed to the side of the wok while fresh food is tossed and turned in the oil.
• Deep-frying uses very hot oil, which seals the outside of the food, preventing moisture escaping and fat soaking in. The fat should come only halfway up the pan to prevent it overflowing.

Griddling

Griddling uses a griddle or ridged stove-top grill pan. The pan is heated before the food is added and no extra fat is used, making it a healthy way of cooking. The food is seared in the hot pan to seal in the juices, then the temperature is reduced and the food is griddled slowly until cooked through. This results in a flavoursome, caramelized surface, known as char-grilled. This method of cooking is ideal for meat, fish and vegetables and the finished results will need little embellishment to make them delicious.

Grilling

Grilling cooks foods under an intense heat source and caramelizes the surface, giving it a good flavour. Select food that is tender, no more than 5 cm (2 inches) thick, and marinate drier and leaner cuts of meat, poultry and thick-fleshed fish. Preheat the grill (not the grill pan) at its highest setting for at least 10 minutes before cooking. Lightly grease the grill rack before placing the food on it. Start with the food at room temperature.
• Start by searing the food under a hot grill to seal the surface and retain the juices, goodness and flavour. Then reduce the temperature and continue cooking until the food is done.
• Use a hot grill to form a thin golden brown crust of melted cheese and breadcrumbs on gratin dishes, potato-topped pies and bakes.
• Add salt just before putting food under the grill. Salting food in advance tends to draw out the juices, leaving the inside dry.
• Grilling is a healthier form of cooking than frying as no extra fat is needed.

Roasting

Roasting takes place in an oven in an open dish or roasting tin. The high temperatures and dry heat result in a deliciously browned exterior, but roasting is suitable only for tender cuts of meat, fish and vegetables which will not become tough with fast hot cooking. See pages 63–64 for roasting tips.

Above Searing meat on a griddle, then cooking slowly locks in the flavour, resulting in delicious, healthy food.

The perfect barbecue

As soon as the good weather comes round, it's out with the charcoal, on with the oven gloves, matches at the ready, and it's barbecue time again!

Outdoor eating

Barbecues have become enormously popular, with the result that outdoor eating has become a much more sophisticated affair than it used to be. Barbecues are the perfect way of entertaining family and friends. Relaxed and informal, they do much to heighten the exhilaration of summer. There's nothing quite like the taste of charcoal-cooked food, with that delicious smell wafting in the balmy night air, to make any occasion seem like a special one.

Barbecues can be as simple or elaborate as you like. It's a great way to share a family supper on a midweek evening in the summer. You can leave some chicken or steak marinating in the refrigerator as you go off to work, then light the coals as soon as you get home, toss a simple salad together, and dine al fresco with very little effort indeed.

Equally, you can make a barbecue a grand occasion for family and friends with a wide selection of different dishes and several courses. If you have the space and confidence, a three or four course meal can all be cooked on a barbecue, although you will need to do some careful planning. To make life simpler, prepare marinades, sauces and salads well in advance so that you have time to enjoy yourself as much as your guests.

Did you know?
A barbecue is ready for cooking when the coals have been burning for about 30 minutes and all the flames have died down. The coals should be covered with a layer of grey ash, but they should still be glowing inside.

Above A brush of oil and a sprinkle of herbs and chopped garlic will transform plain fish, poultry, meat or vegetables of all kinds.

Barbecue hints and tips

A simple barbecue of sausages, steaks or burgers can make an easy informal supper, but with a little planning you can include some unusual dishes.

• Vegetables, such as mushrooms, courgettes, peppers and aubergines, do not need long cooking. Thread them on to skewers and marinate in seasoned oil for 30 minutes, before barbecuing for about 15 minutes.

• Corn on the cob in its husk cooks perfectly on a barbecue. Peel back the husks and remove the silky threads, brush the corn with melted butter, then replace the husks around the cobs. Barbecue for 30–45 minutes.

• Pitta breads are great for filling with barbecued meats and salads. Grill briefly on the barbecue before filling.

• Vegetables that are ideal for barbecuing include potatoes with rosemary and mint; skewers crammed with a mixture of tomato, onion, yellow pepper and mushrooms; red peppers stuffed with feta cheese coated in pesto; or try a fruit kebab.

• Herb butters and oils (see page 95) are perfect for melting or drizzling over simple barbecued meat, fish and vegetables and transform them into something really quite special.

• Consider barbecuing a whole fish, such as bass or salmon, or a larger joint of meat, such as a boneless leg of lamb, and carving it at the table.

• For vegetarian options, barbecue courgette slices (sliced lengthways) and top with slices of haloumi cheese with a drizzle of herb oil. Or wrap goats' cheese in foil parcels with some herbs and seasoning, then bake until soft.

• A marinade of flavoured oil, wine and herbs can transform a simple piece of chicken or pork, and helps to keep the meat tender and moist. Or you could try the following marinade to impart a rich and fruity flavour to your meat.

Red wine marinade

Mix together:

1 onion, thinly sliced

1 carrot, thinly sliced

1 celery stalk, finely chopped

1 garlic clove, crushed and finely chopped

125 ml (4 fl oz) red wine

2 tablespoons lemon juice

6 black peppercorns, bruised

1 bay leaf

sprig of parsley

sprig of thyme

TOP TIP

Mini vegetables are perfect for cooking whole on the barbecue, as they are sweet and tender and cook quickly. Little aubergines and pattypan squashes are usually available in ethnic markets, and in some supermarkets.

Above Try combining chunks of swordfish with vegetables and fruit such as peppers, onions and mango to make tasty kebabs.

Food safety

Cooking on a barbecue is a safe and enjoyable experience when it is done sensibly, but there are a few extra precautions you should bear in mind.

• Always marinate food, especially meat, fish and shellfish, in a cool place. If you intend to marinate for longer than an hour, place the food in a refrigerator and bring it back to room temperature before you begin cooking it.

• Keep foods refrigerated until you are ready to cook, especially in warm weather.

• Keep foods that are waiting to be cooked covered with plastic wrap or in sealed plastic boxes to prevent flies getting to them.

• Make sure that food is cooked through before you serve it. This is particularly important with pork, chicken and sausages. Pierce the thickest part of the meat with the point of a sharp knife. If the juices run clear, it is cooked. If there are traces of pink in the juices – even if the outside is well browned – continue cooking the meat for a little longer and check again before serving.

• Keep raw and cooked foods separate to prevent the possibility of contamination. Never put cooked foods on plates or platters that have had raw foods on them unless the plates have been thoroughly washed in the meantime.

• Don't leave sauces and dips, particularly those like mayonnaise that contain raw egg, standing in hot sunshine for a long time.

Left Wrapping burgers in pancetta gives the meat a lovely smoky taste and prevents the meat from drying out.

Spiced Pumpkin Wedges with Coconut Pesto

1 tsp cumin seeds

1 tsp coriander seeds

2 cardamom pods

1 kg (2 lb) pumpkin, cut into wedges 1 cm (½ inch) thick

3 tbsp sunflower oil

1 tsp caster sugar

Coconut pesto

25 g (1 oz) coriander leaves

1 garlic clove, crushed

1 green chilli, deseeded and chopped

pinch of sugar

1 tbsp shelled pistachio nuts, roughly chopped

6 tbsp coconut cream

1 tbsp lime juice

salt and pepper

Creamy coconut pesto makes a perfect foil to the soft, nutty wedges of barbecued pumpkin dusted with curry spices.

Preparation time 10 minutes **Cooking time** 15–18 minutes **Serves** 4

1 Dry-fry the whole spices until they have browned, then grind them to a powder in a spice grinder. Place the pumpkin wedges in a dish. Toss with the oil, sugar and spice mix to coat.

2 Cook the pumpkin wedges on a barbecue for 6–8 minutes on each side, until they are charred and tender.

3 Meanwhile, make the pesto. Work the coriander, garlic, chilli, sugar, nuts, salt and pepper in a food processor until fairly finely ground. Add the coconut cream and lime juice and process again. Transfer to a bowl and serve with the pumpkin.

Barbecued Fruits with Palm Sugar

25 g (1 oz) palm sugar

grated rind and juice of 1 lime

2 tbsp water

½ tsp cracked black peppercorns

500 g (1 lb) mixed prepared fruits

To serve

cinnamon or vanilla ice cream

lime slices

Many fruits lend themselves to barbecuing, especially those with a high sugar content – try pineapple slices, mango wedges, nectarines and peaches.

Preparation time 10 minutes, plus cooling **Cooking time** 6–8 minutes **Serves** 4

1 Warm the sugar, lime rind and juice, measured water and peppercorns in a small pan until the sugar has dissolved. Plunge the base of the pan into iced water to cool.

2 Brush the cooled syrup over the prepared fruits and barbecue or grill them until they are charred and tender. Serve with scoops of cinnamon or vanilla ice cream and slices of lime.

1 kg (2lb) monkfish fillet, cut into 4 cm (1½ inch) cubes

200 ml (7fl oz) natural yogurt

4 tbsp lemon juice

3 garlic cloves, crushed

2 tsp grated fresh root ginger

1 tsp hot chilli powder

1 tsp ground cumin

1 tsp ground coriander

2 fresh red chillies, finely sliced

sea salt and pepper

To garnish
chopped fresh coriander leaves

lime slices

sliced red chillies

Monkfish Kebabs

Monkfish has firm white flesh which lends itself to barbecuing, since it won't flake and fall apart.

Preparation time 10 minutes, plus marinating **Cooking time** 8–10 minutes **Serves** 4

1 Place the monkfish cubes in a non-metallic bowl.

2 In a small bowl, mix together the yogurt, lemon juice, garlic, ginger, chilli powder, cumin, ground coriander and chillies and season with salt and pepper. Pour this over the fish, cover and marinate in the refrigerator overnight, if time allows.

3 Lift the fish out of the marinade and thread it on to 8 flat metal skewers. Cook over hot coals for 3–5 minutes, turning once, until the fish is cooked through. Serve hot, garnished with chopped fresh coriander, lime slices and chilli slices.

Making pastry

Pastry-making is not an esoteric art, but a matter of following a set of simple rules, the most important of which is to keep everything cool – hands, head, equipment and ingredients.

Ingredients

The following ingredients are the basic ones that you will need to make pastry. Once you get the hang of it, you could always try adding flavourings such as mustard, Worcestershire sauce or cheese, for example.

Flour

Plain white flour is the best choice for most recipes. Wholemeal flour, or a mixture of half wholemeal and half white, can be used for shortcrust pastry but it tends to give a heavy, crumbly dough. Puff pastry is usually made with strong plain flour because its high levels of gluten give the dough more elasticity and strength.

Fat

The type of fat you use will affect the texture as well as the flavour of the pastry. It should be cold so keep in the refrigerator until shortly before use. The best shortcrust pastry is made using equal quantities of butter or margarine (for flavour) with lard or white vegetable fat (for a light, crumbly texture.)

Water

Use as little water as possible to bind the dough. Always try to use cold water and use less if you are adding egg.

Sugar

Some rich pastries use a small amount of sugar to give a crisp texture and golden colour.

Egg

Usually only the yolk of the egg is used to bind rich pastries; it also adds a nice yellow colour. Beat the yolk lightly with a fork before adding to the other ingredients.

> **TOP TIP**
> When you are making pastry, it is vital to preheat the oven thoroughly first, particularly for pastries with a high fat content, which should be cooked at a high temperature for light, crisp results.

Secrets of success

• Measure the right proportions of fat to flour, according to the type of pastry.
• Unless you are making choux pastry, keep everything, including your hands, as cool as possible.
• When you are rubbing in fats, use only the very tips of your fingers to keep the mixture cool. Lift the fingers high and let the crumbs run through them back into the bowl. If you use a food processor pulse the power to make sure that the pastry is not overmixed.
• When you are rolling out and shaping pastry, don't handle it more than necessary as this will make it heavy and tough.
• Don't add the liquid all at once. Flours vary in absorbency, and too much liquid can also make the pastry heavy.

How much pastry?
add other ingredients in proportion to flour

Tart tin diameter	Flour quantity
18 cm (7 inch)	125 g (4 oz)
20 cm (8 inch)	175 g (6 oz)
23 cm (9 inch)	200 g (7 oz)
25 cm (10 inch)	250 g (8 oz)

Above When rolling out pastry, make sure it is larger than the tart tin, then remove any surplus using a rolling pin.

Rolling out

Dust a cool work surface, and your rolling pin, lightly with flour. Roll lightly and evenly in one direction, always away from you, moving the pastry around by a quarter turn occasionally. Try to keep the pastry even in shape and thickness. Avoid stretching the pastry, which will cause it to shrink during cooking. Depending on the recipe, shortcrust pastry is usually rolled to about 3 mm (⅛ inch) thick; puff pastry can be rolled slightly thicker, to about 5 mm (¼ inch).

Lining a tart tin

Put the tart tin on a baking sheet and roll out the pastry to about 5 cm (2 inches) larger all round than the diameter of the tin. Roll the pastry loosely around the rolling pin, lift it over the tin, then carefully unroll it into the tin. Next, gently ease the pastry into the tin, pressing it into the flutes with your finger and taking care not to stretch it or leave air gaps underneath. Turn any surplus pastry outwards from the rim, then roll the rolling pin over the top so that the surplus pastry is cut away to leave a neat edge.

Baking blind

This is the process of part-baking pastry in the tin before the filling is added, to ensure crisp results. The pastry is weighted down to prevent it from bubbling up or falling down around the sides.

To begin with, line the tart tin with the rolled-out pastry as usual and prick the base with a fork so that any air trapped underneath can escape, rather than cause the pastry to bubble up. Place a square of nonstick baking paper or foil in the pastry case and half-fill the paper with dried beans or ceramic baking beans. Bake as instructed in the recipe, usually for 10–15 minutes, then remove the paper and beans. Return the pastry case to the oven for about 5 minutes to crisp the base if necessary.

Filo pastry

Filo pastry is difficult to make so it's not really worth trying to make your own, especially as it is so readily available to buy. However, even shop-bought filo pastry has a reputation for being difficult to handle, but if you follow these simple guidelines you will find that it is no more difficult to use than any other pastry. To keep filo soft and workable, make sure that the pastry is covered all the time you are not actually working on it. Lay a sheet of clingfilm or a damp cloth over it, or keep it wrapped otherwise it will become brittle and break easily if it dries out.

Make sure your hands aren't hot and work quickly, using up any broken or torn pieces of filo between whole sheets – no one will notice once the pastry is cooked. Do not moisten filo pastry with water as this will make the sheets stick together and disintegrate; keep the work surface dry for the same reason. Use fat, such as melted butter, to seal edges and to brush the pastry for crisp results.

Did you know?
With the exception of choux, pastry benefits from chilling and resting for about 30 minutes before baking. This reduces shrinkage during cooking. Wrap the pastry in clingfilm to prevent it from drying out and put it in the refrigerator.

Above Use your fingertips to rub the fat into the flour until the mixture resembles fine breadcrumbs.

Shortcrust pastry

The classic choice for savoury and sweet everyday dishes, shortcrust pastry is easy to handle and holds its shape well for pies and tart cases. It has a medium to high proportion of fat to flour and a low moisture content. Handle shortcrust pastry lightly and quickly, with the minimum of rolling, to give a crumbly texture when baked. This type of pastry does not rise during cooking.

Makes 300 g (10 oz)
200 g (7 oz) plain flour
pinch of salt
100 g (3½ oz) fat, such as equal quantities of butter and white vegetable fat
2–3 tbsp iced water

1 Sift the flour and salt into a mixing bowl. Cut the fat into small pieces and add it to the bowl with the flour.
2 Using your fingertips, rub the fat into the flour very lightly and evenly until it begins to resemble fine breadcrumbs.
3 Sprinkle the water over the surface and stir with a palette knife until the mixture begins to clump together but is not too moist.
4 Turn out the pastry on to a lightly floured surface and press it together lightly with the fingers. Chill for about 30 minutes before use.

Sweet shortcrust

A sweet shortcrust pastry has a rich, biscuit-like texture due to the addition of sugar and egg yolk, which helps to bind it. Sweet shortcrust pastry is used for desserts such as sweet tarts and pastries. The quantity given in this recipe makes enough pastry to line a 20 cm (8 inch) tart tin.

Makes 300 g (10 oz)
175 g (6 oz) plain flour
pinch of salt
75 g (3 oz) unsalted butter, slightly softened
2 egg yolks
1 tbsp cold water
40 g (1½ oz) caster sugar

1 Sift the flour and salt into a neat pile on a cold, clean work surface and make a well in the centre with your fingertips.
2 Add the butter, egg yolks, water and sugar to the well and use the fingertips of one hand to work them together into a rough paste. The mixture should resemble scrambled egg.
3 Making sure your hands are reasonably cool, gradually work in the flour with your fingertips to bind the mixture together until it has formed a smooth dough. Press together lightly and form into a ball. Try not to handle the dough too much. Wrap in clingfilm and chill for about 30 minutes before use.

Below Adding an egg yolk to the pastry ingredients helps to bind the pastry together as well as giving it a richer taste.

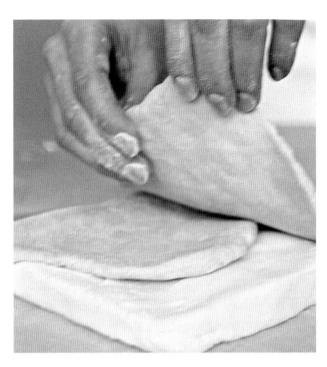

Above Folding the pastry over onto itself will trap air, which will help to make the pastry rise up.

Rough puff pastry

This deliciously rich and crisp flaky pastry is ideal for single-crust pies, pasties or sweet pastries. It does not rise as much as real puff pastry, but it is far simpler to make.

Makes 500 g (1 lb)
250 g (8 oz) plain flour
pinch of salt
175 g (6 oz) butter, thoroughly chilled, until almost frozen
about 150 ml (1/4 pint) iced water mixed with
2 teaspoons lemon juice

1 Sift the flour and salt into a bowl. Holding the butter with cool fingertips or by its folded-back wrapper, grate it coarsely into the flour. Work quickly before the butter softens from the heat of your hand.
2 Stir the grated butter into the flour with a palette knife, then sprinkle with just enough iced water to start binding the ingredients into a dough. Press the dough lightly together with your fingertips.
3 Turn out the dough on to a lightly floured surface and roll it out into an oblong about three times longer than it is wide.
4 Fold the bottom third of the pastry up and the top third down, then press around the sides with a rolling pin to seal the layers together lightly. Chill for about 30 minutes before use.

Choux pastry

This breaks all the rules for pastry making: it needs lots of heat and firm handling for good results. Use it for sweet or savoury buns, profiteroles and éclairs.

Makes 250 g (8 oz)
75 g (3 oz) plain flour
pinch of salt
50 g (2 oz) unsalted butter
150 ml (1/4 pint) water, or equal quantities of water and milk
2 large eggs, lightly beaten

1 Sift the flour and salt on to a large sheet of greaseproof paper.
2 Place the butter and measured water in a saucepan and heat gently until the butter melts, then bring quickly to the boil. Do not bring to the boil before the butter has completely melted.
3 Take the pan off the heat and immediately add the flour. Beat with a wooden spoon until the mixture forms a smooth ball that leaves the sides of the pan clean. Do not overbeat at this stage or the paste will become oily.
4 Cool the mixture for 2 minutes. Gradually add the eggs, beating hard after each addition, and continue to beat until the mixture is smooth and glossy. The paste should be just soft enough to fall gently from the spoon. Use the pastry immediately or cover tightly and chill until needed.

Below Choux pastry paste should be smooth and glossy and just soft enough to fall off the spoon.

Prawn and Courgette Tart

Use small courgettes with dark green, glossy skin for this tart. As they age, the skin of courgettes becomes duller and the flavour is less intense.

Preparation time 25 minutes, plus chilling **Cooking time** 40 minutes **Serves** 4–6

1 quantity Shortcrust Pastry (see page 146)

40 g (1½ oz) butter

1 courgette, cut into matchsticks

25 g (1 oz) plain flour

300 ml (½ pint) hot milk

175 g (6 oz) peeled cooked prawns, defrosted if frozen

2 eggs, beaten

75 g (3 oz) mature Cheddar cheese, grated

salt and pepper

1 Roll out the pastry and line a 23 cm (9 inch) tart tin. Chill for 30 minutes, then bake the pastry case blind in a preheated oven for 15 minutes.

2 Melt the butter in a saucepan, add the courgette matchsticks and cook gently for about 5 minutes until softened. Stir in the flour and cook for 1 minute. Gradually stir in the hot milk, cooking until the sauce is thick and smooth.

3 Let the sauce cool slightly, then stir in the prawns and eggs with 50 g (2 oz) of the grated cheese. Season to taste with salt and pepper. Pour the filling into the pastry case and sprinkle with the remaining grated cheese.

4 Bake the tart in a preheated oven at 190°C (375°F), Gas Mark 5, for about 25 minutes, until the filling is golden brown. Serve warm.

Caramelized Brie Parcels

Cut open these crisp, buttery pastry parcels and reveal the melting cheese within. Choose cheese which is ripe but still firm for best results.

Preparation time 20 minutes, plus chilling **Cooking time** 20 minutes **Serves** 2–4

½ quantity Rough Puff Pastry (see page 147)

2 small wheels of Brie or a Camembert-style cheese

1 small egg

1 tbsp milk

pinch of salt

50 g (2 oz) whole almonds, toasted, to garnish (optional)

To serve
flat leaf parsley sprigs

shredded beetroot

1 Divide the pastry into 4 and roll out each piece on a lightly floured surface to form a thin round, 5 cm (2 inches) larger than the cheeses.

2 Make an egg glaze by beating together the egg, milk and salt in a small bowl. Place each cheese wheel in the middle of a pastry round. Brush the pastry around the cheese with a little of the egg glaze and then top each with a second pastry round. Press all around the edges of the pastry rounds to seal the pieces together well, then trim the pastry to give a 2.5 cm (1 inch) border.

3 Transfer the 2 pastry-covered cheeses to a baking sheet and leave them to chill for about 30 minutes. Brush the tops and sides with more of the egg glaze and score the tops with a sharp knife to form a pattern. Cut 2 small slits in each top to allow steam to escape.

4 Bake in a preheated oven at 220°C (425°F), Gas Mark 7, for 20 minutes, until the pastry is puffed up and golden. Allow to stand for 10 minutes before garnishing with toasted almonds, if using, and serving with flat leaf parsley and shredded beetroot.

Spinach and Feta Filo Pie with Pine Nuts

This is Mediterranean cooking at its best. Cooked in a crisp shell of filo pastry, this pie is ideal for a picnic.

Preparation time 25 minutes, plus cooling **Cooking time** about 1 hour **Serves** 6

750 g (1½ lb) fresh spinach leaves, cleaned

250 g (8 oz) feta cheese, roughly crumbled

½ tsp dried chilli flakes

75 g (3 oz) Parmesan cheese, finely grated

50 g (2 oz) pine nuts, toasted

15 g (½ oz) dill, chopped

15 g (½ oz) tarragon, chopped

3 eggs, beaten

1 tsp grated nutmeg

250 g (8 oz) fresh filo pastry

5–8 tbsp olive oil

1 tbsp sesame seeds

salt and pepper

1 Place the spinach in a large saucepan with just the water left on the leaves after rinsing. Cook gently until wilted and soft. Drain well. When cooled slightly, wring all of the water out of the leaves. Mix the feta into the spinach with the chilli flakes, Parmesan, pine nuts and herbs. Add the beaten eggs to the mixture, along with plenty of salt, pepper and grated nutmeg. Combine together well.

2 Unwrap the filo pastry and, working quickly, brush the top sheet of pastry with a little olive oil. Lay the sheet in the bottom of a lightly greased 20 cm (8 inch) loose-bottomed cake tin with the edges overlapping the rim. Brush the next sheet of pastry and lay it in the opposite direction to the first sheet to completely cover the base of the tin. Repeat this brushing with oil and layering in the tin until 6–8 sheets of pastry have created a shell and there are at least 3 sheets of pastry left for a 'lid'.

3 Spoon the spinach mixture into the filo pastry shell, pushing it in well with the back of the spoon and levelling the surface. Brush the next sheet of pastry with oil and then cut the length of the remaining stack of filo pastry into 5 cm (2 inch) wide strips. One by one, place these strips of pastry over the top of the spinach in a casual folded arrangement, remembering to brush all the strips of pastry with oil.

4 Once all the strips are in place, fold in the overhanging filo. Sprinkle with sesame seeds and bake in a preheated oven at 190°C (375°F), Gas Mark 5, for 1 hour. Cool for 15 minutes, then gently push the pie out of the tin. Serve warm or cold.

Peach and Raspberry Tartlets

These tempting tartlets are simple to make. They can be cooked several hours ahead, but should be filled just before eating to prevent the pastry going soft.

Preparation time 15 minutes **Cooking time** 8-10 minutes **Serves** 4

15 g (½ oz) butter, melted

4 sheets filo pastry, each about 25 cm (10 inches) square

125 ml (4 fl oz) double cream

1 tbsp soft brown sugar

2 peaches, peeled, halved, stoned and diced

50 g (2 oz) raspberries

icing sugar, to dust

1 Grease 4 deep muffin tins with the melted butter. Cut a sheet of filo pastry in half, then across into 4 equal-sized squares. Use these filo squares to line each muffin tin, arranging them at slightly different angles. Press them down well, tucking the pastry into the tin neatly. Repeat with the remaining pastry.

2 Bake the filo pastry tartlets in a preheated oven at 190°C (375°F), Gas Mark 5, for 8–10 minutes or until golden. Carefully remove the tartlet cases from the tins and leave to cool on a wire rack.

3 Pour the cream into a bowl and add the sugar. Whip lightly until it holds its shape. Spoon the cream into the tartlet cases and top with the peaches and raspberries. Dust with icing sugar. Serve at once.

French Apple Flan

For a special occasion, sprinkle a few drops of Calvados (the brandy made from distilled cider) over the apple slices when you arrange them in the tart.

Preparation time 30 minutes, plus chilling **Cooking time** 45–50 minutes **Serves** 8

Sweet Shortcrust, made with 250 g (8 oz) flour (see page 146)

750 g (1½ lb) eating apples

3 tbsp lemon juice

4 tbsp warmed, sieved apricot jam

175 ml (6 fl oz) single cream

2 eggs, beaten

50 g (2 oz) caster sugar

1 Roll out the pastry and line a 25 cm (10 inch) tart tin. Chill the pastry case in the refrigerator for 30 minutes.

2 Peel and core the apples. Slice them finely into a bowl and toss with the lemon juice. Drain the apples and arrange them in concentric circles over the base of the pastry case to cover it.

3 Brush the apricot jam over the apple slices and bake the tart in a preheated oven at 200°C (400°F), Gas Mark 6, for 10 minutes.

4 Whisk the cream, eggs and sugar in a bowl. Pour the mixture carefully over the apples. Return the flan to the preheated oven and bake at 190°C (375°F), Gas Mark 5, for 30–35 minutes until the pastry is golden and the filling cooked. Serve warm.

Lemon Curd Tartlets

These crisp little pastry shells contain a generous spoonful of tangy lemon curd, topped with a rich curd cheese filling, rather like cheesecake. They are especially good warm.

Preparation time 20 minutes, plus chilling **Cooking time** 20–25 minutes **Makes** 9

1 quantity Sweet Shortcrust (see page 146)

4 tbsp lemon curd

250 g (8 oz) curd cheese, softened

2 eggs, beaten

50 g (2 oz) caster sugar

grated nutmeg, for sprinkling

icing sugar, for dusting

1 Roll the pastry out thinly and cut nine 10 cm (4 inch) rounds. Line a 9 hole muffin tin with the dough, then chill the muffin tin for about 15 minutes.

2 Put a teaspoon of lemon curd in the base of each pastry case.

3 Mix together the curd cheese, eggs and sugar in a bowl. Divide the filling between the pastry cases and sprinkle with grated nutmeg.

4 Bake the tartlets in a preheated oven at 190°C (375°F), Gas Mark 5, for 20–25 minutes until the filling has risen and the pastry is crisp. Dust with sifted icing sugar and serve warm or cold.

Profiteroles

Everyone loves profiteroles. These have a mocha icing drizzled over the top rather than the traditional chocolate, making them a little less sweet and a little more sophisticated.

Preparation time 20 minutes **Cooking time** 20–25 minutes **Serves** 8–10

1 quantity Choux Pastry (see page 147)

250 ml (8 fl oz) double cream

1 tbsp strong cool coffee

Mocha icing
125 g (4 oz) plain chocolate

1 tbsp instant coffee dissolved in 1½ tablespoons hot water

200 g (7 oz) icing sugar, sifted

1 Place 8–10 spoons of the choux pastry on a greased baking sheet. Bake in a preheated oven at 200°C (400°F) Gas Mark 6, for 20–25 minutes. Split each profiterole horizontally to let out the steam and leave to cool on a wire rack.

2 Combine the cream and coffee and whip until stiff. Use to fill the profiteroles.

3 To make the mocha icing, break the chocolate into a heatproof bowl and place over a saucepan of very hot water until melted. Make sure the bowl does not touch the water. Remove from the heat and beat in the dissolved coffee, then the icing sugar. Use the icing to decorate the tops of the profiteroles.

Homemade bread

Anyone can make bread – it is no longer the domain of experienced cooks or master bakers. Fast-action dried yeast has made baking bread child's play.

By hand or machine

Making and baking bread by hand or in a machine is immensely satisfying and relaxing, and with the stresses of modern living, that must surely be a good thing.

For those who are really short of time, a bread machine will effortlessly and efficiently mix, knead, rise and bake your bread. All you need to do is measure out the ingredients, turn it on and walk away. When you do have more time, it can be fun to make dough in the bread machine and then shape it by hand into a plait, ring, twist or tiny shaped rolls.

Ingredients

The better the ingredients you use, the better the finished loaf will be. Also, it will contain none of the extra ingredients that manufacturers add to prolong the shelf life of shop-bought bread.

Flours

White flours Choose strong white flour, sometimes known as bread flour, for breadmaking. This has a higher gluten content for added stretch. Use plain flour or self-raising flour in yeast-free breads only. To avoid additives use choose organic, unbleached strong white flour.

Wholewheat or wholemeal flour Milled from the whole wheat kernel it contains the bran and wheat germ, making it more nutritious with a nuttier flavour and coarser texture. Again, choose wholemeal flour marked 'strong', or 'bread'. Loaves will be denser and heavier as the bran inhibits the release of gluten, so they take longer to rise. To make a lighter bread, mix half wholewheat flour with half strong white flour.

Strong brown flour Since this contains only 80–90 per cent of the kernel it produces a lighter brown loaf.

Granary flour A sweet, nutty flour made with wholemeal, white and rye flours mixed with malted wheat grains. Malthouse flour is similar.

Yeast

There three types of yeast: fresh yeast; traditional dried yeast that requires frothing in water before use; and fast-action dried yeast, which is by far the easiest and needs only to be stirred into the dry ingredients.

Recipes made in a bread machine have to be made with fast-action dried yeast. This can be used straight from the sachet. If you are making bread by hand, any of the three types of yeast can be used.

Yeast works through a fermentation process. As it feeds on the sugar and later the starches in the flour, it produces a gas (carbon dioxide), and it is this gas that causes the bread to rise.

Sugar

Sugar is a vital food for the yeast and without it fermentation cannot take place. Choose from white, light brown or dark brown sugars. In a 500 g (1 lb) loaf, just 1 teaspoon of sugar is enough to activate the yeast, but more can be added to flavour the bread.

Salt

Salt acts as a seasoning to make the bread taste good, but if used in large quantities can inhibit the yeast.

Water

There is one main difference between making bread in a bread machine and by hand: the temperature of the water. Cold water is required for a bread machine – unless a bread is being made on a rapid or fastbake programme – whereas warm water must always be used when making bread by hand. Too hot and the yeast will be killed, too cold and the yeast won't be activated. Milk may also be used for a tender crumb. Use powdered milk in a machine if using the timer facility.

Using a machine

There is a wide range of bread machines to choose from. Lower- and medium-priced machines make surprisingly good loaves, so you don't need to make a big investment. Check the capacity before buying: some make loaves of 500 g (1 lb) only, others will make loaves up to 1 kg (2 lb). Not all machines are the same, so check your machine manual before you try a recipe for the first time. You may need to alter the amounts of ingredients or add them in the order that the manufacturers specify.

Enriching ingredients

Butter, oil and eggs all add richness to the finished bread, giving a softer, more tender crumb. Butter and oil also act as a preservative and keep bread fresh for longer. Breads made without butter or oil, such as French bread, must be eaten on the day they are made.

Basic Techniques

There is a basic procedure to follow when making bread, from mixing together the ingredients through to baking the loaf in the oven.

Mixing (1)

Measure the flour into a large bowl, then add the butter (if using) and rub it in with the fingertips until the mixture resembles fine breadcrumbs. Stir in the salt, milk powder (if using), sugar and fast-action dried yeast. Make a well in the centre of the flour then, using a wooden spoon, gradually mix in enough warm water to make a soft dough, then begin using your hands.

Kneading (2)

Begin by turning the dough out on to a lightly floured surface. Stretch the dough by pushing the front half away with the heel of one hand while holding the back of the dough with the other hand. Fold the stretched part of the dough back on itself, give it a quarter turn and repeat until the dough has been turned full circle several times and is a smooth and elastic ball.

First rising

Dust the mixing bowl with a little extra flour, put the kneaded bread back into the bowl and cover the top loosely with oiled clingfilm. Leave in a warm place to rise, or 'prove', for about 1 hour, or until the dough

has doubled in size. This may take more or less time, depending on the temperature in the kitchen.

Knocking back (3)

Remove the clingfilm and save for the next rising. Knock back or punch the risen dough in the bowl with your fist to deflate it, then pull it out of the bowl. Turn the dough out on to a lightly floured surface and knead well, as before.

Shaping (4)

Roll the dough back and forth with the palms of your hands in a rocking action until a rope of dough begins to form – about half as long again as the length of the loaf tin. Fold the end of the dough under so that it is an even width and the exact length of the tin then lay it in the greased tin. Cover loosely with oiled clingfilm.

Second rising and glazing

Leave the bread in a warm place for 30 minutes for a second and final proving, or until the dough rises to just above the top of the tin. It is crucial not to over prove the dough at this stage or the bread may collapse in the oven. The dough is ready if, when pressed lightly with a fingertip, the dent springs back slowly but surely. If the dent stays as it is, the bread is over proved. Remove the clingfilm and sprinkle with flour.

Baking and testing

Bake bread in a preheated oven at 200°C (400°F), Gas Mark 6, for 25 minutes for a 500 g (1 lb) loaf, 30 minutes for a large 750 g (1½ lb) loaf or 35 minutes for an extra large 1 kg (2 lb) loaf. The bread should be well risen, golden brown and sound hollow when tapped with the fingertips. Turn out on to a wire rack to cool.

Farmhouse White Loaf

This is the ideal everyday loaf – light, fluffy and easy to slice, perfect for packed lunches and toast, or simply spread with butter and jam for tea.

Preparation time 15 minutes, plus proving **Cooking time** 25 minutes
Makes 1 small loaf

300 g (10 oz) strong white flour
1 tbsp butter
1 tsp sugar
½ tsp salt
1 tsp fast-action dried yeast
175 ml (6 fl oz) warm water

1 Put the flour into a large bowl, add the butter and rub it in with the fingertips until the mixture resembles fine breadcrumbs. Stir in the sugar, salt and yeast. Gradually mix in enough warm water to make a soft dough.

2 Knead well on a lightly floured surface for 5 minutes until the dough is smooth and elastic. Put the dough back into the bowl, cover loosely and leave in a warm place to rise for 45 minutes, or until doubled in size.

3 Tip the dough out on to a lightly floured surface, knead well, then put into a greased 500 g (1 lb) loaf tin. Cover loosely with oiled clingfilm and leave in a warm place to rise for 30 minutes, or until the dough reaches the top of the tin.

4 Remove the clingfilm, sprinkle with flour and bake in a preheated oven at 200°C (400°F), Gas Mark 6, for 25 minutes, covering with foil after 20 minutes to prevent overbrowning. Transfer to a wire rack to cool.

Rapid Light Wholemeal Loaf

This loaf is a good halfway stage for children who are reluctant brown bread eaters, since it is made with half wholemeal and half white flour. Great for sandwiches and toast.

Preparation time 15 minutes, plus proving **Cooking time** 25 minutes
Makes 1 small loaf

175 g (6 oz) strong wholemeal flour

150 g (5 oz) strong white flour

2 tsp caster sugar

½ teaspoon salt

1¾ tsp fast-action dried yeast

1 tbsp sunflower oil

200 ml (7 fl oz) warm water

1 Mix the flours, sugar, salt and yeast in a large bowl. Add the oil and gradually mix in enough warm water to make a soft dough.

2 Knead well on a lightly floured surface for 10 minutes until the dough is smooth and elastic. Put into a greased 500 g (1 lb) loaf tin.

3 Cover loosely with oiled clingfilm and leave in a warm place to rise for 45 minutes, or until the dough reaches just above the top of the tin.

4 Remove the clingfilm and bake in a preheated oven at 200°C (400°F), Gas Mark 6, for 25 minutes, or until the bread is browned and sounds hollow when tapped. Cover with foil after 15 minutes if overbrowning. Transfer to a wire rack to cool.

Couronne

Traditionally, this loaf is made with a yeast starter that is left for two days, but this cheat's version is made with natural yogurt instead, to give it the characteristic sourdough flavour.

Preparation time 20 minutes, plus proving **Cooking time** 20–25 minutes
Makes 1 loaf

500 g (1 lb) unbleached
strong white flour

1½ teaspoons salt

2 tsp caster sugar

1¼ tsp fast-action
dried yeast

200 g (7 oz) natural yogurt

175 ml (6 fl oz) warm water

1 Put the flour into a large bowl then stir in the salt, sugar and yeast. Add the yogurt then gradually mix in enough warm water to make a soft dough. Knead on a lightly floured surface for 5 minutes, or until the dough is smooth and elastic. Put it back into the bowl, cover loosely with oiled clingfilm and leave to rise in a warm place for 1 hour, or until it has doubled in size.

2 Tip the dough out on to a lightly floured surface and knead well. Shape into a round, then make a small hole in the centre with the fingertips; enlarge the hole with your fist until the hole is about 12 cm (5 inches) wide and the bread a ring of about 20 cm (8 inches) in diameter.

3 Transfer to a greased baking sheet and mark with 3 or 4 cuts if liked. Grease the base of a small basin and put it into the centre of the bread to keep the 'hole' intact. Cover the bread and basin loosely with oiled clingfilm and leave in a warm place for 30 minutes, or until it is half as big again.

4 Remove the clingfilm and basin, sprinkle the dough with flour and bake in a preheated oven at 220°C (450°F), Gas Mark 7, for 20–25 minutes until it is well risen and browned and the bread sounds hollow when tapped with the fingertips. Cover with foil after 15 minutes if overbrowning. Transfer to a wire rack to cool.

Tomato Focaccia

This classic Italian flat bread is studded with cherry tomatoes and olives, then sprinkled with fresh rosemary and crunchy salt flakes. Serve warm or cold.

Preparation time 20 minutes, plus proving **Cooking time** 15 minutes
Makes 2 loaves

475 g (15 oz) strong white flour

1 teaspoon sugar

1 teaspoon salt

1½ teaspoons fast-action dried yeast

3 tablespoons olive oil

275 ml (9 fl oz) warm water

Topping
200 g (7 oz) cherry tomatoes

a few rosemary sprigs

a few black olives

1 teaspoon salt flakes

3 tablespoons olive oil

1 Put the flour, sugar, salt and yeast into a large bowl. Add the olive oil, then gradually mix in enough warm water to make a soft dough. Knead the dough well on a lightly floured surface for 5 minutes until it is smooth and elastic. Put the dough back into the bowl, cover loosely with oiled clingfilm and leave in a warm place to rise for 1 hour, or until doubled in size.

2 Tip the dough out on to a lightly floured surface, knead well, then cut into 2 pieces. Press each into a rough oval shape a little larger than your hand.

3 Transfer the loaves to 2 greased baking sheets, then make indentations in the surface of each loaf with the end of a wooden spoon. Remove the green tops from the tomatoes and press them into some of the indentations, add small rosemary sprigs and olives to some of the others. Sprinkle with the salt flakes and leave to rise, uncovered, for 20 minutes.

4 Drizzle the loaves with a little of the oil and bake in a preheated oven at 200°C (400°F), Gas Mark 6, for 15 minutes. Swap shelf positions during cooking, so that both loaves brown evenly. Drizzle with the remaining olive oil and serve warm or cold, torn into pieces.

Making stock

There is nothing to beat the flavour of real homemade stock. It adds depth to soups, casseroles and sauces, and while it may take a while to cook, the results are well worth the effort. It is cheap and simple to make and freezes well.

Above An easy way to remove fat from your stock is to leave it to cool then, using a fork, carefully lift off the layer of fat that has formed.

Rules for good stock

• Do not add salt to the stock during cooking. When the stock is reduced, the flavour will be concentrated, so add salt only to the finished soups, casseroles, sauces and other dishes in which it is used.
• When the stock is simmering, remove the scum frequently. Adding a cup of cold water during cooking will bring froth to the surface where it can be removed.
• Avoid adding potatoes to vegetable stocks, as these tend to break down during boiling and straining and make the stock cloudy.
• Leave to cool in the pan and skim off as much fat as possible before removing bones.
• Strain the cooked stock through a fine sieve. If you do not have a suitable sieve, line an ordinary sieve with muslin and let the stock drain through it. Do not press the vegetables through or they will make the stock cloudy. Remove the remaining fat when cold.
• Raw bones, often available free from a butcher, make a stronger-flavoured stock than the ones that come from the remains of a roast joint.
• Raw meat, with a lot of blood in it, helps to make the liquid rich and clear.

TOP TIP

To make stocks for Oriental dishes, leave out the bouquet garni or other herbs and instead include garlic cloves, lemon grass stalks, slices of fresh root ginger and fresh coriander stalks to create the right character for the stock.

Removing fat from stock

A small amount of fat usually collects on the surface of most stocks as they cook and this should be removed before use. If the stock is still warm, use a large spoon to skim off as much fat as possible, then add a few ice cubes. The fat will set around the ice, making it easy to spoon out. Alternatively, cool and chill the stock until the fat sets in a layer on the surface, then gently lift off.

Clarifying stock

Clarifying stock will get rid of any impurities. When your stock has cooled, in a separate bowl, mix together 3 egg whites with their shells crumbled, and 1 onion, 1 celery stick and 1 carrot, finely sliced. Whisk these ingredients into your stock and slowly bring to a simmer, but be careful not to boil. Simmer for about 10–15 minutes until a layer of scum has formed then leave to stand for 1 hour. Line a sieve with a piece of muslin, push the scum aside and ladle the stock into the sieve.

Storing stock

To store stock, first boil it rapidly, uncovered, until reduced by about half. This concentrates the flavour and saves storage space. For food safety, cool stocks as quickly as possible, then cover and chill them. Stock will keep in the refrigerator for 2–3 days or it may be frozen for longer storage.

To freeze stock in convenient portions for use in sauces, casseroles and similar dishes, pour it into ice cube trays and freeze until solid, then tip the cubes of concentrated stock into polythene bags to store.

Basic beef stock

Makes 1.5 litres (2¾ pints)

750 g (1½ lb) shin of beef, diced, or 375 g (12 oz) shin of beef and 1.5 kg (3 lb) beef bones

2 onions, chopped

2 carrots, chopped

2 celery sticks, chopped

1 bouquet garni (see page 19)

6 black peppercorns

1.8 litres (3 pints) cold water

1 Place all the ingredients in a large saucepan and bring them slowly to the boil.

2 Reduce the heat until the stock simmers slowly. Skim any scum from the surface, then cover the pan and simmer for 4 hours.

3 Strain and cool the cooked stock.

Basic chicken stock

Makes 1 litre (1¾ pints)

1 cooked chicken carcass

chicken giblets (optional)

1 onion, chopped

2 carrots, chopped

1 celery stick, chopped

1 bouquet garni (see page 19)

1 tsp black peppercorns

1.8 litres (3 pints) cold water

1 Cut the chicken carcass into 3–4 pieces and place them in a large saucepan with the remaining ingredients.

2 Bring to the boil and skim off any scum. Reduce the heat, cover and simmer gently for 2–2½ hours.

3 Strain and cool.

Trimmings

- Oily fish trimmings – such as mackerel or herring – will make fish stock greasy and strongly flavoured, so don't use them. Prawn shells or crab legs will add a good flavour so include these if you have some.
- Vegetable trimmings, such as broccoli stalks and the leafy tops of leeks, can be used to make stock if you wash them well.
- Instead of throwing away the chicken carcass after your Sunday lunch, boil it up with a few vegetable trimmings to make your chicken stock.

Above To make straining stock easier, use a strainer that you can either stand in the pan or hook onto the side of the pan.

Basic fish stock

Makes 1 litre (1¾ pints)

1 kg (2 lb) white fish bones and trimmings

1 onion, sliced

2 carrots, sliced

2 celery sticks, sliced

1 bouquet garni (see page 19)

6 white peppercorns

150 ml (¼ pint) dry white wine

1 litre (1¾ pints) cold water

1 Place all the ingredients in a large saucepan and bring slowly to the boil.

2 Skim off any scum, then reduce the heat and cover the pan. Simmer very gently for 20 minutes.

3 Strain and cool the stock.

Basic vegetable stock

Makes 1 litre (1¾ pints)

500 g (1 lb) mixed vegetables, chopped, such as onions, carrots, celery and leeks

1 litre (1¾ pints) water

1 garlic clove

6 black peppercorns

1 bouquet garni (see page 19)

1 Place all the ingredients in a large saucepan and bring slowly to the boil.

2 Skim off any scum, then reduce the heat and cover the pan. Simmer gently for 30 minutes.

3 Strain and cool the stock.

Simple soup

Making soup is rewarding, with scope for creative combinations. Soups are also versatile – they can be quick and simple snacks; hearty, nutritious family main courses; or elegant dinner party starters.

Soup-making secrets

It is a popular myth that soups require hours of preparation; in fact, most take only a few minutes of attention. The secret of most good soups is a well-flavoured stock, so start by either making your own stock (see pages 160–161) or buying a good-quality product. Then choose the freshest vegetables in season for the best flavour and most economical results.

Thickening soups

1 Puréeing chunky vegetable soups in a blender or food processor will naturally result in a thick soup. This is especially true of starchy vegetables, such as potatoes, squash, pumpkins, parsnips and carrots. Thinner soups can be made thick by including a few chunks of potato and puréeing the soup after cooking.
2 Another way to thicken a soup is to use beurre manié. This is a paste of flour and butter which is whisked into simmering liquid. As the butter melts, the flour is incorporated and the liquid is thickened without lumps. Cream equal amounts of butter and plain flour together to form a thick paste. Drop small pieces or teaspoonfuls of the paste into the barely simmering soup, stirring briskly and continuously until each piece has melted before adding the next. Simmer for 2–3 minutes, stirring, until the soup is thickened.

Making croûtons

1 Remove the crusts from sliced bread and use a sharp knife to cut it into 1 cm (½ inch) squares. Alternatively, use small food cutters to stamp out shapes, such as hearts or stars.
2 Quickly stir-fry the pieces in a mixture of butter and oil until crisp and golden brown. Season to taste. Drain on kitchen paper and sprinkle over the soup just before serving.

Above Beurre manié is a paste of flour and butter, which can be used to thicken soup. Incorporate a little piece at a time.

Freezing soups

Most soups freeze successfully for 2–3 months. Highly seasoned or garlic-flavoured soups are best used within 2–3 weeks, as some flavours may be affected by freezing.

Pack soups for the freezer in rigid containers with well-fitting lids, in 300–600 ml (½–1 pint) quantities which will thaw quickly. Allow room for the soup to expand in the container as it freezes – at least 3 cm (1¼ inches) of headspace. Seal and label clearly.

Garnishes and additions

Most soups benefit from finishing touches that add a contrast in colour, texture and flavour to transform even the plainest bowl of soup into your own special creation. These ideas are suitable for most soups.
Cream or crème fraîche Swirl a spoonful into each portion of soup. For an extra flourish, use a cocktail stick to swirl the cream into a delicate feather pattern.
Herbs Scatter a handful of chopped parsley, snipped chives or torn basil leaves over soup just before serving.
Citrus rind Use a zester to pare fine curls of lemon, lime or orange rind and scatter it over soup for colour and flavour. Orange rind goes well in carrot soup, and lime rind is delicious with avocado soup.
Cheese A sprinkling of grated Cheddar, Gruyère or Parmesan adds flavour to vegetable soups. Try crumbled feta or finely diced mozzarella for topping soups with Mediterranean flavours.
Pesto or tapenade A swirl of pesto (see page 170) or tapenade (olive paste), either homemade or bought, adds an intense flavour to simple vegetable soups.
Flavoured oils At the last minute, drizzle a little chilli oil, basil oil or lemon oil on to the soup.

3 tbsp olive oil

1 onion, finely chopped

2 celery sticks, finely sliced

2 garlic cloves, finely sliced

2 x 425 g (14 oz) cans butter beans, rinsed and drained

4 tbsp sun-dried tomato paste

900 ml (1½ pints) Vegetable Stock (see page 161)

1 tbsp chopped rosemary or thyme

salt and pepper

Parmesan cheese shavings, to serve

Butter Bean and Sun-dried Tomato Soup

Although it takes only a few minutes to prepare, this chunky soup resembles a robust Italian minestrone. It makes a worthy main course, served with bread and plenty of Parmesan cheese.

Preparation time 5 minutes **Cooking time** 20 minutes **Serves** 4

1 Heat the oil in a saucepan. Add the onion and fry for 3 minutes until softened. Add the celery and garlic and fry for 2 minutes.

2 Add the butter beans, sun-dried tomato paste, stock, rosemary or thyme and a little salt and pepper. Bring to the boil, then reduce the heat, cover and simmer gently for 15 minutes. Serve sprinkled with the Parmesan shavings.

Broccoli and Cheese Soup

A satisfying and warming soup that is perfect for winter lunches and suppers.

Preparation time 30 minutes **Cooking time** 40 minutes **Serves** 6

1kg (2 lb) broccoli

50 g (2 oz) butter or margarine

1 onion, chopped

1 large potato, peeled and quartered

1.5 litres (2½ pints) Vegetable Stock (see page 161)

125 ml (4 fl oz) single cream

1 tbsp lemon juice

1 tsp Worcestershire sauce

a few drop of Tabasco sauce

125 g (4 oz) mature Cheddar cheese

salt and pepper

watercress sprigs, to garnish

1 Remove all the tough stems and leaves from the broccoli. Cut off the stalks, peel and cut them into 2.5 cm (1 inch) pieces. Break the florets into very small pieces and set them aside.

2 Melt the butter or margarine in a large saucepan. Add the onion and broccoli stalks and cook, covered, for 5 minutes over a moderate heat. Stir frequently.

3 Add the reserved broccoli florets, potato and vegetable stock to the pan. Bring the mixture to the boil. Cook, partially covered, for 5 minutes. Using a slotted spoon, remove 6 or more florets for a garnish and set aside. Season the mixture with salt and pepper and continue to cook over a moderate heat for 20 minutes, or until all the vegetables are soft.

4 Using a blender or food processor, puree the mixture in batches until smooth, transferring each successive batch to a clean saucepan. Add the cream, lemon juice, Worcestershire sauce and a few drops of Tabasco to the pan. Simmer for 3–5 minutes. Do not allow to boil or the soup will curdle. Just before serving, stir in the grated cheese and garnish each portion with the reserved florets and watercress sprigs.

Chunky Carrot and Lentil Soup

Serve this simple soup with a spiced butter, so diners can help themselves at the table and stir in as much as they like.

Preparation time 10 minutes **Cooking time** 30–35 minutes **Serves** 4

1 First make the spiced butter. Put all the ingredients into a bowl and beat together until combined. Transfer to a small serving dish, cover and chill until ready to serve.

2 To make the soup, heat the oil in a large saucepan. Add the onion and celery and cook over a low heat, stirring occasionally, for 5 minutes, or until softened. Add the carrots and garlic then fry for 3 minutes.

3 Add the lentils and stock and bring just to the boil. Reduce the heat, cover the pan and cook gently for 20–25 minutes, until the vegetables are soft and the soup is pulpy. Season lightly to taste. Divide the soup between warmed soup bowls. Serve the spiced butter separately so that diners can stir it in to taste.

2 tbsp vegetable oil

1 large onion, chopped

2 celery sticks, sliced

500 g (1 lb) carrots, sliced

1 garlic clove, crushed

150 g (5 oz) split red lentils, rinsed

1.4 litres (2¼ pints) Vegetable Stock (see page 161)

salt and pepper

Spiced butter
40 g (1½ oz) butter, softened

2 spring onions, finely chopped

¼ tsp dried chilli flakes

1 tsp cumin seeds

finely grated rind of 1 lemon

handful of fresh coriander, chopped

a few mint sprigs, chopped

Sauces and dressings

A good sauce can transform simple meat, chicken, fish or vegetables into a lively and interesting dish. A sauce complements and enhances the food it accompanies, adding flavour, colour, texture and moisture without overpowering it.

Ingredients

There are a few essential ingredients that help make a really good sauce. But there's nothing to stop you from experimenting with more interesting flavours and combinations once you've learnt the basics.

Stock

Any sauce that uses meat, fish or vegetable stock will taste better if you use a homemade one (see pages 160–161). Don't be put off by this, stocks are easy to make, cost very little and it's not difficult to get into the habit of making them. Use the leftover bones from

Below A swirl of single or double cream or crème fraîche can thicken a thin soup and enrich its flavour.

a roast or ask your butcher for bones when you're in the shop, or use a selection of fresh vegetables if you have a surplus in the refrigerator. If you don't need the stock for a few days, freeze it for a ready supply. Cartons or tubs of ready-made stock make a good alternative but are expensive for the amount you get. Concentrated liquid stocks are an adequate standby, as are good-quality cubes and powders. These are often quite salty though, and should therefore be used sparingly. If you are using this type of stock, be sure to taste your sauce before adding any further seasoning.

Butter

Always use unsalted butter for sauce-making, although salted butter will do if you run out. Salted butter has a less creamy flavour and burns more easily.

Oils

You don't need a huge supply of oils in the storecupboard. A richly flavoured, extra virgin olive oil is ideal for Mediterranean-style sauces, while a light olive oil is more suitable for a sauce where you need a good oil but don't want its flavour to dominate, for example in mayonnaise. Choose a mildly flavoured oil, such as sunflower or groundnut oil, for other recipes including Indian and Asian-style sauces. A little sesame oil adds a delicious flavour to Asian dishes although it cannot be used for frying because of its low smoking point. Nut oils such as walnut and hazlenut are particularly good in recipes where you want to emphasize a nutty flavour.

Herbs

Fresh herbs have a far better flavour than dried ones but are best used as soon as possible after buying or picking. Delicate herbs deteriorate after several days in the refrigerator.

Eggs

Use really fresh eggs in sauces, preferably free-range organic ones. This is particularly important in custard where the eggs provide the colour and flavour.

Cream

An essential ingredient, cream is often used to add a velvety-smooth finishing touch to a sauce. Provided it's really fresh, neither double nor single cream should separate even when it's boiled unless it's mixed with a high proportion of acidic ingredients. Crème fraîche, which makes a good alternative when you want a tangier, but still creamy flavour, is best not cooked at high temperatures.

Making a bouquet garni

This is simply a small bundle of herbs tied together with fine string. Add to stocks, sauces, soups or stews to infuse the liquid with the flavour of the herbs, then remove the bundle before serving. Tie the herbs firmly by their stems or tie into a bundle in a small square of muslin. Traditionally, the basic bouquet garni includes a bay leaf, a thyme sprig and 2 or 3 parsley sprigs. This can be varied according to the dish it is to flavour. Add a sprig of fresh rosemary for lamb, a fresh sage sprig for pork, a piece of celery for beef, or a strip of finely pared lemon rind and a sprig of dill or fennel for fish or chicken.

Thickening sauces

There are various ways to thicken a sauce; sometimes it is the first step of a recipe, as in a roux, in other cases it's a finishing step and uses ingredients such as egg yolks, cream and butter. The most important rule is to avoid over-thickening. A sauce made too thick with flour or cornflour is unpalatable and can ruin a dish. As a guide, most sauces are sufficiently thickened when they thinly coat the back of a wooden spoon. Let the sauce cool slightly on the spoon, then run your finger along it – it should leave a clear impression.

Roux

Roux is a blend of butter and flour, lightly cooked together before the liquid is added, as in a Béchamel Sauce (see page 168). If the roux is cooked a little more it forms the base of a Velouté Sauce (see page 168).

Beurre manié

This is also a mixture of butter and flour, which are first kneaded together in a bowl to make a paste and then whisked into the cooked sauce until it thickens. This is a useful method for thickening a disappointingly thin sauce, or a stew or casserole in which the juice is very thin. Use about 15 g (½ oz) each of softened butter and plain flour to 600 ml (1 pint) of liquid.

Cornflour

Cornflour must be blended with a little water, stock or juice before it is added to a sauce. Make sure you don't add too much liquid – just enough to make a paste. It's rarely used in traditional sauces but sometimes crops up in Asian-style ones.

Egg yolks and cream

These are good for adding extra flavour and richness to a thin sauce, particularly those with a stock base. Blend 2 egg yolks with 150 ml (¼ pint) of single cream and add a ladleful of the hot but not boiling sauce. Tip the mixture back into the pan and cook over a very gentle heat, whisking or stirring until the sauce is slightly thickened.

Enriching with butter

Whisking a little chilled butter into a finished sauce thickens it slightly and gives it a lighter flavour and glossier finish. Make sure you take the pan off the heat before adding the butter.

Puréeing

Some sauces, particularly those with fruit or vegetables, can be thickened by puréeing them in a blender or food processor, or using an immersion blender.

Reducing

Provided it doesn't include ingredients such as eggs or yogurt, or any ingredients that are likely to curdle, a thin stock or sauce can be reduced and thickened by rapid boiling. This will concentrate the flavour of the sauce as well as creating the right consistency. If you are reducing a stock, don't start boiling it until you have removed the bones. The reducing time will vary depending on the amount of liquid, so keep an eye on the pan. Leaving the pan uncovered will speed up the time it will take for the liquid to evaporate and the sauce to reduce. If necessary, skim off any froth on the surface and don't season the sauce until it has been fully reduced.

Roux-based sauces

A roux is simply a mixture of flour and fat. Once cooked it will absorb and thicken a liquid giving a smooth consistency without lumps. It is the base for classic white sauces, such as béchamel. It is essential to cook the roux on its own before adding the liquid or the finished sauce will not be smooth.

Melt the butter in a saucepan, then stir in the flour and cook, stirring, for 1–2 minutes. The mixture should bubble and form a honeycomb-like texture. Remove from the heat and gradually stir in the hot or cold liquid. Return to the heat and continue stirring until the sauce boils. Simmer, stirring continuously, for a further 2–3 minutes, until the sauce has thickened and is smooth.

Classic béchamel sauce

This sauce features in so many dishes it is worth getting it right. Spoon over vegetables, layer in baked dishes such as lasagne and fish pie, toss with pasta or use as the basis for a whole host of other sauces.

Makes 300 ml (½ pint)
300 ml (½ pint) milk
½ small onion, sliced
1 small carrot, sliced
1 small celery stick, sliced
6 peppercorns
1 bay leaf
15 g (½ oz) butter
15 g (½ oz) plain flour
salt and pepper
freshly grated nutmeg

1 Pour the milk into a saucepan and add the onion, carrot, celery, peppercorns and bay leaf. Heat the milk and flavouring ingredients over a low heat until it is almost boiling, then remove from the heat. Cover the pan and leave the milk and other ingredients to infuse for 10–15 minutes. Strain the milk through a sieve and discard the flavouring ingredients.
2 Melt the butter in a clean pan, add the flour and cook, stirring, for 1–2 minutes.
3 Remove from the heat and gradually stir in the milk, then stir or whisk continuously over a moderate heat for 2–3 minutes until the sauce boils and is smooth and thickened. Season to taste with salt, pepper and nutmeg.

Variations

Cheese sauce Stir 75 g (3 oz) of grated strong cheese, such as mature Cheddar, and ½ teaspoon of English or Dijon mustard into the finished sauce. Heat gently until the cheese melts.

Above When making roux-based sauces, add the liquid gradually while whisking so that you don't make the sauce too runny.

Parsley sauce Stir 2 tablespoons of finely chopped parsley into the finished sauce.
Mushroom sauce Finely slice 50 g (2 oz) of button mushrooms and cook them in 15 g (½ oz) butter until soft. Stir into the finished sauce, adding a generous dash of Worcestershire sauce.

Velouté sauce

This sauce is made in the same way as bechamel, but uses stock instead of milk for a more savoury flavour. Match the stock to the food the sauce is accompanying.

Makes 300 ml (½ pint)
20 g (¾ oz) butter
20 g (¾ oz) flour
300 ml (½ pint) Chicken or Fish Stock (see page 161)
1 egg yolk
2–3 tbsp cream
salt and white pepper

1 Melt the butter in a saucepan until foaming. Add the flour and cook, stirring, for 5 minutes until the roux is straw-coloured.
2 Bring the stock to the boil and gradually stir it into the roux. Bring to the boil, season with salt and pepper and simmer for 15 minutes, whisking, until the sauce is the correct consistency.
3 When the sauce is thick and smooth, enrich it with egg and cream just before serving. To prevent it curdling, remove the pan from the heat, mix a little of the hot liquid with the egg and cream before stirring it into the sauce. The sauce may be returned to the heat to heat through, but do not let it boil.

Egg-based sauces

Egg yolks will thicken a sauce as they are heated, but can also be used as an emulsifier to thicken a cold sauce. Hollandaise is made with egg yolk and butter and is served hot or cold, while mayonnaise is made with egg yolk and oil and is served cold.

Classic mayonnaise

Mayonnaise is delicious with salads, boiled eggs, cold chicken, cold poached salmon, prawns, lobster and crab, or in sandwiches. The homemade version is fantastic.

Makes 300 ml (½ pint)

2 egg yolks

1 tsp Dijon mustard

2 tsp white wine vinegar

pinch of caster sugar

salt and pepper

300 ml (½ pint) olive oil

1 Place all the ingredients, except the oil, in a mixing bowl and whisk lightly until combined.

2 Gradually add the oil, drop by drop at first, whisking continuously until the mixture begins to thicken.

3 When the mixture has thickened slightly, add the remaining oil in a thin, steady stream, still whisking, until all the oil is incorporated and the mayonnaise is thick. Adjust the seasoning to taste.

Above Add the oil in a thin, steady stream to your mayonnaise, whisking continually to ensure the sauce remains smooth.

Making mayonnaise in a blender

Place the egg yolks, mustard, vinegar, sugar, salt and pepper in a blender and process for a few seconds to mix thoroughly. With the motor running, gradually add the oil in a thin stream through the feeder tube in the lid. Process until the mayonnaise is smooth and thick.

Variations

Aioli Omit the mustard from the basic recipe and add 4 crushed garlic cloves to the yolks.

Herb mayonnaise Stir 3 tablespoons of mixed finely chopped basil, parsley and chives into the mayonnaise.

Blue cheese dressing Stir 50 g (2 oz) of Stilton or Gorgonzola cheese, crumbled, into the mayonnaise.

Lemon mayonnaise Replace the wine vinegar with lemon juice. Stir in 1 teaspoon of finely grated lemon rind and 1 tablespoon of lemon juice to the mayonnaise.

Seafood sauce Add 1 teaspoon of Tabasco sauce and tomato purée to taste to the prepared mayonnaise.

Reduced-fat mayonnaise Use 1 whole egg instead of 2 yolks. Alternatively, mix the prepared mayonnaise with an equal quantity of low-fat natural yogurt.

Quick hollandaise sauce

Hollandaise is a thick, velvety sauce. Spoon it over fresh asparagus, pan-fried fish or poached eggs.

Makes about 200 ml (7 fl oz)

150 g (5 oz) butter

1 tbsp white wine vinegar or lemon juice

3 egg yolks

salt and pepper

lemon juice, to taste

1 Melt the butter then remove the pan from the heat and allow to cool, but not set.

2 Place the wine vinegar or lemon juice, egg yolks, salt and pepper in a blender and process for about 10 seconds on high speed.

3 With the motor running at high speed, add the butter in a thin, steady stream through the feeder tube in the lid of the blender.

4 Add lemon juice to taste and serve at once.

> **TOP TIP**
> If the Hollandaise sauce begins to curdle and separate, place a spoonful of vinegar in a clean bowl and gradually whisk in the sauce until it thickens.

Simple herb sauces

Fresh herbs make delicious sauces that can liven up meat, fish or vegetables. Herb sauces are often very quick and easy to prepare too, making them a fresh, healthy way to add life to mid-week meals.

Pesto

Pesto has numerous uses, most commonly as a pasta sauce but also to flavour soups, stews and risottos.

Serves 4

50 g (2 oz) fresh basil, including stalks

50 g (2 oz) pine nuts

65 g (2½ oz) freshly grated Parmesan cheese

2 garlic cloves, chopped

125 ml (4 fl oz) olive oil

salt and pepper

1 Tear the basil into pieces and put it into a food processor with the pine nuts, Parmesan and garlic.
2 Blend until the nuts and cheese are broken into small pieces, scraping the mixture down from the sides of the bowl if necessary. Add the oil and a little salt and blend to a thick paste. It can be kept, covered in the refrigerator, for up to 5 days.

Variation

Red Pesto Drain 125 g (4 oz) of sun-dried tomatoes in oil, chop them into small pieces and add to the food processor instead of the basil.

Below Harissa is simple to make and transforms roasted or barbecued vegetables with a fiery depth of flavour.

Above Making home-made pesto in a food processor or blender couldn't be easier, and the finished result is delicious.

Hot harissa sauce

A quick and easy spicy sauce with plenty of flavour. Stir into sautéed vegetables and beans, or pep up soups, stews and couscous.

Serves 4–6

1 tbsp coriander seeds

1 tsp caraway seeds

3 tbsp light olive oil

1 red pepper, deseeded and roughly chopped

1 small red onion, roughly chopped

1 red chilli, deseeded and chopped

3 garlic cloves, chopped

4 tbsp coriander leaves, torn into pieces

½ tsp celery salt

150 ml (5 oz) passata

1 Using a pestle and mortar, grind the coriander and caraway seeds until they are lightly crushed. Alternatively, use a small bowl and the end of a rolling pin.
2 Tip the crushed seeds into a small frying pan and add the olive oil, chopped red pepper and onion. Cook the mixture very gently over a low heat for about 5 minutes until the vegetables are softened and the spices smell fragrant.
3 Transfer the mixture to a food processor or blender and add the chopped fresh chilli, garlic, coriander leaves, celery salt and passata.
4 Blend until the mixture is smooth, scraping it down from the sides of the bowl from time to time if necessary. Transfer the harissa to a serving bowl and cover it with clingfilm. Chill in the refrigerator until ready to serve.

Above A simple sauce or dressing can transform salads, plain grilled meats, fish or vegetables, making a memorable meal.

Salsa verde

This intensely flavoured sauce is packed with aromatic ingredients such as fresh herbs, olives, capers and anchovies. Served cold, it's a summery sauce you can make in advance or a dip for cooked or raw vegetables.

Serves 6

25 g (1 oz) flat leaf parsley

15 g (½ oz) mixed basil, chives and mint

2 garlic cloves, roughly chopped

15 g (½ oz) pitted green olives

1 tbsp capers, rinsed

2 tsp wholegrain mustard

3 anchovy fillets

3–4 tsp lemon juice

125 ml (4 fl oz) extra virgin olive oil

salt and pepper

1 Tear the herbs into small sprigs without discarding the stalks. Put them into a food processor or blender with the garlic, olives, capers, mustard and anchovy fillets. Add 3 teaspoons of the lemon juice.

2 Blend the ingredients until finely chopped. Gradually blend in the oil to form a chunky sauce. Season with salt and pepper, adding extra lemon juice to sharpen the flavour if you like. Turn into a small serving bowl and chill until ready to serve.

Salad dressing

A vinaigrette – a mixture of oil and vinegar – is one of the simplest salad dressings to make. Choose good-quality extra virgin olive oil, walnut or hazelnut oil, or a flavoured oil, for example with chilli, garlic or herbs. For a more robust-flavoured vinegar, use white and red wine vinegars, sherry or balsamic vinegars; for a milder flavour, try cider vinegar.

Basic vinaigrette

The usual proportions are 3 parts oil to 1 part vinegar. If you use a straight-sided jar for mixing, you can see the proportions at a glance without having to measure.

Makes 125 ml (4 fl oz)

6 tbsp extra virgin olive oil

2 tbsp red or white wine vinegar

1 tsp Dijon mustard

pinch of caster sugar

salt and pepper

1 Place all the ingredients in a screw-top jar, cover and shake well to combine.

Variations

Honey citrus dressing Replace the vinegar with lemon juice and add 1 teaspoon of honey instead of the sugar.
Herb dressing Omit the mustard and add 2 tablespoons of finely chopped fresh herbs, such as parsley, chives or chervil, or a mixture of herbs.

Below A simple vinaigrette dressing, made with olive oil and vinegar, will enliven all types of salads.

Sweet sauces

Sweet sauces give puddings and desserts of all kinds a mouthwatering finishing touch.

Glossy chocolate sauce

Use a good-quality dark chocolate with about 70 per cent cocoa solids to give a rich flavour and glossy sheen. Take care not to overheat the chocolate or the sauce will develop a grainy texture.

Serves 5–6
125 g (4 oz) caster sugar
125 ml (4 fl oz) water
200 g (7 oz) plain dark chocolate
25 g (1 oz) unsalted butter

1 Put the sugar into a small, heavy-based saucepan with the water. Cook over a low heat, stirring constantly with a wooden spoon, until the sugar has dissolved.
2 Bring the syrup to the boil and boil for 1 minute, then remove the pan from the heat and leave to cool for 1 minute. Chop the chocolate into pieces and tip them into the pan.
3 Add the butter and leave until the chocolate and butter have melted, stirring frequently until the sauce is smooth and glossy. If the last of the chocolate doesn't melt completely or you want to serve the sauce warm, return the pan briefly to the lowest heat setting and warm through.

Above A delicious chocolate sauce can turn the plainest of puddings into a sumptuous dessert.

Butterscotch fudge sauce

Muscovado sugar and evaporated milk give this sauce its distinctive and delicious flavour; great for those who like hot puddings bathed in a sweet, creamy puddle!

Serves 4–6
75 g (3 oz) unsalted butter
150 g (5 oz) light muscovado sugar
175 g (6 oz) can evaporated milk

1 Cut the butter into pieces and place them in a small, heavy-based saucepan with the sugar. Heat very gently, stirring with a wooden spoon, until the butter has melted and the sugar dissolved. Bring to the boil and boil for about 2 minutes until the mixture is bubbling and treacly in consistency.
2 Remove the pan from the heat. Pour in the evaporated milk and stir gently until evenly combined. Return the pan to the heat, bring the sauce to the boil and cook for 1 minute until smooth and glossy. Pour into a jug and serve hot.

Red fruit coulis

Two or three summer fruits, blended and strained to a smooth and colourful purée, make a useful sauce for setting off all sorts of summery desserts. Use the coulis to flood the serving plates or drizzle it around the edges.

Serves 6–8
3 tbsp caster sugar
about 50 ml (2 fl oz) boiling water
500 g (1 lb) ripe summer fruits, such as strawberries, raspberries and redcurrants
2–3 tsp lemon juice

1 Put the sugar into a small jug and make it up to 50 ml (2 fl oz) with boiling water. Stir until the sugar dissolves and leave to cool.
2 Remove the redcurrants, if using, from their stalks by running them through the tines of a fork. Place all the fruits in a food processor or blender and blend to a smooth purée, scraping the mixture down from the sides of the bowl if necessary. Blend in the sugar syrup.
3 Pour the sauce into a sieve set over a bowl. Press the purée with the back of a large metal spoon to squeeze out all the juice.
4 Stir in enough lemon juice to make the sauce slightly tangy, then transfer it to a jug. To serve, pour a little coulis on to each serving plate and gently tilt the plate so it is covered in an even layer. Alternatively, use a tablespoon to drizzle the sauce in a ribbon around the edges of the plates.

Homemade Custard

Smooth, creamy and comforting, custard is always a great favourite and well worth the effort of making from scratch. You can vary the proportions of cream to milk, but this recipe, using half cream and half milk, creates a good balance of flavours.

Preparation time 20 minutes, plus infusing **Cooking time** 20 minutes **Serves** 6

1 vanilla pod, split lengthways

300 ml (½ pint) full cream milk

300 ml (½ pint) single cream

6 egg yolks

25 g (1 oz) caster sugar

1 Put the vanilla pod into a heavy-based saucepan with the milk and cream and bring slowly to the boil. Remove from the heat and leave to infuse for 15 minutes.

2 Whisk together the egg yolks and sugar in a bowl with a balloon whisk until thick and pale. Lift the vanilla pod out of the pan and scrape the seeds into the pan.

3 Pour the milk over the egg mixture, whisking well. Return the mixture to a clean pan and cook over a medium heat, stirring constantly with a wooden spoon, until the sauce thickly coats the back of the spoon. This will take about 5–10 minutes, but don't be tempted to raise the heat or the custard might curdle. Serve warm.

Variations
Chocolate custard Omit the vanilla and stir 50 g (2 oz) chopped plain dark chocolate into the sauce as soon as it has thickened, stirring until melted.
Coffee custard Omit the vanilla and add 1 tablespoon of instant espresso coffee when heating the milk.

Mastering batters

Batters are used to make pancakes, waffles and other sweet desserts, as well as Yorkshire pudding and toad-in-the hole. They are also used as a coating for a variety of different fried foods.

Pancakes

Inexpensive and easy to make from storecupboard ingredients, pancakes are served in countries throughout the world. They can be rolled around all types of fillings, or simply served plain.

It is not essential to let the batter stand before cooking the pancakes but it does make lighter pancakes. Pancakes made with rested batter tend to have a bubbly rather than a flat surface because the starch grains in the flour have had a chance to swell.

The secret of successful pancake batter is to avoid overbeating. Beat the ingredients only until they are combined and smooth. Too much whisking causes the gluten in the flour to develop and, as a result, the pancakes will be tough and chewy.

Basic pancakes

Pancakes can be stuffed with all types of delicious savoury fillings, as well as making a wonderful dessert.

Makes 8
225 g (4 oz) plain flour
pinch of salt
1 egg, beaten
300 ml (½ pint) milk or half milk and half water
light olive oil, vegetable oil or butter, for greasing the pan

1 Put the flour and salt into a mixing bowl and make a well in the centre. Add the egg to the well in the dry ingredients. Gradually stir in half the milk, or milk and water, then beat thoroughly until the batter is smooth and lump-free. Gradually beat in the remaining liquid until the surface is covered in tiny bubbles. Chill the batter for at least 30 minutes before using.
2 Put a little oil or butter into an 18 cm (7 inch) pancake pan or heavy-based frying pan. Heat the oil

until it starts to smoke – or the butter until it is foaming, but not browned. Pour off any excess oil and pour a little batter into the pan, tilting the pan until the base is coated in a thin, even layer. Cook for 1–2 minutes until the underside of the pancake starts to turn golden.
3 Flip the pancake with a palette knife and cook for a further 30–45 seconds until it is golden on the second side. Slide the pancake out of the pan and make the remaining pancakes, oiling the pan as necessary. Set the pancakes aside while making the filling.

Variation

Spinach pancakes Trim the stalks from 250 g (8 oz) washed spinach leaves and put the leaves, with just the water clinging to them, into a heavy-based saucepan. Cover the pan with a lid and cook the spinach over a gentle heat for 2 minutes or until wilted. Drain thoroughly, pressing out any excess water. Chop finely and beat into the batter with the milk.

Coating batter

Use to coat fish fillets, apple rings or vegetable chunks before frying. For a light batter, use beer instead of milk.

Makes 250 ml (8 fl oz)
60 g (2½ oz) self-raising flour
60 g (2½ oz) cornflour
pinch of salt
1 tbsp sunflower oil
150 ml (¼ pint) milk
1 egg white

1 Sift the flour, cornflour and salt into a large bowl and make a well in the centre. Add the oil and milk, then beat until smooth and bubbly.
2 Whisk the egg white in a clean bowl until it holds soft peaks, then fold it quickly into the batter.

Sweet crêpes

Use this sweet pancake mixture when you want a rich, sweet flavour for a special dessert.

Makes 8–10
225 g (4 oz) plain flour
pinch of salt
2 tbsp caster sugar
1 egg, lightly beaten
300 ml (½ pint) milk
25 g (1 oz) unsalted butter, melted
light olive oil, vegetable oil or butter, for greasing the pan

1 Put the flour, salt and sugar into a bowl and make a well in the centre. Pour the egg and a little of the milk into the well. Whisk the liquid, gradually incorporating the flour to make a smooth paste. Whisk in the butter, then the remaining milk until smooth. Pour the batter into a jug and cover. Chill the batter in the refrigerator for at least 30 minutes before using.
2 Put a little oil or butter into an 18 cm (7 inch) pancake pan or heavy-based frying pan and heat until it starts to smoke. Pour off the excess oil and pour a little batter into the pan, tilting the pan until the base is coated in a thin layer. (If you prefer, use a small ladle to measure the batter into the pan.) Cook for around 1–2 minutes until the underside of the pancake starts to turn golden.
3 Flip the pancake over with a palette knife, or the toss of your wrist, and cook for a further 30–45 seconds until it is golden on the second side. Slide the pancake out of the pan and make the remaining pancakes, oiling the pan as necessary. Eat immediately with lemon juice and sugar or stuff with a sweet filling.

Above A coating batter can be used on all types of ingredients. Fried apple rings make a wonderful dessert sprinkled with sugar.

Yorkshire puddings

Everyone loves Yorkshire puddings with their roast beef. With individual small puddings rather than one big one, it is easier to achieve success – the puddings should be well-risen and golden. This batter can also be used for toad-in-the-hole.

Makes 12
125 g (4 oz) plain flour
pinch of salt
2 eggs
150 ml (¼ pint) milk or half milk and half water
oil, for greasing

1 Make the batter as for Coating Batter (above) and leave to stand for 30 minutes.
2 Pour ½ teaspoon of oil into each of 12 deep muffin tins and place in a preheated oven at 220°C (425°F), Gas Mark 7, for 5 minutes until very hot. Quickly pour the batter into the tins until half-full, return them to the oven and bake for about 20 minutes until well-risen, crisp and golden brown.

Did you know?
• Water helps to make a batter light
• Milk will make it smooth and helps to brown
• Melted butter enriches and helps to prevent the batter from sticking

Bacon, Avocado and Soured Cream Pancakes

Smooth avocado, salty bacon and soured cream make a tempting filling. Serve as a light lunch.

Preparation time 15 minutes, plus making the batter **Cooking time** 30 minutes
Serves 4

8 pancakes (see page 174)

250 g (8 oz) thin streaky bacon rashers

2 avocados

300 ml (½ pint) soured cream

1 garlic clove, crushed

3 tbsp snipped chives

½ tsp mild chilli powder

oil, for greasing

125 g (4 oz) Cheddar cheese, finely grated

salt and pepper

1 Make the pancakes according to the instructions on page 174 and keep them warm while making the filling.

2 Dry-fry the bacon in a heavy-based pan until crisp. Leave it to cool slightly then cut it into small pieces. Halve, stone and peel the avocados and slice them thinly. Mix with the bacon. Beat the soured cream with the garlic, chives, chilli powder and salt and pepper. Stir into the bacon and avocado mixture.

3 Divide the filling among the pancakes, spreading it thinly to within 1 cm (½ inch) of the edge. Roll up the pancakes and place them in a lightly greased, shallow ovenproof dish.

4 Sprinkle the pancakes with the cheese and bake in a preheated oven at 190°C (375°F), Gas Mark 5, for about 20 minutes until the cheese has melted.

50 g (2 oz) ground hazelnuts or almonds, toasted

1 tsp almond extract

4 tablespoons milk

1 quantity Sweet Crêpe batter (see page 175)

oil or butter, for frying

300 g (10 oz) chocolate and hazelnut spread

4 tbsp double cream

5 large bananas

2 tbsp lemon juice

icing sugar, for sprinkling

25 g (1 oz) hazelnuts, toasted and roughly chopped

single cream, to serve

Chocolate and Banana Pancake Torte

Although delicious served cold, this dessert can also be heated before serving. Assemble it on a baking sheet and warm in a preheated oven at 200°C (400°F), Gas Mark 6, for 10 minutes.

Preparation time 20 minutes, plus making the batter **Cooking time** 25 minutes **Serves** 6

1 Beat the toasted nuts, almond extract and milk into the pancake batter and cook the pancakes following the instructions on page 175. Set the pancakes aside while making the filling.

2 Put the chocolate spread in a small pan with the cream and heat gently until slightly softened but not liquid. Slice the bananas as finely as possible and toss in the lemon juice.

3 Place a pancake on a flat plate and spread with a little of the chocolate spread. Cover with a thin layer of banana slices. Arrange another pancake on top. Continue layering the ingredients, finishing with a pancake. Sprinkle with icing sugar and scatter with toasted hazelnuts. Serve cut into wedges, with cream.

Buttermilk Pancakes with Blueberry Sauce

Perfect for breakfast on a summer's morning.

Preparation time 10 minutes **Cooking time** 20 minutes **Serves** 4–6

250 g (8 oz) fresh blueberries

2 tbsp clear honey

dash of lemon juice

15 g (½ oz) butter

150 g (5 oz) self-raising flour

1 tsp bicarbonate of soda

40 g (1½ oz) caster sugar

1 egg, beaten

350 ml (12 fl oz) buttermilk

Greek yogurt or crème fraîche, to serve

icing sugar, for dusting

1 Warm the berries with the honey and a dash of lemon juice in a small saucepan for about 3 minutes, until they release their juices. Keep warm.

2 Melt the butter in a small saucepan. Sift together the flour and bicarbonate of soda in a bowl and stir in the sugar. Beat together the egg and buttermilk and gradually whisk the mixture into the dry ingredients. Whisk in the melted butter to make a smooth batter.

3 Heat a nonstick frying pan until hot and drop in large spoonfuls of batter. Cook for 3 minutes, until bubbles appear on the surface. Flip the pancakes over and cook for a further minute. Keep them warm in a low oven while cooking the rest.

4 Serve the pancakes topped with the blueberry sauce and some Greek yogurt or crème fraîche. Dust with a little icing sugar to decorate.

Waffles with Mixed Berries

Waffles are made with a batter that is similar to a pancake mixture, but a little thicker. You will need a waffle iron or electric waffle maker for this dish.

Preparation time 15 minutes **Cooking time** 15 minutes **Serves** 4

75 g (3 oz) unsalted butter

2 eggs

125 ml (4 fl oz) milk

125 g (4 oz) self-raising wholemeal flour

3 tbsp icing sugar, sifted

grated rind and juice of ½ lemon

450 g (14½ oz) pack of frozen mixed berries, defrosted

1 sprig of mint, plus extra to garnish

crème fraîche, to serve

1 Melt the butter, then allow it to cool a little. Separate the eggs. Add the yolks to the milk and whisk lightly. Add 1 tablespoonful of the melted butter to the milk and work in lightly with a fork.

2 Heat a waffle iron on the hob or preheat an electric one while you sift the flour into a bowl. Make a well in the flour and gradually beat in the milk and the remaining butter. Whisk the egg whites until stiff enough to hold firm peaks, then fold into the batter with 2 tablespoons of icing sugar and the lemon rind.

3 Grease the waffle iron and pour in about one-eighth of the waffle batter. Close the lid and cook for 4–5 minutes, turning the iron once or twice if using a hob model. When the waffle is golden brown and cooked, cover and keep warm while you cook the remaining waffles.

4 Put the lemon juice and fruit into a saucepan with the mint and heat gently until the juices run, stirring to prevent the fruit sticking. Put two waffles on each plate and top with some of the fruit. Shake over a little sifted icing sugar and add a sprig of mint to decorate. Serve with crème fraîche.

Ice creams and sorbets

Ice creams are universal favourites, appealing to people all over the world – in cold countries as well as hot. Such is their appeal that they have been made from almost every possible ingredient.

Above If making sorbet by hand, rather than in an ice cream machine, beat it regularly as it freezes to keep the texture smooth.

The science behind ices

When making iced desserts, it helps to know a little about the freezing process. Without any additions, a fruit purée, the basis of many ices, would freeze to the solid consistency of an ice lolly, but when other ingredients, such as sugar, cream, gelatine, eggs, alcohol and air, are added to the purée they prevent it from freezing quite so hard.

In general, the higher the ratio of cream to the basic flavouring, the less beating is necessary. This means that if an ice contains a high proportion of water (a sorbet made with fruit juice, for example), then ice crystals will form easily and, for a smooth finish, the ice will need a considerable amount of beating and stirring.

The quantity of sugar is critical for both ice creams and sorbets. Too much sugar and the ice won't freeze properly; not enough and it will be hard to scoop.

A simple dessert

Iced desserts have the enormous advantage for the busy host or hostess in that they must be made in advance and that, on the whole, they don't require very much of the cook's time, merely a lengthy wait while the mixture freezes.

Basically, there are only two types of ice. First, sorbets, which include water ices and granitas, and are generally light and refreshing. Second, cream ices, which should be smooth, rich and sumptuous.

Granitas

These are usually made with fruit juice or coffee, sugar and, sometimes, alcohol and served ice cold in tall glasses. They are sometimes layered with cream, to be eaten with a spoon. Unlike sorbets and ice creams, they have a grainy texture.

Sorbets and water ices

Like granitas, sorbets and water ices are made with a sugar syrup base, but they often also include lightly beaten egg whites to lighten the mixture and give a smoother texture. Sorbets are often served in sundae glasses or in tall glasses like granitas.

Ice creams

These contain fats, usually in the form of cream and/or egg custard. Some ice creams are frozen to the correct consistency without further beatings, but although custard-based ice creams may include whipped cream, the custard base does not contain sufficient air to prevent ice crystals from forming, so these ices must be beaten during freezing to get rid of any graininess, which would spoil the texture of the finished dish.

This applies only if you are making the ice cream by hand. If an ice cream maker is being used, the machine will do the beating for you while it is churning and freezing.

Ice cream machines

The main work involved in making ice creams and sorbets by hand is regularly beating the mixture as it freezes to ensure a light, smooth texture. Ice cream machines will do all this work for you, and are a worthwhile investment if you want to make a lot of frozen desserts. You simply pour the mixture into the machine and it will beat continuously as it freezes, giving you perfect ice cream or sorbet in 20–30 minutes. What could be easier?

Coffee Granita

This is a simple and elegant recipe, which cannot be made in an ice cream machine. Serve after dinner instead of coffee.

Preparation time 10 minutes, plus cooling and freezing **Serves** 4

4 tbsp freshly ground strong coffee

125 g (4 oz) caster sugar

450 ml (¾ pint) boiling water

whipped cream, to serve (optional)

1 Put the ground coffee and sugar into a jug and stir in the boiling water. Stir until the sugar has dissolved, then leave to cool.

2 Strain the coffee liquid into a freezer container, cover and chill in the refrigerator for about 30 minutes. Transfer to the freezer and freeze for at least 2 hours, or until completely solid.

3 Remove the granita from the container, then quickly chop it into large chunks with a large heavy knife. Return it to the container and freeze again until required. Serve straight from the freezer, with whipped cream if you like.

Old-fashioned Vanilla Ice Cream

The original and best – just taste the homemade version.

Preparation time 10 minutes, plus cooling and freezing **Cooking time** 25 minutes
Serves 6

300 ml (½ pint) single cream

1 vanilla pod

4 egg yolks

50 g (2 oz) caster sugar

300 ml (½ pint) double or whipping cream

redcurrants coated in icing sugar, to serve (optional)

1 Put the single cream and vanilla pod into a heavy-based saucepan, set over a low heat and bring to just below boiling point. Remove from the heat and leave to infuse.

2 Meanwhile, put the egg yolks and sugar into a heatproof bowl and set it over a pan of gently simmering water. Stir with a wooden spoon until thick and creamy, then gradually stir in the scalded single cream, discarding the vanilla pod. Continue stirring for 15 minutes until the custard thickens sufficiently to coat the back of a spoon. Remove the bowl from the heat and leave to cool.

3 Pour the vanilla mixture into a freezer container, cover and transfer to the freezer for about 45 minutes or until slushy. Whip the cream until it just holds its shape. Remove the vanilla mixture from the freezer, beat thoroughly, then fold in the cream. Return the mixture to the container, cover and freeze for a further 45 minutes, then beat again until smooth. Freeze the ice cream for at least 1–2 hours. Transfer to the refrigerator for about 30 minutes to soften slightly before serving. Decorate with redcurrants coated in icing sugar, if desired.

Cherry Almond Ice Cream

Another custard-based ice cream, but this one is flavoured with sweet cherries and fragrant almonds.

Preparation time 20 minutes, plus cooling and freezing **Cooking time** 20 minutes
Serves 6

150 ml (¼ pint) milk

50 g (2 oz) ground almonds

1 egg and 1 extra yolk

75 g (3 oz) caster sugar

2–3 drops almond essence

500 g (1 lb) red cherries, pitted, or 500 g (1lb) cherry compôte

25 g (1 oz) slivered almonds

150 ml (¼ pint) double cream

1 Pour the milk into a small saucepan and stir in the ground almonds. Bring to the boil, then set aside.

2 Put the egg and the extra yolk into a heatproof bowl with the sugar and beat until pale and thick. Pour on the milk and almond mixture. Place the bowl over a pan of gently simmering water and stir until thickened sufficiently to coat the back of a spoon. Stir in the almond essence and cool.

3 Put the cherries into a food processor or blender and whizz to a purée, then stir them into the custard. Toss the slivered almonds in a dry heavy-based frying pan over a low heat to toast them. Leave to cool.

4 Whip the cream until it forms soft peaks. Fold the whipped cream into the cherry mixture. Transfer the mixture to a freezer container, cover and freeze until firm, beating twice at hourly intervals. Stir the slivered almonds into the mixture at the last beating. Serve the ice cream in individual glasses.

Fresh Melon Sorbet

Other flavoursome melons, such as honeydew or watermelon, may also be used for this sorbet. For a dinner party, make three sorbets using different types of melon: the different colours and subtly different flavours make a special dessert.

Preparation time 15 minutes, plus freezing **Serves** 4–6

1 Cantaloupe melon, weighing 1 kg (2 lb)

50 g (2 oz) icing sugar

juice of 1 lime or small lemon

1 egg white

1 Cut the melon in half and scoop out and discard the seeds. Scoop out the melon flesh with a spoon and discard the shells.

2 Place the flesh in a food processor or blender with the icing sugar and lime or lemon juice. Process to a purée, then pour the mixture into a freezer container, cover and freeze for 2–3 hours.

3 Whisk the melon mixture to break up the ice crystals. Whisk the egg white until stiff, then whisk it into the half-frozen mixture. Return to the freezer until firm.

4 Transfer the sorbet to the refrigerator 20 minutes before serving to soften slightly. Scoop the sorbet into glass dishes to serve.

Note If using an ice cream machine, follow the recipe until midway through step 2. Pour into the machine and churn and freeze until half-frozen. Whisk the egg white until it forms soft peaks and add to the machine. Continue to freeze until completely frozen.

Sweet treats

Although they have a reputation for being tricky, homemade cakes and biscuits are within every cook's ability, as long as the ingredients are weighed accurately and the instructions followed carefully. Grasp these skills, and you will find your popularity increases no end among family and friends.

Ingredients

The range and quality of ingredients you use obviously play a vital role in successful baking.

Eggs

For baking, eggs should be used at room temperature so that they hold the maximum amount of air and give a good rise to cakes and bakes. Very cold eggs tend to curdle in creamed mixtures, making the cake heavy and tough.

Sugars and sweeteners

The type depends on the individual recipe.

Caster sugar is the most useful for general baking, and golden caster is a good choice for adding colour to simple sponges.

Below Homemade cakes are not difficult to make if you follow the recipes carefully, and are so much nicer than shop-bought cakes.

Granulated sugar is coarser than caster sugar and it tends to give baked sponges a speckled appearance. You can grind granulated sugar for just a few seconds in a food processor to make it finer and produce a good substitute for caster sugar.

Soft light and dark brown sugars are coloured and flavoured fine crystal sugars which can be used instead of caster sugar for adding extra colour. Break up small lumps before adding them to mixtures, or they may not mix evenly.

Dark and light muscovado sugars are natural brown sugars with fine crystals and a natural coating of molasses, giving a distinctive rich flavour and colour. The darker ones tend to be sticky, so these can give cakes a moist, soft texture.

Demerara sugar has very large crystals which are too coarse for use in creamed mixtures, but it can be used for cakes made by the melting method. It also makes an attractive crunchy topping when sprinkled on cakes, muffins or biscuits.

Icing sugar is the finest-textured sugar. It is used for making smooth icings and meringues, but because of its fine texture, it gives a poor volume to cake and biscuit mixtures.

Honey and golden syrup can be used instead of some of the sugar in many cakes. They are very good in cakes made by the melting method.

Flours

Self-raising and plain white flour are the usual choice, although some recipes may use wholemeal plain or self-raising flours. Self-raising flour has a balanced amount of raising agent already mixed in, making it convenient for many cakes. In some recipes it is necessary to add extra raising agent.

If a recipe calls for self-raising flour and you have only plain flour in the house, add 2½ teaspoons of baking powder to each 250 g (8 oz) of plain flour. Sift the baking powder and flour together thoroughly to mix them evenly before use.

Fats

Butter and block margarine are the most commonly used fats in baking and are generally interchangeable. Bring these hard fats to room temperature before use and, if necessary, beat them with a wooden spoon to soften them slightly, making them easier to mix.

Soft or tub margarines, reduced-fat and low-fat spreads cannot be used successfully in standard recipes, since they have a high water content. Light-flavoured oils, such as sunflower or corn oil, are good in some cakes, especially those made by the melting method.

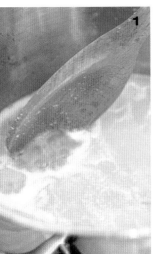

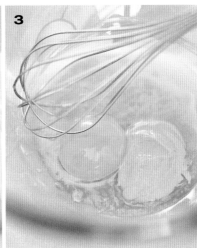

Dried fruit

Dried fruit of all kinds are useful storecupboard standbys for cakes and bakes. Make sure you store them in airtight containers and use them up regularly, since they can become dry and tasteless when old.

Ready-to-eat, semi-dried fruits, such as apricots or figs, are useful because they do not require soaking before use. Smaller fruits, such as currants and sultanas, do not need soaking.

Nuts

Many cake recipes use chopped or ground nuts for added texture and flavour. Nuts should always be as fresh as possible. Whole nuts keep better than cut nuts, so if you can, grind or chop your own rather than buying them ready prepared. For example, freshly ground almonds prepared in a food processor have a far better, fresher flavour than those ready ground.

Techniques

There are four basic methods used in baking. If you are familiar with these, you will be able to tackle just about any cake recipe.

Melting method (1)

This is one of the easiest methods for cakes. It is used for moist mixtures such as gingerbread. Melt the fat and sugar in a saucepan with other liquid ingredients, but not the eggs. Keep the heat low to dissolve the ingredients without boiling. Remove from the heat and cool slightly before stirring in the eggs followed quickly by the flour and spices. Mix to combine evenly. The heat starts to activate the raising agent straight away, so the quicker you put the mixture in the oven, the better it will rise.

Creaming method (2)

This is the most popular way to make sponges. Cream or beat the fat and sugar together, either by hand or with an electric whisk or processor, until pale in colour and fluffy and light in texture. Add the eggs gradually, beating hard after each addition – if they are added too quickly the mixture may curdle and the cake will be heavy in texture. Finally, fold the flour into the creamed mixture, together with any other additions, such as fruit or nuts.

Whisking method (3)

In all whisked mixtures, the air trapped when whisking expands in the heat of the oven to act as the main raising agent. The simplest mix is a light sponge without added fat. Whisk the eggs and sugar together in a bowl standing over a saucepan of hot water. The heat speeds up the whisking process. The water should not be boiling, but just kept at a low simmer, so that the gentle heat melts the sugar and begins to set the eggs – if the heat is too high then the eggs will begin to cook. When the mixture forms a pale, thick, mousse-like consistency, remove the bowl from the heat. The mixture should be thick enough to hold a clear trail on the surface when the whisk is lifted. Finally, lightly fold in the well-sifted flour.

Rubbing-in method (4)

Scones and teabreads are the most common examples of bakes made by this simple method. This usually uses less than half fat to flour. Rub the fat into the dry ingredients with the fingertips or in a food processor as for Shortcrust Pastry (see page 146). Add the eggs and any other liquid ingredients and mix lightly to combine the ingredients evenly.

Choosing the right tin

Always use the size of tin recommended in the recipe. You can change a round tin for a square tin, or the reverse, but remember that a square tin should be 2.5 cm (1 inch) smaller than a round tin. So, if the recipe is for a 23 cm (9 inch) round tin, you can use a 20 cm (8 inch) square tin instead.

How to prepare cake tins

For most simple cakes, the only preparation that is needed for the tin is greasing by brushing oil or melted butter over the base and sides. Placing a piece of non-stick baking paper in the base ensures that the baked goods turn out easily. For richer cakes, which tend to stick or burn at the edges, you should line the sides of the tin with baking paper.

Lining a round tin

1 Grease the base and sides of the tin by brushing with melted butter or oil.
2 Cut a long strip of non-stick baking paper slightly longer than the circumference of the tin and about 4 cm (1½ inch) deep. Fold over about 1.5 cm (¾ inch) along one long edge, then unfold it leaving a crease.
3 With scissors, snip the folded edge of the paper up to the fold. Make diagonal cuts so that the paper can be eased into the tin and overlapped to fit around the curve at the base of the tin.
4 Place the tin on a piece of non-stick baking paper and draw around it to mark the size of the base. Cut out just inside the line to give a round that will fit snugly inside the tin. Place the round of paper in the tin to cover the overlapping snipped edge of the side lining paper.

Flouring tins

To prepare sandwich tins for cooking whisked sponges, grease the tins by brushing the base and sides with oil or melted butter. Next sprinkle a little flour into the tin. Tilt the tin, tapping it lightly to make sure the flour coats the base and sides evenly, then tip out the excess flour and discard.

Preventing dryness

When cooking rich fruit cakes, the long, slow cooking process tends to dry out or overcook the edges of the cake. To prevent this from happening, wrap a double thickness of brown paper or newspaper around the outside of the cake tin – the paper should be slightly higher than the sides of the tin. Tie the paper firmly in place with string.

Start with something simple

If you have never made a cake before, start with small cakes such as fairy cakes or muffins, since they are virtually foolproof. You don't need to line tins as the cakes are cooked in paper cases, and the mixtures are usually a simple all-in-one affair.

Above Lining a cake tin will ensure that your cakes don't stick to the bottom of the tin and will be much easier to turn out.

TOP TIP

To make lining tins quicker and easier, it is possible to buy ready-cut rounds of non-stick baking paper in all the standard cake tin sizes. You can also buy long strips of paper of different widths to line the sides. If you are cooking cakes in loaf tins, look out for loaf tin liners too.

It is worth buying good-quality cake tins and baking sheets. Not only will they last a lifetime, but your cakes will be noticeably better than those cooked in poor-quality tins. The thicker metal will conduct the heat better. Cheap tins and baking sheets quickly buckle, making them useless. Baking sheets that are pale and dull-coloured are preferable to dark or shiny ones as these can cause the food to over-brown.

Is it cooked?

To check a sponge, press the surface lightly with your fingertips – it should feel springy to the touch and spring back without leaving an impression. Whisked sponge cakes should have shrunk slightly away from the side of the tin.

To check a rich fruit cake, lift the tin from the oven and listen closely to the cake – if you can hear the mixture sizzling, it is not fully cooked. Alternatively, insert a metal skewer into the centre of the cake and pull it out immediately. If it comes out clean without mixture on it, the cake is cooked. If there is sticky mixture on the skewer, the middle of the cake is not cooked and you will need to put it back in the oven. If you do need to cook the cake for a little longer, make sure you don't leave it in the oven for too long – an overcooked cake will be dry and hard and all your hard work will be wasted!

Sugarpaste icing

Use this traditional white icing to cover fruit cakes and sponges for special occasions. It can be rolled out and cut to fit any cake. The glucose stops the icing becoming too brittle so the cake will be easy to cut.

Makes enough for a 20cm (8 inch) round cake
900 g (1 lb 12 oz) icing sugar, plus extra for dusting
2 egg whites
4 tablespoon glucose, warmed

1 Sift the icing sugar into a bowl. Make a well in the centre, add the egg whites and warmed glucose and mix the sugar into the moist ingredients with a wooden spoon.
2 Continue until all the sugar has been incorporated.
3 Turn the icing out of the bowl and knead it on a cold work surface dusted with icing sugar until it is smooth and pliable.

Victoria Sponge

Preparation time 15 minutes
Cooking time 15–25 minutes
Serves 8

125 g (4 oz) butter, at room temperature
125 g (4 oz) caster sugar
2 eggs
½ tsp vanilla essence
125 g (4 oz) self-raising flour
1 tsp baking powder (optional)
2 tbsp milk

1 If you are making the mixture in a food processor, beat together all the ingredients, except the milk, until the mixture is thick, creamy and well combined. Add the milk a little at a time while you pulse the machine. When all the milk has been added the mixture should have a soft dropping consistency.
2 If making the mixture by hand, use a wooden spoon to beat the butter and sugar together until pale and creamy. Gradually beat in the eggs and vanilla extract, a little at a time, adding a tablespoon of flour with each addition – this will help prevent the mixture from curdling. Sift the remaining flour into the bowl and fold gently into the creamed mixture with a metal spoon, taking care not to knock out the air.
3 Divide the mixture between the prepared tins or paper cases and bake in a preheated oven at 180°C (350°), Gas Mark 4, for 15–20 minutes for small cakes, or 20–25 for the large cakes. Turn the cakes on to a wire rack to cool.

Variations

Chocolate Substitute 2 tablespoons cocoa powder for 2 tablespoons of the flour.
Coffee Add 1 tablespoon espresso or strong instant coffee granules.
Citrus Add the finely grated zest of 1 lemon or 1 small orange, or combine the zest of ½ lemon and ½ orange.
Cranberry or blueberry Add 75 g (3 oz) dried cranberries or blueberries, chopped if large.
Ginger Add 2 teaspoons ground ginger and use light brown sugar instead of caster sugar.

Rich Fruit Cake

Long cooking at a low temperature results in a rich, moist cake ideal for icing for a special occasion, such as Christmas, a birthday or even a wedding. Spread the top with apricot jam, then cover with marzipan and icing if you like.

Preparation time 10–15 minutes **Cooking time** 3½ hours **Serves** 12

1 Line a deep 20 cm (8 inch) round cake tin with greaseproof paper and grease well. Cream the butter and sugar together until fluffy and light in colour. Beat in the eggs, one at a time. Sift the flour with the spice and cocoa and fold in. Add all the remaining ingredients and mix well.

2 Spoon the mixture into the prepared tin and spread evenly. Bake in a preheated oven at 160°C (325°F), Gas Mark 3, for 30 minutes. Reduce the oven temperature to 150°C (300°F), Gas Mark 2, and bake for a further 1 hour. Reduce the oven temperature to 140°C (275°F), Gas Mark 1, and bake for a further 2 hours, or until cooked (see page 187).

3 Turn the cake out to cool on a wire rack. Wrap the cake in greaseproof paper and foil and store for at least 1 month before using.

250 g (8 oz) butter

250 g (8 oz) soft brown sugar

6 eggs

250 g (8 oz) plain flour

1½ tsp ground mixed spice

1 tbsp cocoa powder

grated rind and juice of 2 oranges

grated rind and juice of 1 lemon

250 g (8 oz) currants

250 g (8 oz) sultanas

250 g (8 oz) raisins

175 g (6 oz) chopped mixed peel

175 g (6 oz) glacé cherries, chopped

50 g (2 oz) blanched almonds, chopped

Strawberry Layer Gâteau

This cake, made by the creamed method, both looks and tastes wonderful. The sponge layers can be made up to three days in advance and stored in an airtight container.

Preparation time 15–20 minutes **Cooking time** 25–30 minutes **Serves** 8

250 g (8 oz) butter

250 g (8 oz) caster sugar

4 large eggs, beaten

50 g (2 oz) ground almonds

150 g (5 oz) self-raising flour

250 g (8 oz) strawberries, halved

200 ml (7 fl oz) double cream, lightly whipped

chocolate curls, to decorate

1 Grease two 22–23 cm (8½–9 inch) sandwich tins and line the bases with greaseproof paper. Cream the butter and sugar until fluffy and light in colour. Gradually beat in the eggs, adding a tablespoon of the ground almonds with the last amount. Sift in the flour and fold it into the mixture with the remaining almonds.

2 Turn into the prepared tins and bake in a preheated oven at 180°C (350°F), Gas Mark 4, for 20–25 minutes, or until the cakes are golden brown. Leave in the tins for 2–3 minutes, then turn out on to a wire rack to cool.

3 Halve or, if they are very large, quarter the strawberries. Reserve a few halves for decoration, with their green tops in place, if liked. Spread three-quarters of the cream on one of the sponges and top with the strawberries. Sandwich the cakes together and spread the remaining cream on the top sponge. Decorate the top with the reserved strawberries and chocolate curls.

Blueberry and Vanilla Muffins

Muffins are simple to make and quite delicious – serve for breakfast or tea. To keep the muffins light and soft, avoid overmixing the ingredients – mix until only just combined.

Preparation time 5 minutes **Cooking time** 15 minutes **Makes** 10

150 g (5 oz) ground almonds

150 g (5 oz) golden caster sugar

50 g (2 oz) self-raising flour

175 g (6 oz) unsalted butter, melted

4 egg whites

1 tsp vanilla extract

150 g (5 oz) blueberries

1 Line 10 sections of a muffin tray with paper cases, or grease the sections. Mix together the ground almonds, sugar, flour and butter. Add the egg whites and vanilla extract and mix to a smooth paste.

2 Spoon into the cases and scatter with the blueberries. Bake in a preheated oven at 220°C (425°F), Gas Mark 7, for 15 minutes until just firm in the centre. Leave for 5 minutes, then transfer the muffins to a wire rack to cool.

Cranberry, Oatmeal and Cinnamon Scones

Like all scones, these sweet, fruit-specked ones are best served fresh, or frozen ahead and then thawed and warmed to serve.

Preparation time 10 minutes **Cooking time** 12 minutes **Makes** 10

175 g (6 oz) self-raising flour

1 tsp baking powder

1 tsp ground cinnamon

75 g (3 oz) unsalted butter

75 g (3 oz) caster sugar

50 g (2 oz) oatmeal, plus extra for sprinkling

75 g (3 oz) dried cranberries

5–6 tbsp milk

beaten egg or milk, to glaze

1 Grease a baking sheet. Place the flour, baking powder and cinnamon in a food processor. Add the butter, cut into small pieces, and process until the mixture resembles breadcrumbs. Add the sugar and oatmeal and blend briefly. Alternatively, with your fingertips, rub the butter into the flour, baking powder and cinnamon in a bowl, then add the sugar and oatmeal. Add the cranberries and milk and blend briefly until the mixture forms a soft dough, adding a little more milk if necessary.

2 Turn out on to a floured surface and roll out to 1.5 cm (¾ inch) thick. Cut out rounds using a 5 cm (2 inch) cutter. Transfer to the prepared baking sheet and re-roll the trimmings to make more scones.

3 Brush with beaten egg or milk and sprinkle with oatmeal. Bake in a preheated oven at 220°C (425°F), Gas Mark 7, for 10–12 minutes until risen and golden. Transfer to a wire rack to cool. Serve split and buttered.

Quick Hazelnut Melts

These hazelnut cookies literally melt in the mouth. Serve on their own as a scrumptuous snack or cook a batch to accompany a mousse or ice cream dessert.

Preparation time 10 minutes **Cooking time** 12 minutes **Makes** 20

50 g (2 oz) blanched hazelnuts

125 g (4 oz) butter, softened, plus extra for greasing

50 g (2 oz) caster sugar

150 g (5 oz) plain flour

1 Grind the hazelnuts in a food processor until fairly smooth, but still retaining a little texture. Dry-fry in a heavy-based frying pan over a low heat until evenly golden. Tip into a bowl and stir until cool.

2 Blend together the butter and sugar in the food processor until creamy. Add the flour and cooled nuts and process again to make a soft dough.

3 Take walnut-size pieces of dough and shape it into rolls, then pat them into flat ovals. Place the biscuits on a greased baking sheet and bake in a preheated oven at 190°C (375°F), Gas Mark 5, for 12 minutes, until just golden. Cool on a wire rack.

Traditional Shortbread

Shortbread is delicious at any time of year, but it is a traditional Christmas teatime treat. It makes a wonderful gift for friends and family, especially if packaged in pretty boxes.

Preparation time 15 minutes, plus chilling **Cooking time** 45 minutes–1 hour
Serves 6–8

250 g (8 oz) plain flour

125 g (4 oz) ground rice

125 g (4 oz) caster sugar, plus extra for dusting

pinch of salt

250 g (8 oz) unsalted butter

1 Sift the plain flour, ground rice, sugar and salt into a mixing bowl. Soften the butter slightly, cut it up, and rub it into the dry ingredients with your fingers. When the mixture starts to bind, gather it together with one hand into a ball. Knead it on a lightly floured surface to a soft, smooth and pliable dough.

2 Place a 20 cm (8 inch) flan ring on a greased baking sheet and put in the dough, pressing it out evenly with your knuckles to fit the ring. With the back of a knife, mark the shortbread into triangles. With a fork, prick right through to the baking sheet in a neat pattern. Cover the shortbread and chill for at least 1 hour before baking, to firm it up.

3 Bake the shortbread in a preheated oven at 150°C (300°F), Gas Mark 2, for 45 minutes–1 hour, or until it is a pale biscuit colour but still soft. Remove the shortbread from the oven and leave to cool and shrink before lifting off the ring, then dust lightly with caster sugar. When cold, cut it into triangles and store in an airtight container until required.

Jams and preserves

For centuries, the surplus fruits and vegetables of summer have been preserved by turning them into juicy jams, jellies and syrups.

Above All manner of fruit and vegetables can be transformed into preserves, jams, pickles and marmalades.

What are they?

Preserving is a method of keeping food, in this case fruit and vegetables, for a longer time than it would last if fresh, and it can cover a multitude of processes. The most familiar are jams, jellies and marmalades. A jam is made from crushed or whole fruit and is runnier than jelly, which is made from strained fruit juices. Marmalade is jam made exclusively from citrus fruit.

What you will need

The following basic equipment are essential for making preserves and are worth investing in.

Preserving pan

A preserving pan should be made of aluminium or tin-lined copper. It should have a thick base and be narrower at the bottom than the top. If a preserving pan is not available, use a large saucepan, but you may need to boil the jam longer to get it to set. Jars should be very clean and free of cracks and chips. You can use special preserving jars, or the jars from commercial jams. The 450 g (1 lb) size is best. Always have more jars ready than you think you will need to avoid a last-minute rush. After washing and drying, put them into a preheated cool oven, and fill them while they are hot to prevent them cracking.

Jam covers

These are necessary to seal the preserve. Waxed paper discs are the best. Place them wax-side down on the hot jam. These in turn are covered with dampened cellophane covers which are secured with elastic bands.

Labels

Only apply labels when the jam is cool. Store jars in a dark cupboard or larder.

Slotted spoon

Useful to skim the surface of the jam, especially for fruits with stones, when the stones come to the surface.

Jelly bag

As jellies are made with unpeeled, uncored fruits, straining through a bag is crucial for crystal clear juice. Traditionally made of white cotton flannel, jelly bags are now more commonly made from fine nylon mesh.

Jam funnel

A jug and special jam funnel are useful for filling the jars.

Sugar thermometer

Useful if an accurate test is to be done for setting, although you can manage without.

Requirements for setting

Jams, jellies and marmalades are made by boiling fruit or fruit juices with sugar, until the sugar, fruit, pectin and acid combine to set the mixture when it is cold. A combination of all four is essential for successful setting: pectin is a substance contained in the cell walls of most fruit and it reacts with the natural acids of the fruit to form a jelly-like set; the sugar, which is a natural preservative, also helps the pectin to form a set.

Fruits that contain little pectin and acid require the addition of a fruit which is high in both of these; the juice of 1–2 lemons, for instance, can be used per 1.75 kg (4 lb) of fruit. Alternatively, commercial pectin is easily available and, if you use it, you should follow the manufacturer's instructions. There is also a special preserving sugar available with pectin already added to help set jam made with fruits such as strawberries.

Sugar

Basically, any sugar can be used in preserves. Preserving sugar gives the clearest result, but it is more expensive than granulated. Brown sugar will give a darker colour. Sugar has a hardening effect on fruit, so it should only be added to fruit which have been softened by cooking. The exception is soft fruit such as strawberries, which can be 'hardened' by the sugar to help them retain their shape and remain whole.

Testing for set

There are three ways of testing for a set.

Wrinkle test Place about 1 teaspoon of jam on a cold saucer. Cool it quickly – in the freezer, perhaps – then push the tip of your finger through the surface of the jam or jelly. If the surface of the jam wrinkles while it is still tepid, the jam will set when it is cold.

Temperature test This is the most accurate method. Place a sugar thermometer in the preserving pan. When the temperature reaches 104°C (220°F) a set will be obtained. Some fruit, needs a degree above or below this, so it is best to combine this test with one of the others.

Flake test Stir the jam with a long-handled wooden spoon. Hold a spoonful of jam horizontally above the pan to cool it a little, then tip the spoon to allow the jam to run off it. If the jam sets partly on the spoon and falls away in large flakes rather than drops, it is ready. If the jam runs in an unbroken single stream, it needs further boiling before being tested again.

Jam

Making your own jam has distinct advantages in that you can adapt the recipe to suit your own taste. Commercially produced jams are aimed at everyone so you rarely find those that include some of the more unusual ingredients such as cloves, for example. In addition, when making your own preserves you are in control of how sweet you make your jam. Shop-bought jams are often incredibly sweet due to their juice-extracting process which requires extra pectin to be added. Consequently, extra sugar is then added in order to get the correct set.

Choose fruit that is firm and slightly under-ripe to just ripe, with absolutely no blemishes. Never use over-ripe fruit as this will contain less pectin and acid and therefore will not set very well.

It is a good idea to pick over the fruit and prepare it according to type. Wipe if it is dusty and be sure to dry it thoroughly. Do not wash unless absolutely necessary, since water will dilute the pectin and acid. The boiling process will purify the fruit.

Making jam

If you are not following a recipe then the general guidelines for making jam are as follows:

1 Lightly crush the fruit with your hands and put into the preserving pan. If the fruit you are using is fairly dry, for example apricots, then you may need to add a little water. Bring to the boil and simmer until the fruit is tender, stirring frequently to prevent the fruit from sticking to the bottom of the pan and burning.

2 The proportions of sugar to fruit varies according to the type of fruit you are using. A rough starting point is to use equal measures.

3 Heat the sugar in a cool oven, 140°C (275°F), Gas Mark 1, for 10 minutes, to help it dissolve more quickly when added to the fruit. Stir it into the pan and heat gently, stirring occasionally, until the sugar has dissolved.

4 Now boil the jam rapidly, uncovered, stirring occasionally, until it sets when tested. This varies from 3–20 minutes, depending on the type of fruit and quantity. Start timing when the jam reaches a fast boil.

5 Once a set has been reached, take the jam off the heat and skim off any scum.

6 Arrange the hot jars on a baking sheet. Using a jam funnel, pour the hot jam into the jars right up to the neck. Be very careful because the jam will be extremely hot. Whole fruit jams should be cooled for 15 minutes before potting so that the fruit does not rise in the jars.

7 Cover the hot jam with the waxed discs, then wipe the rim of the jars with a slightly damp hot cloth.

8 Dampen the top of the cellophane covers, making sure that the underside is dry, then stretch them over the tops of the jars. Secure with elastic bands.

9 When cool, label the jars with the name and date and store in a cool, dry, dark place.

Below The fruit will need to be boiled rapidly for up to 20 minutes, or until the correct set has been reached.

Above Seville oranges produce excellent marmalade but have a short season. Alternatively choose other tart oranges.

Marmalade

Marmalade-making is very similar to jam-making but the cooking time is longer for two reasons. Firstly, the rind of citrus fruit is much tougher and thicker and therefore it requires longer cooking to soften it. Secondly, the water content is so much higher than for making jam. The liquid should be reduced by half by the end of the first cooking stage, by which time the fruit rind should be really soft. A pressure cooker is ideal for speeding up this process – allow about 15 minutes.

The pectin in marmalades is contained in the white pith of the fruit and in the pips. If you want to make a clear, delicate jelly marmalade, use only the rind of the fruit and its juice. Carefully save the pith and pips and tie them in a muslin or gauze bag; attach to the handle of the preserving pan and suspend in the marmalade. It is vital that the bag is totally submerged in the liquid at all times during the cooking.

Making marmalade

1 Finely chop the fruit, discarding the pips. For each measure of fruit, add two measures of water and put into a large pan.
2 Bring to a boil and simmer gently until the liquid has reduced by half and the fruit is very soft.
3 Measure the fruit with its liquid and add an equal measure of sugar. Boil rapidly until setting point.
4 Using a slotted spoon, remove any scum then leave the marmalade to stand for 15 minutes to allow the fruit to settle.
5 Stir well, then transfer to warm, dry jars. Pot, cover the jars and store in the usual way.

Jellies

The rules for making jelly are similar to those for jam, but the amount of sugar should be calculated from the yield of strained juice from the fruit. Choose fruits that are high in pectin and acid as these are obviously the best for making jellies.

Ready-made jelly bags with stands are available for straining jellies, but you can improvise with a doubled fine cloth or tea towel. Turn a stool or chair upside down, and secure the corners of the cloth firmly to each leg. Place a bowl underneath to catch the jelly as it drips through. The bag or cloths must be completely sterile. To achieve this, pour boiling water through them twice, allowing it to drip through.

Making jellies

1 Check over the fruit, discarding any that are damaged or bruised. Large fruit such as apples and plums need to be roughly chopped. There is no need to peel, core or stone the fruit because they will be separated from the juice when it is strained.
2 The fruit should be covered with water, but the juicier the fruit the less liquid required. Soft fruits may be cooked without a lid, but hard fruit should be covered. Cook the fruit very slowly to extract as much juice as possible – this will take about 45–60 minutes.
3 Have ready the sterilized jelly bag, or cloth, with a bowl underneath. Pour the cooked fruit and water into it and allow it to drip through. Do not squeeze the bag or touch it in any way – this will cloud the jelly.
4 When the bag has stopped dripping the juice is measured then mixed with the appropriate amount of sugar. Allow 500 g (1 lb) of sugar for every 600 ml (1 pint) of juice. The process is finished as for jam.
5 When setting point is reached, remove the scum, and if necessary strain the jelly. Pot and cover the jars in the usual way, but do not move the jars until the jelly is completely cold. Store jellies in a cool, dry, dark place to retain their vibrant colours.

Did you know?
Fruits vary in their pectin and acid content.
- Gooseberries, currants, damsons, apples, Seville oranges, lemons, limes and some plums are high in both and give a good set.
- Greengages, some plums, raspberries, apricots and loganberries give medium set.
- Strawberries, melon, rhubarb, cherries, blackberries and pears give a poor set.

Strawberry and Champagne Conserve

This timeless favourite has been given star treatment with the addition of a glass of dry Champagne.

Preparation time 10 minutes **Cooking time** 20 minutes, plus standing
Makes 2.25 kg (5 lb)

1.5 kg (3 lb) strawberries, hulled

150 ml (¼ pint) dry Champagne or sparkling white wine

1½ tsp citric acid

1.5 kg (3 lb) preserving sugar with added pectin

1 Pick over the strawberries and discard any bruised or very soft ones. Halve or quarter them, depending on size, then put half into a large pan and roughly crush them with a potato masher. If the strawberries are difficult to mash, warm them a little in the pan and then try again.

2 Add the Champagne or wine, citric acid and sugar and heat gently for 10 minutes, stirring continuously, until the sugar has completely dissolved.

3 Increase the heat and boil rapidly for 5–10 minutes, testing at 5-minute intervals until a set is reached. Using a slotted spoon, carefully skim off any scum, then leave the conserve to stand for 15 minutes to allow the fruit to settle.

4 Transfer to warm, dry jars. Cover the surface of each with a disc of waxed paper, waxed-side down, and leave until cold. Top the jars with airtight lids or cellophane covers. Label and store in a cool, dark place. It will keep for 6–12 months.

Dark Orange and Lemon Marmalade

Muscovado sugar gives this marmalade a good, rich flavour. For a tangy marmalade, use Seville oranges when in season.

Preparation time 10 minutes **Cooking time** 2 hours, plus standing
Makes about 2 kg (4 lb)

2 large oranges, finely chopped and pips discarded

4 large lemons, finely chopped and pips discarded

1.8 litres (3 pints) water

1 kg (2 lb) sugar

250 g (8 oz) muscovado sugar

1 Put the fruit into a large pan and add the water. Bring to the boil, reduce the heat and cover the pan. Simmer for 1½ hours.

2 Add all the sugar to the pan and cook over a low heat, stirring continuously, until the sugar has completely dissolved. Increase the heat and bring to a rolling boil, then boil hard to setting point. Using a slotted spoon, carefully skim off any scum, then leave the marmalade to stand for 15 minutes to allow the fruit to settle.

3 Stir the marmalade, then transfer to warm, dry jars. Cover the surface of each with a disc of waxed paper, waxed-side down, then leave until cold. Top the cold jars with airtight lids or cellophane covers. Label and store in a cool, dark place. It will keep for 3-4 months.

Mint and Apple Jelly

This is a traditional way of preserving mint for use in the winter or very early spring months. You can also try using rosemary instead of mint, or a selection of mixed herbs.

Preparation time 10 minutes **Cooking time** 1½ hours, plus straining and standing
Makes about 1.5–2 kg (3–4 lb)

2 kg (4 lb) cooking apples, roughly chopped

300 ml (½ pint) white vinegar

600 ml (1 pint) water

1.5 kg (3 lb) sugar

125 g (4 oz) fresh mint stalks

1 Put the apples into a pan with the vinegar and water. Bring to the boil, lower the heat and cover the pan. Simmer for 1 hour until reduced to a pulp. Allow to cool, then strain the mixture overnight through a jelly bag suspended over a large bowl.

2 The next day, pour the resulting juice into a large pan and add the sugar. Cook over a low heat, stirring continuously, until the sugar has completely dissolved. Increase the heat and bring to a rapid boil, then boil hard to setting point.

3 Pick the leaves from the mint and chop them finely. Using a slotted spoon, carefully skim off any scum from the jelly, then stir in the mint. Leave to stand for 10 minutes, then stir well and transfer to warm dry jars.

4 Cover the surface of each with a disc of waxed paper, waxed side down, then leave until cold. Top the cold jars with airtight lids or cellophane covers. Label and store in a cool, dark place. It will keep for 3–4 months.

Green Tomato Chutney

If you grow tomatoes why not chop up the unripened ones at the end of the season and make this tempting chutney.

Preparation time 15 minutes **Cooking time** 1 hour 40 minutes **Makes** 2 kg (4 lb)

1 Put the tomatoes, onions, apples and chillies into a large pan and mix together. Add the garlic, ginger, cloves and turmeric, then stir in the raisins, sugar and vinegar.

2 Bring to the boil, reduce the heat and cover the pan. Simmer, stirring frequently, for 1¼–1½ hours or until the chutney has thickened.

3 Transfer the chutney to warm, dry jars and cover the surface of each with a disc of waxed paper, waxed-side down, then top with an airtight lid. Label and leave to mature in a cool, dark place for at least 3 weeks before using, or store, unopened, for 6–12 months.

1 kg (2 lb) green tomatoes, finely chopped

500 g (1 lb) onions, finely chopped

500 g (1 lb) cooking apples, peeled, cored and chopped

2 fresh green chillies, halved, deseeded and finely chopped

2 garlic cloves, crushed

1 teaspoon ground ginger

generous pinch of ground cloves

generous pinch of ground turmeric

50 g (2 oz) raisins

250 g (8 oz) soft dark brown sugar

300 ml (½ pint) white wine vinegar

putting it
into practice

Meal planning and menus

Now you have learned all the basic techniques for preparing and cooking food, how do you put it all together and plan a meal? Most people find that meal planning is good fun and it allows you to use your creativity and ingenuity.

What to choose

The dishes you choose will depend on the occasion – a simple family supper for four, or a buffet for ten, for example – the time of year, and the tastes of those eating the meal. Unless it is a very special occasion, it is a good idea to limit the number of courses to two or three – or four, perhaps, if you are serving cheese – with coffee to finish. Choose one interesting course to impress everyone, and keep the rest simple. When planning a barbecue, choose three or four main courses and serve them with bread and a variety of salads, followed by a simple cold dessert.

Getting the balance right

The most important thing when you are planning a menu is to aim for overall variety and balance. Variety is self-explanatory, but what exactly does balance mean? Above all, it means not serving too much of any one thing and being careful about the overall spread of different ingredients, flavours, colours, temperatures, textures and even shapes.

Hot or cold?

Try, for example, not to serve every course hot. If there are to be three courses, it is probably best to serve one hot course and two cold ones. The hot dish generally makes the heart of the meal, especially during the winter months, although in summer this need not be the case. Then you might like to ring the changes by providing your guests with a surprise – you might serve the first and dessert courses hot, for example, and the main course cold, which is not only unusual but also has the added advantage of being prepared in advance.

Similarly, it is usually better not to serve every course cold. One exception to this is where you are eating al fresco, in which case cold food throughout the meal might seem more summery and more appropriate.

There's nothing wrong, either, with mixing hot and cold in the same course. Serve a hot main dish with a cold dressed salad instead of hot vegetables; or serve cold salmon, say, with hot new potatoes. Combining hot and cold within the same dish can also be interesting: serve ice cream with hot chocolate sauce; or make a warm salad with hot bacon or chicken livers. All these things can add an interesting surprise.

Dos and don'ts

• Don't serve two runny dishes in the same meal: for example, soup, followed by another fairly liquid main course, such as a casserole. Similarly, don't serve a creamy soup if you are planning to offer a creamy dessert to finish. As a general rule, it's a good idea not to serve two courses that are eaten with a spoon.

• Don't serve two complicated courses, both with elaborate sauces. Make sure that at least one of them is a simple dish, which isn't 'messed about'.

• Don't serve two pastry dishes in the same meal, even if the type of pastry is different: for example, chicken filo parcels as a starter, followed by a vegetable tart, or steak and kidney pie, followed by apple tart.

• Many people believe that it is wrong to serve more than one fish course in a meal, but others think that as long as your guests like fish, there's no bar to serving it twice. Fish is a healthy option and you can't really eat too much of it. Think about a light fish pâté to open with, for example, or a smoked fish or prawn starter, then follow this with a bold, fleshy fish such as grilled fresh tuna or roasted monkfish. Two fish courses are probably better than two meat courses. It would not be a good idea, for instance, to serve chicken satay followed by roast lamb.

TOP TIP

Make sure that the meal you are serving contains a variety of both colours and textures. Don't choose a menu consisting of a succession of all brown dishes – or all bright orange ones, or all beige.

Sample menus

The following menus, using the recipes in this book, will give you an idea of how to put together a meal for any occasion.

Summer lunch al fresco

Celeriac and Potato Remoulade (page 101)
Tabbouleh with Fruit and Nuts (page 124)
Green salad
Fresh Melon Sorbet (page 183)

Winter warmer

Chilli Bean Soup (page 245)
Eggs Florentine (page 130)
Tomato Focaccia (page 159)

Birthday breakfast

Waffles with Mixed Berries (page 179)
Scrambled eggs on toast
Fresh coffee

Afterwork supper with friends

Tomato and Aubergine Parmigiano
  (page 96)
Green salad
Crusty bread
Crêpes Suzette (page 211)

Family supper

Griddled Liver and Bacon (page 68)
French beans
Baked Apples, stuffed with raisins (page 103)

Dinner for two

Valentine Martini (page 223)
Cherry Tomato Tartlets with Pesto (page 208)
Fillet Steak with Roquefort and
  Horseradish (page 66)
Parsnip purée (page 94)
Grilled tomatoes
Tiramisu with Raspberry Surprise (page 133)

Elegant dinner party

Caiparinha (page 221)
Scallops with Ginger and Asparagus
  (page 235)
Salmon in Banana Leaves (page 215)
New potatoes
Mixed leaf salad
Coffee Granita (page 181)
Dolcelatte, Camembert and goats' cheese

Sunday lunch

Broccoli and Cheese Soup (page 164)
Roast Pork with Bulgar and Celery Stuffing
  (page 68)
Carrots and spinach
French Apple Flan (page 152)
Homemade Custard (page 173)

Vegetarian supper

Chunky Carrot and Lentil Soup (page 165)
Couronne (page 158)
Sweet Potato, Rocket and Haloumi Salad
  (page 203)
White Bean and Sun-dried Tomato Salad
  (page 210)
Bananas with Palm Sugar Toffee Sauce
  (page 108)

Barbecue party

Hummus (page 116)
Pitta breads
Monkfish Kebabs (page 143)
Chicken with Herb and Lemon Marinade
  (page 72)
Spiced Pumpkin Wedges with Coconut Pesto
  (page 142)
Barbecued sweetcorn (page 140)
Panzanella (page 100)
Green salad
Mayonnaise (page 169)
Barbecued Fruits with Palm Sugar (page 142)
Old-fashioned Vanilla Ice Cream (page 182)

One dish feast

Moroccan Lamb Couscous (page 204)

Starters

Starters are just that: they are only the opening paragraph, the introduction to the meal, not the main part. As such, they should arouse interest while not providing the complete answer: they should whet the appetite rather than satisfy it. Your guests should still be hungry and eager for the delights that the meal will have to offer next. Starters should also be quick and easy to serve so you can concentrate on the next course.

Main courses

Whether you choose fish, meat, poultry or a vegetarian dish, the main course should be the heart of the meal. When planning your menu, choose your main course first and pick a starter and dessert to complement it. If you are entertaining, choose something fairly innocuous, or check first that your guests like what you have chosen. If someone does not eat what you are serving for starter or dessert, it is embarrassing, but if they won't eat the main course it is a disaster.

Desserts

The dessert provides the finishing touch to a meal. Plan your menu so that you choose the appropriate dessert for the meal. Try to balance a rich main course with a light dessert, such as a fruity concoction or refreshing sorbet. The time of year plays a part, too, in your choice of dessert. The winter months demand something hot, warming and satisfying, allowing you to forget the big freeze outside, while hot summer days call for ice creams, sorbets and frozen desserts to make the most of the sunshine. Make generous amounts of dessert so that everyone can enjoy it to the full.

Write it down

All these suggestions may sound glaringly obvious, but it is surprising how easy it is to forget and to do it without thinking, which is why it is so important to write down your proposed menu and to look at it carefully before you make any firm decisions and do your shopping. Sometimes things suddenly become more obvious when they are written down.

Above Organisation and simplicity are the keys to enjoyable, relaxed entertaining.

Modern entertaining

Sharing food with friends should be relaxing and sociable. It doesn't have to be a formal event or a meal on a grand scale. A simple supper or lunch with a glass or two of wine is all that is required. Gone are the days when cooks were expected to turn out course after course of complicated dishes to show their culinary worth. These are the three cardinal rules of entertaining:

1 Make it easy No one will care whether you've spent all day or just an hour in the kitchen, so pick food that is easy. These days, just one course is sufficient if you serve drinks and nibbles beforehand. Think big, filling casseroles, sumptuous risottos, a large platter of pasta, or a big dish of curry. Make it really delicious and offer bread with it. If you want to serve a dessert, buy some good-quality ice cream and biscuits.

2 Enjoy yourself You've invited friends or family round for a meal because you want to see them, so don't spend all evening in the kitchen. Choose dishes you have tried before and you are comfortable making, so the stress levels are low. Pick dishes that require no last-minute cooking – cold dishes are often the answer because they can be made well ahead, or long-cook dishes which go in the oven before your guests arrive.

3 Do it with flair Whatever you decide to cook, do it with flair and offer no apologies for food you have not painstakingly made yourself. So what if you bought the bread, or the sauce comes out of a tub? Equally, don't draw everyone's attention to the fact that the cake didn't rise quite evenly or the sauce has a few lumps. No one will even notice unless you tell them.

TOP TIP

Take care when serving a spicy or strongly flavoured dish as part of a meal. Don't follow it with something more delicate or your guests will simply not be able to taste the next course.

1 kg (2 lb) sweet potatoes, sliced

6 tablespoons olive oil

500 g (1 lb) haloumi cheese, patted dry on kitchen paper

150 g (5 oz) rocket

Dressing
10 tablespoons olive oil

3 tablespoons clear honey

4 tablespoons lemon or lime juice

3 teaspoons black onion seeds

2 red chillies, deseeded and finely sliced

1 tablespoon chopped lemon thyme

salt and pepper

Sweet Potato, Rocket and Haloumi Salad

This simple salad is a meal in itself, served with plenty of crusty bread – the perfect dish for summer entertaining. The combination of firm, salty cheese, sweet potato and a honeyed, spiced citrus dressing is absolutely delicious.

Preparation time 10 minutes **Cooking time** 15 minutes **Serves** 4

1 Mix together all the ingredients for the dressing in a small bowl.

2 Cook the sweet potatoes in lightly salted boiling water for 2 minutes. Drain well. Heat the oil in a large frying pan, add the sweet potatoes and fry for about 10 minutes, turning once, until golden.

3 Meanwhile, thinly slice the cheese and place on a lightly oiled foil-lined grill rack. Cook under a preheated moderate grill for about 3 minutes until golden.

4 Pile the sweet potatoes, cheese and rocket on a large serving platter and spoon over the dressing.

500 g (1 lb) lean lamb, cut into large cubes

900 ml (1½ pints) water

2 onions, quartered and thickly sliced

2 garlic cloves, crushed

pinch of saffron threads, crushed

1 tsp ground cinnamon

½ tsp paprika

1 fresh red chilli, deseeded and finely chopped

½ tsp ground ginger

250 g (8 oz) small carrots, quartered lengthways

250 g (8 oz) small turnips, quartered

250 g (8 oz) kohlrabi or celeriac, cut into large chunks

250 g (8 oz) courgettes, quartered lengthways

250 g (8 oz) broad beans

4 tomatoes, quartered

large bunch of coriander, chopped

large bunch of parsley, chopped

500 g (1 lb) couscous

40 g (1½ oz) butter

salt and pepper

Moroccan Lamb Couscous

This dish is a substantial feast that requires no accompaniments or other courses. Lamb and vegetables are cooked in liquid, then served with plain couscous. The fragrant cooking broth is served separately so that diners can moisten their couscous throughout the meal.

Preparation time 25 minutes **Cooking time** 50 minutes **Serves** 4

1 Put the lamb into a large saucepan. Add the measured water, onions, garlic, saffron, cinnamon, paprika, chilli, ginger, salt and pepper. Bring to the boil, remove the scum from the top, cover and simmer very gently for about 30 minutes. Add the carrots, turnips, kohlrabi or celeriac, cover and simmer for 15 minutes.

2 Add the courgettes and broad beans to the lamb in the pan. Add the tomatoes, coriander and parsley and cook for a further 5 minutes until the lamb and all the vegetables are really tender.

3 Cook the couscous according to packet instructions. Turn it on to a large serving platter, dot the butter over the top, stir in, and season with salt and pepper. Form it into a large mound with a well in the centre and place the lamb in the well. Use a slotted spoon to lift the vegetables from the cooking broth and arrange them on and around the lamb. Serve the broth in a separate warmed bowl.

Chicken Biryani

A wonderful one-pot dish that is impressive and substantial enough to stand alone as a meal in itself. Serve poppadums and chutney as a predinner nibble.

Preparation time 30 minutes, plus marinating **Cooking time** 1¼ hours **Serves** 4–6

1.5 kg (3 lb) chicken, cut into 8 joints

2 tbsp vegetable oil or ghee

10 saffron threads

300 ml (½ pint) hot milk

500 g (1 lb) basmati rice

15 g (½ oz) cinnamon stick, broken up

2 bay leaves

6 cardamom pods, bruised

150 ml (¼ pint) Chicken Stock (see page 161)

75 g (3 oz) sultanas

50 g (2 oz) toasted almonds

Marinade
5 garlic cloves, crushed

7.5 cm (3 inch) piece of fresh root ginger, peeled and chopped

1 onion, chopped

1 tsp cloves

1 tsp black peppercorns

3 cardamom pods, bruised

1 tbsp coriander seeds

1 tbsp cumin seeds

½ tsp turmeric

2 pieces of mace

2 tbsp vegetable oil or ghee

300 ml (½ pint) thick Greek yogurt

To serve
2 onions, sliced and deep-fried

1 tablespoon toasted almonds

½ tablespoon sultanas

edible silver leaf, to garnish (optional)

1 First make the marinade. With a pestle and mortar or food processor, blend the garlic, ginger, onion, cloves, peppercorns, the seeds from the cardamom pods, coriander and cumin seeds, turmeric and mace to make a spice paste. Fry the paste in the oil for 2–3 minutes. Leave the spice paste to cool, then stir the mixture into the yogurt and spread over the chicken pieces. Cover and leave to marinate for a minimum of 3 hours, or overnight.

2 Heat the oil in a large casserole. Remove the chicken from the marinade and brown on all sides, remove from the heat and add the leftover marinade.

3 Soak the saffron in the hot milk. Put the rice into a large saucepan. Cover with water and bring to the boil, then reduce the heat and simmer for 5 minutes – the rice will not be cooked. Drain well and place on top of the chicken. Add the cinnamon stick, bay leaves, and the bruised cardamom pods.

4 Pour the saffron threads and milk and the stock over the rice, cover the casserole with a tight-fitting lid and cook in a preheated oven, 150°C (300°F), Gas Mark 2, for 1 hour. About 10 minutes before the dish is ready, put the sultanas and almonds on top of the rice.

5 To serve, spoon the rice and chicken on to a warm plate and serve with the fried onion, extra toasted almonds and sultanas, and garnish with silver leaf, if liked.

Shortcuts and cheats

None of us can be a slave to the kitchen all the time, and that's where shortcuts and cheats come in. There is no guilt in buying pastry if you don't have the time or inclination to make it, and there are many ready-prepared foods that are well worth buying. The trick is to choose the best and make the most of them.

Choosing the best

Although a huge range of convenience foods is on offer, many are disappointing and not as good as you could make yourself, but sometimes we have to compromise. It may be because we don't have the time, but often it is because we just don't fancy cooking. All is not lost, however. Many supermarket products are very good and offer the cheat's version of a great meal. Be selective and get to know your brands and products.

Prepared vegetables

The ultimate in shortcuts are ready peeled and diced fresh vegetables, such as carrots and sprouts. They may contain fewer vitamins than vegetables that are prepared immediately before cooking, but if you are short of time, why not use them?

The same applies to bags of salad leaves which make a great garnish or instant salad. Make sure they are well within their sell-by date so they are really fresh.

Frozen vegetables can be worth buying, too: they don't lose their vitamin content. Frozen leaf spinach is useful for pies, flans and curries and does not need to be precooked. Frozen peas and sweetcorn are also good products. Frozen chopped herbs are superior to dried herbs and save time on washing and chopping.

Pastry

Ready-made pastry can be almost as good as homemade. People buy filo pastry because it is so hard to make, so why not other pastries too? Choose a good-quality brand, made with butter rather than margarine. Most types are available fresh and frozen. You can even buy ready-rolled pastry – simply get it out of the box and use to line a tin for a quick tart or pie.

Fresh sauces

Most supermarkets sell fresh sauces, including white sauce, bread sauce, cheese sauce, tomato sauce, and pasta sauces. Shop around to find the best.
• Tomato sauce is especially useful – use with pasta,

Above Filo pastry is the ultimate in convenience. While you work with one sheet, keep the others covered with a damp cloth.

Shortcuts to avoid
• Ready-grated cheese can be tasteless. How difficult can it be to grate your own?
• Bought bolognese sauce generally lacks flavour, as well as meat.
• Many canned vegetables are flaccid and flavourless. Avoid canned asparagus, peas, spinach, potatoes and carrots.
• Dried packet soups are not a patch on fresh cartons.
• Ground black pepper loses its taste very quickly. Buy whole peppercorns and a pepper grinder.
• Jars of crushed garlic or garlic paste taste little like freshly crushed garlic.
• Quick-cook dried pasta can have a soggy texture. If you really need to save those extra few minutes, buy fresh pasta instead.

pizza, lasagnes, as a base for casseroles, or simply serve it as an accompaniment to plain meat or fish.

• Pesto is better fresh in a tub than in a jar, but shop around to find a good one. Use to top pasta, drizzle over grilled vegetables or stir into risotto.

• Cheese sauce makes a good base for a vegetable or fish pie. Stir in chunks of raw fish with a few prawns, or a selection of cooked vegetables for a vegetable pie, then top with potato and bake until golden on top.

• Fresh sweet sauces, including custard, brandy butter, rum sauce and fresh fruit coulis are usually quite good and will liven up shop-bought pies, fruit puddings or ice cream.

Pasta pronto

Fresh pasta comes in all shapes and sizes. It tastes as if you've made it yourself, often with delicious cheese, herb or tomato fillings and is faster to cook than dried.

Fresh filled pastas, such as ravioli and tortelloni, come with a wide selection of fillings, including spinach and ricotta, pumpkin and smoked salmon. They make a fine instant dinner with melted butter and freshly grated Parmesan. You can make a really respectable lasagne by browning some minced beef in a frying pan, then adding a tub of fresh tomato sauce. Layer in an ovenproof dish with sheets of fresh lasagne and fresh cheese sauce, then bake in the oven.

Shortcut stocks

Ready-made stock is available in the form of cubes and powders and is more convenient than homemade. Choose quality brands; powders are often better than cubes, especially the organic ones. Tubs of fresh stock are the best choice. This is an expensive way to buy stock, but the flavour is usually very natural.

Instant staples

Some forms of couscous and bulgar wheat are already cooked and need only to be soaked in boiling water to make them ready to eat – check the packet before you buy. This is a simple and quick base for a meal. These starchy staples can accompany a casserole or other moist dish, or make a base for a salad with herbs, chopped onions and tomatoes, for example.

Stress-free soup

Fresh soups bought in cartons are, on the whole, very good indeed. There is usually a wide range to choose from and most are made from only natural ingredients, as you would make them yourself. They usually have a good flavour and texture and make a great starter or light lunch.

Above A quick-cook lasagne made from minced beef, a tub of fresh tomato sauce, a tub of cheese sauce and fresh lasagne sheets.

Canned beans

Beans and other pulses suffer little during the canning process and make a useful, protein-rich convenience food. Dried pulses take an age to soak and cook, so canned are best for the shortcut cook. The wide range on offer includes kidney beans, cannellini beans, haricot beans and lentils. Stir into stews and soups to add weight, mix into tubs of ready-made pasta sauces for an instant casserole, or mix with herbs, a little oil and lemon juice for a fast bean salad.

Deli-cious

While a lot of ready-prepared foods aren't quite up to scratch, a visit to a high class delicatessen will show you what heights convenience food can reach. Succulent hams and wonderful antipasti make a great no-fuss starter or supper, with some salad leaves and fresh bread, or you can toss them with pasta or use to top a pizza. Delis also often stock fresh pasta, homemade pesto and other delights, so browse around and cheat as much as you can afford to.

Dressing it up

While there is no shame in convenience foods, there's also no harm in adding some finishing touches yourself to make them that little bit more appealing. A sprinkling of freshly chopped herbs, a bed of mixed leaves, some juicy wedges of lemon, a dish of grated Parmesan cheese or some sliced red chilli can really make a difference and give your shop-bought food that lovingly prepared aura.

Cherry Tomato Tartlets with Pesto

These crispy tartlets make use of shop-bought puff pastry and pesto, and are simple to assemble and cook. If you buy ready-rolled pastry they will be even quicker to make.

Preparation time 10 minutes **Cooking time** 18 minutes **Serves** 4

2 tbsp extra virgin olive oil

1 onion, finely chopped

375 g (12 oz) cherry tomatoes

2 garlic cloves, crushed

3 tbsp sun-dried tomato paste

325 g (11 oz) ready-rolled puff pastry

beaten egg, to glaze

150 g (5 oz) crème fraîche

2 tbsp ready-made pesto

salt and pepper

basil leaves, to garnish

1 Lightly grease a large baking sheet and sprinkle with water. Heat the oil in a frying pan, add the onion and fry for about 3 minutes until softened. Halve about a third of the tomatoes. Remove the pan from the heat, add the garlic and sun-dried tomato paste, then stir in all the tomatoes, turning until they are lightly coated in the oil.

2 Cut out four 12-cm (5-inch) rounds from the pastry using a cutter or small bowl as a guide. Transfer them to the prepared baking sheet and, using the tip of a sharp knife, make shallow cuts 1 cm (½ inch) from the edge of each round, to form a rim. Brush the rims with beaten egg.

3 Pile the tomato mixture on to the centre of each pastry, making sure the mixture stays within the rim. Bake the tartlets in a preheated oven at 220°C (425°F), Gas Mark 7, for about 15 minutes until the pastry is risen and golden.

4 Meanwhile, lightly mix together the crème fraîche, pesto and salt and pepper in a bowl so that the crème fraîche is streaked with the pesto. When cooked, transfer the tartlets to serving plates and spoon over the crème fraîche and pesto mixture. Serve scattered with basil leaves.

1 tsp chilli powder

1 tbsp paprika

½ tsp ground turmeric

4 garlic cloves, crushed

2 tsp grated fresh root ginger

2 tbsp ground coriander

1 tsp ground cumin

2 tsp soft brown sugar

300 ml (½ pint) water

400 ml (14 fl oz) can coconut milk

2 tsp sea salt

1 tbsp tamarind paste

625 g (1¼ lb) raw tiger prawns

boiled white rice, to serve

Goan Prawn Curry

There's no grinding of spices and long, slow cooking with this curry – it's an all-in-one affair that's straightforward to make but extremely good to eat.

Preparation time 10 minutes **Cooking time** 15 minutes **Serves** 4

1 Put the chilli powder, paprika, turmeric, garlic, ginger, coriander, cumin, the sugar and the measured water into a bowl. Mix well and transfer to a large saucepan. Bring to the boil, then reduce the heat, cover and simmer the mixture gently for 7–8 minutes.

2 Add the coconut milk, salt and tamarind paste and bring to a simmer.

3 Stir in the prawns and cook briskly until they turn pink and are just cooked through. Serve hot, accompanied by boiled white rice.

White Bean and Sun-dried Tomato Salad

2 tbsp olive oil

1 garlic clove, crushed

425 g (14 oz) can cannellini beans, drained and rinsed

1 red onion, sliced

125 g (4 oz) sun-dried tomatoes in oil, drained and roughly chopped

1 tbsp chopped black olives

2 tsp chopped capers

2 tsp chopped thyme

1 tbsp parsley leaves

1 tbsp extra virgin olive oil

2 tbsp lemon juice

salt and pepper

Canned pulses are the perfect shortcut ingredient, requiring none of the overnight soaking and long cooking of their dried counterparts. Here, they form the basis of a flavoursome salad.

Preparation time 10 minutes **Cooking time** 2 minutes **Serves** 2–4

1 Heat the oil in a frying pan. Add the garlic and sauté over a high heat, stirring, to gain a little colour. When it is light golden, remove from the pan.

2 Place the beans in a mixing bowl and stir in the garlic. Add the onion, sun-dried tomatoes, olives, capers, thyme, parsley, extra virgin olive oil, lemon juice and salt and pepper to taste; mix well. Check the seasoning and serve.

Warm Ravioli Salad with Beetroot and Bitter Leaves

4 tbsp extra virgin olive oil

2 red onions, finely sliced

2 garlic cloves, finely sliced

500 g (1 lb) fresh spinach and ricotta ravioli

375 g (12 oz) cooked beetroot in natural juices, drained and diced

2 tbsp capers in brine, drained and rinsed

2 tbsp balsamic vinegar

packet of mixed bitter salad leaves (such as chicory, radicchio, rocket and frisée)

parsley sprigs

basil leaves

salt

Pecorino cheese shavings, to serve

Shop-bought ravioli is dressed up with a few simple ingredients and some prepared salad leaves to make a sophisticated supper dish. Buy the ravioli from an Italian delicatessen if you can.

Preparation time 10 minutes **Cooking time** 12 minutes **Serves** 4

1 Heat 1 tablespoon of the oil in a large pan and fry the onions and garlic over a medium heat for 10 minutes, until golden.

2 Meanwhile, cook the pasta in a pan of lightly salted boiling water for 3 minutes, until it is tender but still firm to the bite. Drain and toss with the remaining oil.

3 Add the beetroot to the onions with the capers and vinegar and heat through. Stir into the ravioli and transfer to a large bowl to cool for 5 minutes, pouring in all the juices from the pan. Arrange the ravioli in bowls or on plates with the salad leaves and herbs. Serve topped with Pecorino shavings.

Crêpes Suzette

Most supermarkets stock ready-made pancakes and they are really quite good. Choose either sweet or plain pancakes for this well-known and much-loved dessert.

Preparation time 10 minutes **Cooking time** 10 minutes **Serves** 4

50 g (2 oz) butter

50 g (2 oz) caster sugar

grated rind and juice of 2 oranges

8 ready-made pancakes

2 tablespoons Grand Marnier (orange liqueur)

2 tablespoons brandy

crème fraîche, to serve

1 Melt the butter in a frying pan, add the sugar, orange rind and juice and heat until bubbling. Dip each pancake into the sauce to warm it through, fold it into quarters and place on a warmed serving dish.

2 Add the Grand Marnier and brandy to the pan; heat gently, then ignite. Pour the flaming liquid over the pancakes and serve immediately with crème fraîche.

Keeping up appearances

Food that looks wonderful creates expectations in people and is more likely to taste good, too. Presentation is, therefore, an important aspect of cooking, and it goes a long way towards making food enticing to all.

Colour and contrast

However good it tastes, roasted cod with boiled potatoes, cauliflower and white sauce will never look appealing. Choose naturally colourful foods for a vibrant effect and avoid too many white or brown foods in a meal. Aim for colour contrasts to get the senses really going – red with green is always a happy combination. Don't forget that garnishes can add colour, too. Lime or lemon wedges, a sprinkling or a sprig of fresh herbs, sliced or chopped red chilli, chopped red or orange sweet peppers, or a slice of orange can set off a dish.

Novel serving ideas

Some foods are always popular because of the way they look. Somehow kebabs served on skewers are more exciting than the same cubes of food cooked in a stove-top griddle pan, even though the flavour is the same.

Parcels have a similar effect. Food cooked in parcels made from banana leaves, greaseproof paper or foil is intrinsically interesting, just because it is novel. And there is the added bonus of the wonderful aroma of the food as each guest opens their parcel at the table.

Serving up

Choose attractive plates, dishes or platters to set off food to best advantage. Think about the styles and colours of the serving dishes, as well as the practical aspects of their size and shape. Choose larger plates than you think you need to give the food space and make it look more elegant – overfilled plates just don't look as good.

Right, top to bottom Make your food look more interesting by making little parcels with interesting fillings or wrapping prosciutto around bite-sized pieces of food and garnishing with watercress.

Garnishes and decorations

A simple decoration or garnish always adds a little extra something. Above all, choose a garnish that marries well with the food.

Chocolate

This is excellent for decorating puddings and cakes. Use it grated or shaved, or melt and drizzle it over the top. You can also melt it, spread it out on nonstick baking paper then leave it to set. When set, cut out shapes or make curls with a sharp knife.

Citrus fruits

Orange, lemon and lime slices, wedges and rind can add colour to sweet and savoury dishes and drinks. Remove the rind with a parer, or cut off pieces using a vegetable peeler and slice it into fine strips.

Flowers

Edible flowers or petals can be used to decorate both sweet and savoury foods. Chive flowers, pot marigolds, primroses, violets and nasturtiums all make pretty decorations, as well as tasty salad ingredients. They can be used either fresh as they are, or can be frosted with egg white and sugar for a pretty coating.

Fruit

Fruit can be very pretty: try raspberries, redcurrants, kumquats or strawberries to decorate summer cakes and desserts, or kiwi fruits and physalis for a change.

Herbs

Most herbs have pretty leaves, particularly chervil, sage, dill, coriander and parsley. Sprinkle chopped fresh herbs generously over a dish, or garnish it with a sprig of whatever herb you have used to flavour it.

> **TOP TIP**
> If you spill any food on the rim of a plate while you are dishing up, wipe it off with a damp cloth. A meal looks so much nicer on a clean plate.

Icing sugar

Sieve through a tea strainer to dust over all types of sweets, desserts and cakes, since it will give them a highly decorative finish.

Salad leaves

Many dishes look good served on a bed of salad leaves. Choose rocket for its distinctive peppery flavour and its prettily shaped leaves, watercress for its rounded leaves, and lollo rosso for its frilly effect, tinged with red. Lime-green curly frisée is also very decorative and has a pleasingly bitter taste.

Toasted seeds

Toasted sesame, pumpkin or sunflower seeds add flavour and texture to a dish, and look very attractive when they are sprinkled over the top. Pine nuts can also be used in the same way.

Vegetables

Whole or sliced chillies and diced sweet peppers can look very attractive. Courgette or carrot ribbons, made with a potato peeler, also make a handsome and effective garnish.

Below, left to right Frosted rose petals are perfect for a cake or dessert; lemon wheels are simple but attractive; lime rind adds a bright green touch; and chocolate curls are delicious and effective.

Laksa

This Singapore noodle dish is a feast for the eyes as well as the appetite. It is finished with chopped spring onion, bright red chilli and roasted peanuts, which contrast nicely with the golden yellow broth.

Preparation time 25 minutes **Cooking time** 30 minutes **Serves** 4

3 tbsp groundnut oil

2 large onions, finely chopped

4 garlic cloves, crushed

3 red bird's eye chillies, finely chopped

75 g (3 oz) roasted peanuts, chopped

1 tbsp ground coriander

1 tbsp ground cumin

2 tsp turmeric

1.2 litres (2 pints) coconut milk

1–2 tbsp sugar, to taste

375 g (12 oz) cooked chicken, shredded

175 g (6 oz) bean sprouts

500 g (1 lb) fresh rice noodles

4 spring onions, chopped

3 tablespoons chopped coriander leaves

salt and pepper

To serve

spring onions, chopped

1 large red chilli, finely sliced

1–2 tablespoons chopped roasted peanuts

1 Heat the oil and fry the onions until golden brown. Add the garlic, chillies, peanuts, ground coriander, cumin and turmeric and fry for 2–3 minutes, or until the spices have cooked through and released a strong aroma.

2 Stir the coconut milk into the spice mixture, cover the pan and leave to simmer for 15 minutes. Season the spiced coconut with salt, pepper and sugar to taste. Add the shredded chicken and half of the bean sprouts to the coconut mixture and simmer for 5 minutes.

3 Blanch the fresh noodles in boiling water and divide between 4 large bowls. Sprinkle with the spring onions and chopped coriander and divide the remaining raw bean sprouts between the bowls.

4 Ladle the chicken and coconut mixture over the noodles and serve with chopped spring onions, red chilli and roasted peanuts.

large bunch of fresh coriander leaves, roughly chopped

3 tbsp chopped mint leaves

2 garlic cloves, crushed

1 tsp grated fresh root ginger

4 fresh red chillies, deseeded and chopped

2 tsp ground cumin

1 tsp ground coriander

2 tsp soft brown sugar

2 tbsp lime juice

150 ml (¼ pint) coconut milk

4 thick salmon fillets, skinned

4 squares of banana leaf or baking paper, each 30 x 30 cm (12 x 12 inches)

salt and pepper

Salmon in Banana Leaves

Banana leaves make great parcels for cooking delicate fish, and look impressive too. To make the banana leaves supple, hold them over an open flame until they go bright green; they will then be easier to handle. They can be bought in Asian stores; if you can't find any, use baking paper instead.

Preparation time 10 minutes **Cooking time** 15 minutes **Serves** 4

1 Put the fresh coriander, mint, garlic, ginger, chillies, cumin, ground coriander, sugar, lime juice and coconut milk into a food processor or blender and blend until fairly smooth. Season with salt and pepper and set aside.

2 Place each salmon fillet on a square of banana leaf or baking paper and spoon some of the herb and spice mixture over it. Carefully cover the fish with the leaf to make a neat parcel and secure with wooden skewers.

3 Place the parcels on a large baking sheet and bake in a preheated oven at 200°C (400°F), Gas Mark 6, for 15 minutes. Remove the parcels from the oven, place on a serving plate and open the packages at the table.

600 ml (1 pint) Vegetable
Stock (see page 161)

1 kg (2 lb) mixed baby
squash, such as gem,
butternut or acorn

125 g (4 oz) baby spinach

rice, to serve

Sauce
4 tbsp olive oil

4 garlic cloves, finely sliced

1 red pepper, cored,
deseeded and finely
chopped

2 tomatoes, chopped

425 g (14 oz) can red
kidney beans, rinsed and
drained

1–2 tbsp hot chilli sauce

small handful of fresh
coriander, chopped

salt

Baby Squash with Red Bean Sauce

This is a great dish to make during the autumn, when various
baby squashes and pumpkin are at their most plentiful. The
brilliant contrasting colours will blow away the autumn blues.

Preparation time 10 minutes **Cooking time** 15 minutes **Serves** 4

1 Bring the stock to the boil in a large saucepan. Peel, quarter and deseed the
squash. Add to the pan, reduce the heat and cover. Simmer gently for about
15 minutes or until the squash are just tender.

2 Meanwhile, make the sauce. Heat the oil in a frying pan, add the garlic and
pepper and fry for 5 minutes, stirring frequently, until very soft. Add the tomatoes,
red kidney beans, chilli sauce and a little salt and simmer for 5 minutes until pulpy.

3 Drain the squash from the stock, reserving the stock, and return to the pan.
Scatter over the spinach leaves, cover and cook for about 1 minute until the spinach
has wilted in the steam.

4 Pile the vegetables on to cooked rice on serving plates. Stir 8 tablespoons of the
reserved stock into the sauce with the coriander. Spoon over the vegetables and serve.

Chocolate Swirl Tart

This tart is so easy to make and yet will look incredibly impressive when you present it at a dinner party. The amaretti biscuits add a delicious almond flavour.

Preparation time 20 minutes, plus chilling **Serves** 6–8

Crumb shell
125 g (4 oz) digestive biscuits

50 g (2 oz) amaretti biscuits

6 tablespoons butter

Filling
200 g (7 oz) plain chocolate

250 ml (8 fl oz) double cream

1 Put the biscuits in a plastic bag and crush them with a rolling pin. Melt the butter in a saucepan and stir in the biscuit crumbs. Press the mixture into a greased 23 cm (9 in) pie dish. Chill until firm.

2 Put the chocolate in a heatproof bowl over a pan of simmering water, stir gently until melted. Cover a rolling pin with foil and brush lightly with oil. Drizzle some chocolate on to the rolling pin in zigzag lines, about 2.5 cm (1 in) long. Chill until set.

3 Beat the cream until it makes soft peaks and fold into the remaining melted chocolate. Spoon into the crumb case and chill for 2 hours until set.

4 Just before serving, carefully peel the chocolate decorations from the foil and arrange them in the centre of the tart.

Drink anyone?

Whatever you serve to your guests – be it a few chilled beers, a wonderful fruit punch, a well-chosen wine or a cup of tea – it is important to realize that the drinks you offer deserve every bit as much attention as the food.

What drinks should I serve?

The drinks that you serve will probably be dictated by two things: the type of occasion and the drinking patterns of your guests. Some of your friends may be teetotallers, others may only drink wine, while still others are happy to drink absolutely anything that is put in front of them. But in the end it is most likely to be the type of party you are having that will be the deciding factor in your choice.

• If you're having a cocktail party, you will obviously serve cocktails, with a choice of exciting and colourful concoctions, both alcoholic and non-alcoholic. Be sure to have a good range of non-alcoholic drinks for the teetotallers, the drivers and the children so you don't make them feel unwanted. It won't be hard to make the non-alcoholic cocktails just as interesting and delicious as the alcoholic ones.

• If you're giving a drinks party, you can serve just about anything you like. Basically, you have two main choices. Either stick to a choice of wines or offer a full bar with a choice of spirits and mixers, plus the usual non-alcoholic options, such as mineral water, fizzy drinks and fruit juices for those not drinking alcohol.

• If you're giving a formal dinner party, you may offer a range of drinks as the evening wears on. You may start with a predinner apéritif, then offer wine throughout the meal. Port with the cheese and a liqueur after the meal with coffee are optional extras, perhaps more likely at the smarter, more elaborate end of the dinner party spectrum.

• At a buffet party, which is a busy, bustling occasion, the simplest options are probably the best. You might, therefore, restrict the choice of liquid refreshment to wine throughout the evening – except, of course, for non-drinkers, who can drink mineral water, fruit juice or soft drinks. Offer guests a choice of red or white wine, and leave it at that.

Non-alcoholic drinks

Don't forget to cater for those who don't drink alcohol, as well as those who are driving. A cold and constant supply of mineral water and fruit juices or non-alcoholic or low alcohol wines and beers is essential for any gathering.

Mineral water is a fashionable, healthy thing to drink, so offer your guests a glass of sparkling water with some ice cubes and a twist of lemon or lime. A lot of people like to drink water as well as wine throughout a meal, since this both helps to keep their heads clear, as well as warding off any morning-after hangover. It also helps the food go down.

Below Decorations make cocktails and other drinks look really special. A simple sprig of mint or a slice of lemon is enough.

TOP TIP

When alcohol is used in food but is not cooked, it lends not only flavour but also a warming kick. Rum-soaked raisins are a good addition to stewed apples or cheesecakes; use sherry, brandy or apricot brandy to soak the sponge for trifles; orange liqueurs go particularly well with strawberries and chocolate desserts, or try fresh melon with a little Port.

Wine, beer and spirits

Some of the world's finest wines are best enjoyed after 30 or more years in the bottle, but the great majority are designed to be drunk young, usually with food. In some countries, notably Germany and Belgium, beer plays the same role, being made in several styles and drunk as an important part of the meal. Spirits and liqueurs are too strong or too sweet to make good partners for food, but they have a big part to play in cooking.

Which wine with which food?

Many serious words have been written about finding the perfect food and wine partnership, but while it is true that some foods go particularly well with certain wines, there are often other, less obvious possibilities.

In general, simple dishes demand straightforward, uncomplicated wines, while more elaborate dishes ask for the more expensive classics. A richly sauced dish goes extremely well with a wine that has enough natural acidity to cut through the sauce and balance it.

The basic principle of white wine with fish and red wine with meat is a sound one, but it is not an exciting one and – as with all the best rules in life – there are many exceptions. Fish is sometimes better accompanied by a rosé wine, and a red wine can on occasion be better still. The colour of the meat is usually best matched by the colour of the wine – a full-bodied claret or Burgundy with roast beef; a light white wine to complement the light flavours of chicken or turkey; and a full-flavoured wine to match the high intensity of goose, duck, pheasant and other game birds, and venison.

How much wine?

Half a bottle of wine per person is a good rule of thumb, but a whole bottle is probably a safer estimate as it ensures that you will not run short – which is one of the most embarrassing things that can happen. If the food is good and the company congenial, the wine will always slip down with remarkable ease, so be sure not to run out.

Did you know?

Wine is made in more than 50 countries around the world, from well over 1,000 grape varieties. The choice is much greater than that between red and white. White wines include still and sparkling, dry and sweet, light-bodied and full-bodied. Much the same applies to red wines, with a full range of light, medium- and full-bodied wines.

Above Red wine is a favourite with many and, if you choose a light one, can happily be served with fish or salads.

Cooking with alcohol

Alcohol can be put to many good uses in the kitchen. It evaporates during cooking, leaving the essential flavours of the wine or spirits in the dish. Or it can be used as a marinade.

• Sherry or brandy adds richness to clear soups and creamy shellfish bisques.

• A wine marinade for meat will tenderize it as well as adding a rich flavour.

• Red wine is often used to poach fruit, such as pears or peaches, for a dessert.

• Use dry white wine or vermouth in the poaching liquid for fish or chicken and it can form the basis of a good sauce.

• White wine is commonly used in risottos, or you could try a splash of sherry which adds a surprisingly warm and rich flavour.

• A good cheese fondue contains dry white wine and a dash of Kirsch.

• To create an almost instant sauce for fried fish or meat, first transfer the food to a warm plate, then pour off excess fat from the pan. Add a little wine, dry vermouth, sherry, Madeira or brandy to the pan, and place over high heat for a few minutes, stirring constantly to deglaze the pan. Increase the amount of sauce with a little stock or water, bring it back to a rapid boil, then, if you like, whisk in a little butter, cream or chopped fresh herbs.

Cocktails

Cocktails are short mixed drinks, usually spirit-based, which are generally drunk before a meal. A true cocktail is an iced alcoholic drink, with a subtle and harmonious blend of ingredients and a powerful kick, though there is an increasing range nowadays of non-alcoholic cocktails for drivers and non-drinkers.

Cocktails had their beginnings during the Prohibition era in the US, between 1920 and 1933, when alcohol was banned. They were designed to create something drinkable from the infamous bootleg liquors. When Prohibition ended, a lot of the more acceptable concoctions were refined and many new cocktails appeared. It was then that the cocktail became popular among the smart set in the more sophisticated cities of America and Europe, and soon no trendy hotel or club was without a cocktail bar.

The 1920s and '30s produced, some of the cocktails we enjoy today, including the Bloody Mary, Gimlet, Mai Tai, Tequila Sunrise, Corpse Reviver, Buck's Fizz and Zombie. But the most famous cocktail of all, the Dry Martini, originated in the nineteenth century, although it has become steadily drier over the years. Many other classic cocktails originated then, such as the Daiquiri, Mint Julep, Manhattan, Old-fashioned and Planter's Punch. The Harvey Wallbanger and Piña Colada belong to the cocktail revival of the late '70s and early '80s, while the B52 and other shooters (short, layered drinks served in a shot glass, to be downed in a single throw) are part of the latest cocktail age.

Making cocktails

It is surprisingly easy to make cocktails. But if they are to be at their most successful, there are a few simple rules that provide the key to success.
• Work on a wipeable surface that will not be spoiled if it is marked by bottles, glasses or drips.
• Keep all drinks in a cool place. Ideally keep all mixers and fruit juices in the refrigerator.
• Clear drinks are usually stirred, while cloudy drinks (those containing egg white, cream or fruit juices) are shaken with ice or mixed in a blender. Because of the ice, frost forms, so shaken drinks are usually strained to remove bits of the ice and fragments of fruit.
• Always wash a shaker or mixing glass and stirrer between using it for different drinks.
• Iced drinks should be served in chilled glasses, while mulled wine and hot punches should be served in warmed glasses which are easy to hold.
• When you are serving hot drinks, first put a metal spoon into the glass, and pour the drink over the spoon to prevent the glass from cracking.

Which glass?
A cocktail glass has a V-shaped bowl on a long stem. Use for cocktails.
A liqueur glass is small for small potent drinks. If you want ice, use a bigger glass.
A brandy balloon is large with a rounded, bowl-shaped cup on a short stem.
An old-fashioned glass is a straight-sided tumbler which holds 175–250 ml (6–8 fl oz). Use for an Old-fashioned or for whisky.
A highball glass is a straight-sided tumbler which holds 250 ml (8 fl oz), perfect for longer cocktails over ice.
A coupette glass has a two-tiered bowl on a long stem, with a wide rim for salt.
A wine glass is made in a variety of shapes and sizes, narrowing slightly at the top.
A hurricane glass is a tall, curved glass on a short stem. Use for long cocktails over ice.
A Champagne flute is tall and slim with a narrow bowl on a long stem, designed for retaining Champagne bubbles.
A rocks glass is a short tumbler, much like an old-fashioned glass.

Caiparinha

The main ingredient in this famous Brazilian cocktail is the local liquor, cachaça.

1 lime, quartered

2 tsp cane sugar

2 measures cachaça

Muddle the lime quarters and sugar together in the base of a rocks glass. Fill it with crushed ice and pour over the cachaça. Stir and add more ice as desired.

The Original Bloody Mary

A classic cocktail, this is more than just vodka and tomato juice.

2 measures vodka

dash of lemon juice

Worcestershire sauce, to taste

tomato juice, to top up

½ tsp cayenne pepper

salt and black pepper

lime wedges, to garnish

Pour the vodka and lemon juice over ice in a highball glass, add a little Worcestershire sauce and top up with tomato juice. Season with salt and both peppers, stir to chill and garnish with lime wedges.

Frozen Mango Daiquiri

Made frappé-style this concoction is a reviving antidote to summer sunshine.

½ mango, peeled and stoned, plus slices to decorate

1 measure lime juice

1 tsp powdered white sugar

2 measures white rum

Place all the ingredients in a blender and process with a small scoop of crushed ice until smooth. Serve in any large glass, and decorate with slices of ripe mango.

Gin Garden

Elderflower cordial adds a delicate fragrant, flowery note.

¼ cucumber, peeled and chopped, plus slices to decorate

½ measure elderflower cordial

2 measures gin

1 measure pressed apple juice

Muddle the cucumber in the bottom of a cocktail shaker with the elderflower cordial. Add the gin, apple juice and some ice cubes. Shake and double strain into a chilled Martini glass and decorate with peeled cucumber slices.

Margarita

Triple Sec is an orange-flavoured liqueur. You could also use Cointreau or Grand Marnier.

1 lime wedge, plus extra to decorate

rock salt

2 measures tequila

1 measure lime juice

1 measure Triple Sec

Rub the rim of a coupette glass with the lime wedge, then dip it into rock salt. Pour the tequila, lime juice and Triple Sec into a cocktail shaker and add some ice cubes. Shake and strain into the salt-rimmed glass. Decorate with a wedge of lime.

Slinky Mink

Raspberry purée can be made by rubbing fresh raspberries through a fine sieve.

½ measure raspberry purée

dash of sugar syrup

2 tsp lime juice

Champagne, to top up

Build the purée, syrup and lime juice in the bottom of a chilled flute glass. Add Champagne to top up, stir lightly and decorate with a lime twist.

Grappa Manhattan

Grappa is a clear Italian brandy made from distilled grape husk. The Martini adds sweetness.

2 measures grappa

1 measure Martini Rosso

½ measure Maraschino liqueur

2 dashes of Angostura bitters

olives, to decorate

Stir together all the ingredients with ice in a mixing glass. Strain into a chilled Martini glass and decorate with an olive.

Strawberry and Hazelnut Lassi

Frangelico adds a hazelnut flavour to this unusual cocktail.

3 strawberries

⅓ banana

1 measure Frangelico

1 measure Baileys

2 measures yogurt

3 mint leaves, plus sprigs to decorate

Place all the ingredients in a blender and process with a small scoop of crushed ice until smooth. Serve in a tall sling glass and decorate with a mint sprig.

Bellini

Prosecco is an Italian sparkling wine, but any dry sparkling wine will do.

1 measure white peach purée

Prosecco, to top up

Pour the peach purée and Prosecco into a flute, stir and decorate with a peach wedge.

'White' Sangria

A white wine punch that is a modern take on the traditional Spanish sangria.

2 large glasses of dry white wine

2 measures lemon vodka

2 measures peach schnapps

2 measures peach purée

slices of apple, lime, lemon and peach

1 measure lemon juice

1 measure lime juice

lemonade, to top up

At least 12 hours before serving, place the wine, vodka, schnapps and peach purée in a jug with the fruit slices and chill. Just before serving, add some ice cubes, the fruit juices and top up with lemonade. Serve from the jug into rocks glasses.

Mojito

The mint and lime make this long, cool drink extremely thirst-quenching.

8 mint leaves, plus sprigs to decorate

½ lime

2 tsp cane sugar

2½ measures white rum

soda water, to top up

Muddle the mint leaves, lime and sugar in the bottom of a highball glass and top with crushed ice. Add the rum, stir and top up with soda water. Decorate with mint sprigs.

Valentine Martini

A daring scarlet drink for that special romantic occasion. It tastes just divine.

2 measures raspberry vodka

6 raspberries, plus extra to decorate

½ measure lime juice

dash of sugar syrup

lime twists, to decorate

Place all the ingredients in a cocktail shaker and add some ice cubes. Shake and double strain into a chilled Martini glass. Decorate with 2 raspberries on a swizzle stick, and a lime twist.

Great meals on a budget

Cooking well on a budget is challenging, but if you master a few basic principles you can create some really good meals for little expense. All that is required is some planning, know-how and ingenuity.

Above Markets can offer great ingredients at budget prices. Feel free to inspect the produce carefully before buying.

What to buy

While oven chips and frozen chicken nuggets may seem good value in the supermarket, they are full of fat and salt and contain little in the way of nutrients (see page 246). In fact, few ready meals and processed foods contain much in the way of fresh ingredients such as meat or vegetables, so they don't really constitute value for money. For the same price, you can produce a much more filling and nutritious meal, and one that tastes better, too.

Meat

Many people consider meat the main part of a meal but most of us eat far too much of it. We really don't need much protein each day; it is better to buy less and really make the most of it.

If you are serving a range of accompaniments, simply buy less meat. Buy smaller chops and serve them with a larger pile of mash or chunky homemade chips; buy a smaller roasting joint and increase the amount of roast potatoes or stuffing; or make Yorkshire puddings to go with it. And don't forget plenty of vegetables. If you buy cheaper cuts of meat, breast of lamb for instance, and cook them slowly, they will be tender and delicious; and a bacon joint can go a long way.

Another way is to choose meals that require less meat. Make lasagne, stews, curries or chilli con carne, all of which contain plenty of other less expensive ingredients to supplement the meat content.

Seasonal produce

Seasonal produce is usually cheaper than foods grown out of season, especially if you shop in markets or farm shops. Enjoy apples and pears in late summer and autumn, strawberries and asparagus in early summer,

for example. These seasonal foods will have a much better flavour than produce that is forced out of season or has been stored for some months.

Local produce

Avoid expensive exotics and make use of fresh local produce, which should be cheaper because it hasn't had to travel so far. Local food is also likely to have been picked more recently, so it will contain more nutrients and generally be fresher and more appealing. Plus you will be avoiding the environmental impact from food miles, something many people are now campaigning against.

Below Fresh vegetables are cheap, nutritious and delicious. Try new inventive ways to cook them for a varied diet.

Good-value ingredients

1 Pulses are nutritious and filling. Dried pulses are especially good value and although they have to be soaked and cooked for a long time, it is not a fiddly or difficult process.

2 Many vegetables are very good value and can make a wonderful meal in themselves. Think warming winter stews with dumplings, vegetable bakes swathed in rich cheese sauce, spicy curries and crusty pies. Root vegetables especially – potatoes, carrots, parsnips, turnips and beetroot – are cheap to buy; so are cabbages, squashes and cauliflower. Be imaginative!

3 Staples such as pasta, rice, couscous and bulgar wheat make a great basis for a meal and don't need a lot of additional ingredients. Try risotto, couscous, pilau, biryani and tabbouleh, all great dishes and cheap to make. Avoid eating white pasta or rice every night, though – choose nutty brown rice or wholemeal pasta for some meals.

4 Canned fish, such as tuna, sardines and mackerel fillets, are not expensive but go a long way in terms of flavour and nutrients. Use them in pasta dishes, risottos, on pizzas, or in salads.

5 Fresh oily fish, such as herring and mackerel, are bursting with flavour and very good value. Nutritionists recommend eating oily fish twice a week, so you'll be healthier too. Try grilling, frying, baking or coating them in tandoori spices.

6 Some cuts of meat are very good value and simply require the right kind of cooking to create a sumptuous meal. Think braising steak in a rich meaty gravy, lamb shanks slowly simmered in stock and wine until the meat falls off the bone, minced lamb made into crispy samosas, or chicken thighs cooked in a Moroccan tagine. Bacon joints can also be good value, giving leftovers for salads and sandwiches.

7 Liver and kidneys are also cheap to buy and are packed with flavour. Consider steak and kidney pie, liver and onions, or a warm salad of pan-fried chicken livers – all very fashionable and quite delicious.

Desserts on a shoestring

Choose desserts that use flour as a major ingredient, such as crumbles, baked sponges, cakes and pancakes – everyone loves these traditional rib-sticking puddings anyway. Rice pudding and bread and butter pudding are also inexpensive and wonderful. If you want something a little healthier, try baked apples or Poached Pears (see page 103).

Right A humble jacket potato makes a wonderful and satisfying meal or accompaniment. Everyone has their favourite topping.

Shopping tips

- Make a list before you go out and buy only what you have planned for the week. You don't want to end up with a random selection of ingredients you can't use up before they go off.
- Don't buy more than you need of any ingredient. Buy just enough for the meal you are planning. Leftovers, especially small quantities, are difficult to use up.
- Look out for special offers in supermarkets. Be guided by what is on special offer and plan your meals around it. If you were planning a chicken curry, but turkey thighs are on offer, go for turkey instead. Be flexible.
- If you have a freezer, make use of 2-for-1 offers and store the excess for next week. But buy only stuff you can use, not products you wouldn't usually buy or which are in addition to your basic needs.
- If you live in the country, visit farm shops for good-value vegetables. They are often much cheaper than supermarkets and the quality can be much better.
- If you live in town, go to markets for your fruit and vegetables. You don't have to buy the discounted produce that is past its best – even the good stuff will be cheaper than in the supermarket.

Pea and Prawn Risotto

A creamy risotto made with fresh prawns, peas, mint and a splash of white wine. This recipe is ideal as a simple yet delicious main course for a dinner party.

Preparation time 10 minutes **Cooking time** 40–45 minutes **Serves** 4–6

500 g (1 lb) raw prawns

125 g (4 oz) butter

1 onion, finely chopped

2 garlic cloves, finely chopped

250 g (8 oz) risotto rice

375 g (12 oz) shelled peas

150 ml (¼ pint) dry white wine

1.5 litres (2½ pints hot Vegetable Stock (see page 161)

4 tablespoons chopped mint

salt and pepper

1 Peel the prawns, reserving the heads and shells.

2 Melt half the butter in a large frying pan. Add the prawn heads and shells and stir-fry for 3–4 minutes. Strain the butter and return it to the pan.

3 Add a further 25 g (1 oz) of the butter to the pan. Add the onion and garlic and sauté for 5 minutes, until softened but not coloured. Add the rice and stir well to coat the grains with the butter. Add the peas, then pour in the wine. Bring to the boil and cook, stirring, until reduced by half.

4 Add the hot stock, a large ladleful at a time, stirring until each addition is absorbed into the rice. Continue adding stock in this way, cooking until the rice is creamy, but the grains are still firm. This should take about 20 minutes.

5 Melt the remaining butter and stir-fry the prawns for 3–4 minutes, then stir them into the rice with the pan juices and mint and season to taste with salt and pepper. Cover the pan and leave the risotto to rest for a few minutes before serving.

25 g (1 oz) butter

2 tbsp olive oil

1 onion, finely chopped

2 celery sticks, finely chopped

2 garlic cloves, crushed

500 g (1 lb) minced beef

300 ml (½ pint) red or white
wine, or water

400 g (13 oz) can chopped
tomatoes

1 tsp caster sugar

2 bay leaves

1 tsp dried oregano

2 tbsp tomato purée

salt and pepper

spaghetti, to serve

Spaghetti Bolognese

Allow time for long, gentle cooking to tenderize the meat and let the flavours mingle. Homemade Bolognese is truely divine and only needs freshly boiled spaghetti as an accompaniment.

Preparation time 15 minutes **Cooking time** 1¼ hours **Serves** 4

1 Melt the butter with the oil in a large, heavy-based saucepan and gently fry the onion and celery for 5 minutes. Add the garlic and beef and cook until they are lightly coloured, breaking up the beef with a wooden spoon.

2 Add the wine or water and let it bubble for 1–2 minutes until slightly evaporated. Add the tomatoes, sugar, bay leaves, oregano, tomato purée and a little salt and pepper and bring just to the boil. Reduce the heat to its lowest setting, cover the pan with a lid and cook for about 1 hour, stirring occasionally, until thick and pulpy.

3 Meanwhile, cook the spaghetti according to packet instructions and serve with the bolognese sauce.

Potato Cakes with Cheese and Bacon

Good wholesome home cooking at its best. The grilled tomatoes finish the dish perfectly.

Preparation time 20 minutes **Cooking time** 30 minutes **Serves** 4

7–10 tbsp vegetable oil

6 spring onions, finely chopped

750 g (1½ lb) floury potatoes, peeled

25 g (1 oz) butter

1 small egg, beaten

125 g (4 oz) strong Cheddar, coarsely grated

handful of chives, snipped, plus extra to garnish

flour, for dusting

50 g (2 oz) dry white breadcrumbs

8 thick rashers of smoked bacon

12–16 cherry tomatoes or 8 medium tomatoes, halved

salt and pepper

1 Heat 2 tablespoons of the oil in a large saucepan. Quickly fry the spring onions until softened. Add the potatoes and enough water to cover. Add a pinch of salt and bring to the boil. Boil until the potatoes are tender and most of the water has evaporated. Drain well and return to the pan. Mash with the butter to make a rough texture. Set aside to cool.

2 Mix the beaten egg and half of the grated cheese into the mashed potatoes with plenty of salt and pepper and the snipped chives. Divide the mixture into 8 and, with floured hands, shape the potato into small patties. Flour lightly, then coat lightly in the breadcrumbs.

3 Heat the remaining oil in a large frying pan until very hot. Cook the patties, 4 at a time, on both sides for 2–3 minutes, or until golden brown and heated through.

4 Remove the patties from the frying pan and place on a baking sheet. Sprinkle the tops of the patties with the remaining cheese and keep hot in the bottom of a preheated grill while cooking the remaining patties and the bacon and tomatoes.

5 Grill the bacon rashers and tomatoes until the bacon is golden brown and crisp and the tomatoes have just burst their skins. Serve the potato cakes topped with the rashers of bacon and with the tomatoes. Garnish with chives and serve immediately.

Tuna Kedgeree

A quick and easy kedgeree that uses canned tuna, rather than the traditional smoked haddock.

Preparation time 10 minutes **Cooking time** 25 minutes **Serves** 4

1 Cook the rice in plenty of lightly salted boiling water for about 8 minutes until almost tender. Add the broad beans and cook for a further 3 minutes, then drain.

2 Melt the butter in a large frying pan, add the onion and curry paste and fry gently for 3 minutes. Add the drained rice, broad beans and tuna.

3 Stir in the parsley and season the kedgeree with salt and pepper to taste. Stir gently over a low heat for 1 minute, then transfer to serving plates. Top with the boiled eggs and garnish with parsley, then serve immediately.

250 g (8 oz) basmati rice

100 g (3½ oz) frozen broad beans

25 g (1 oz) unsalted butter

1 small onion, finely chopped

1 tsp medium curry paste

4 eggs, hard boiled, shelled and quartered

400 g (13 oz) can tuna in oil or brine, drained

small handful of flat leaf parsley, plus extra sprigs, to garnish

Cooking to impress

There are times when you want to pull out all the stops and create a fantastic meal, whether it is a special occasion or you just want to impress your guests. Cooking is an easy way to impress or flatter people, as long as you are artful and plan carefully.

Above Fresh mussels make a simple starter or an impressive main course served in a white wine sauce.

The ingredients

The key to an impressive meal is to use impressive ingredients. If you start with something wonderful and do little to it, it is likely you will end up with something wonderful. And of course this also means you will have less complicated cooking to do. Consider dressed crab with homemade mayonnaise, pan-fried scallops, ribbons of succulent Parma ham served with juicy ripe figs, quails' eggs with seasoned salt for dipping, or plain roasted partridge. All these dishes are difficult to get wrong but will certainly create an impression.

The wow factor

There are a few things that seem to impress people out of all relation to the effort involved.

Serve fish Everyone seems to be impressed by seafood, partly because most people are nervous of dealing with it. However, it requires little preparation, especially if you get your fishmonger to do most of the work for you, and hardly any time cooking at all.

> **TOP TIP**
> Cooking something with a French name is sure to impress – try Crème Caramel (see page 236), Crêpes Suzette (see page 211), a Couronne (see page 158) or a Hot Chocolate Soufflé (see page 135). Even Italian sounds good – try a Frittata (see page 132), Tiramisu (see page 133) or Tomato Focaccia (see page 159).

Homemade bread Although making a loaf can span several hours, there is little actual preparation involved – it is mainly waiting for the dough to rise.

Homemade pasta Pasta is very easy to make, if a little bit fiddly. A simple starter of fresh linguine with homemade pesto and grated Parmesan shows real style.

Serve extra courses A meal becomes a special occasion if you include plenty of courses. Include a cheese course, or serve sorbet (preferably homemade) between the fish course and main course, or between the main course and cheese.

Homemade nibbles before dinner Welcome your guests with a warm tray of something from the oven and they will be eating out of your hand.

Pastry Serve a dish that includes pastry, and people seem to think you are an expert chef, even if you bought the pastry.

Serve a predinner cocktail Choose just one type of cocktail and offer it to your guests as they arrive.

Fresh herbs, especially more unusual ones such as tarragon and chervil, always give off the right vibes.

Planning and preparation

If you want to impress your guests, everything must run extremely smoothly, and that means plenty of advance planning. You want guests to think that organizing and cooking such a meal is well within your reach and has been very little effort for you.

If you're contemplating a very complicated meal with several courses, and you know that time is going to be tight on the day, it is useful if you can prepare some of the dishes in advance and put them in the refrigerator or freezer for a day or two. Choose your menu carefully (see page 200).

You may want to write a list of all the tasks you need to do and the times you should do them: such as when to switch the oven on; what food to start cooking when; when to put on the vegetables; and when to take the dessert out of the freezer or the cheese out of the refrigerator. There will be many tiny but all-important details to remember, and it is impossible not to forget something. A list of everything you need to do and when will eliminate this possibility and reduce anxiety.

Plan every detail and leave nothing to chance. Work out your time schedule with military precision, making it as accurate and detailed as possible, and then stick to it rigidly. List every single task you have to do, including such things as arranging the flowers, laying the table, making the salad dressing, taking things out of the freezer to give them to time to thaw, lighting the oven, garnishing the starter or carving the meat.

Above all, don't forget to allow time for yourself. There's no point in managing to serve the most glorious meal if your hair is a mess and you haven't had time to change. Taking a bath and dressing attractively are as important as anything else, if you are going to be a relaxed and happy host or hostess.

Presentation

The way food looks makes a huge difference. If you've gone to the effort of cooking a really good meal, take the time to make it look as appealing as you can (see page 212). And don't just stop at the garnishes – think about which plates to use, napkins, table cloths and even flowers for the table. These are great ways to make a real occasion of a meal.

Below There are a whole range of pretty table accessories available these days to brighten up your table setting.

Above Name places are a good idea and add an element of sophistication to a dinner party.

A cheese course

With a little thought and care, a cheese course can be one of the highlights of a meal and makes it seem more special, as well as prolonging the enjoyment.

There is a great choice of different cheeses, some of them home-produced and many others imported from all over the world. Always choose a supplier who has a good reputation, and try to make sure that the cheeses you buy are in prime condition. Avoid buying any cheese that looks either too dry or sweaty, or that has any blue mould visible on the surface (unless, of course, it's a blue cheese).

When you are planning what cheeses to buy, try to make sure that the flavours and textures are well balanced. Three cheeses are usually enough for a good selection – choose one hard cheese, such as a good mature Cheddar; one semi-soft cheese, such as a mild, washed-rind cheese like Pont l'Evêque, which has a rich creamy flavour; and one soft cheese such as a ripe Brie or a goats' cheese. If you want to add a fourth cheese, a blue cheese such as Stilton, Gorgonzola or Roquefort would be a good choice, or you could opt for a semi-hard cheese like Caerphilly or Jarlsberg. Whatever your preferences, your choice will also depend on what looks good in the shop and what is ripe enough to eat on the day that you need it.

Tandoori Chicken Poppadums

Mini poppadums can be found in most large supermarkets. If they are not available, use large popadums and carefully break them into bite-sized pieces.

Preparation time 20 minutes, plus marinating and cooling **Cooking time** 8 minutes
Makes 20

1 Score the chicken fillets several times with a sharp knife and place them in a shallow bowl. Mix together the garlic, ginger, yogurt, honey, tandoori powder and salt, then spoon over the chicken. Toss well and set aside to marinate for 10 minutes.

2 Grill or griddle the marinated chicken for 3–4 minutes on each side, then leave it to cool for about 5 minutes.

3 Meanwhile, make the coconut pesto. Slice the chicken and serve on the poppadums with a spoonful each of the pesto and mango chutney and garnish with a coriander sprig.

2 skinless chicken breast fillets

1 small garlic clove, crushed

2.5 cm (1 inch) piece of fresh root ginger, peeled and grated

50 ml (2 fl oz) Greek yogurt

1 tsp clear honey

1 tsp tandoori spice powder

1 teaspoon salt

½ quantity Coconut Pesto (see page 142)

20 mini poppadums

To serve
mango chutney

coriander sprigs

Griddled Asparagus with Frazzled Eggs and Parmesan

A very stylish starter, which makes use of tender seasonal asparagus. The eggs are fried in very hot olive oil, which gives them a crisp, brown lacy edge but a soft yolk.

Preparation time 10 minutes **Cooking time** 10 minutes **Serves** 4

500 g (1 lb) thin asparagus, trimmed

olive oil, for frying

4 fresh eggs, chilled

salt and black pepper

Parmesan cheese shavings, to serve

1 Blanch the asparagus for 2 minutes in salted boiling water. Drain and refresh under cold running water. Drain again and toss in a little olive oil, to coat.

2 Cook the asparagus in a preheated stove-top grill pan or under a preheated grill for 1–2 minutes on each side until tender but still with a bite. Set aside to cool slightly.

3 Pour enough olive oil into a large frying pan to coat the base generously and heat it until almost smoking. Crack each egg into a cup and carefully slide it into the pan. Watch out – the oil will splutter! Once the edges of the eggs have bubbled up and browned, turn the heat right down and cover the pan with a lid. Leave for about 1 minute, then lift out the eggs and drain them on kitchen paper. The yolks should have formed a skin but remain runny inside.

4 Divide the asparagus among 4 warmed serving plates and top each pile of asparagus with an egg. Sprinkle with black pepper and Parmesan shavings. Serve with a little pot of salt for the eggs.

1 large orange

1 garlic clove, crushed

2 large tomatoes, skinned, deseeded and diced

2 tbsp chopped basil

50 g (2 oz) pitted black olives, chopped

5 tbsp extra virgin olive oil

4 cod fillets, about 175 g (6 oz) each

1 tbsp jerk seasoning

salt and pepper

basil leaves, to garnish

green salad, to serve (optional)

Blackened Cod with Orange and Tomato Salsa

This is a visually stunning dish to make your guests gasp. Choose thick fillets of cod from the head end of the fish.

Preparation time 15 minutes **Cooking time** 8 minutes, plus resting **Serves** 4

1 Peel and segment the orange, holding it over a bowl to catch the juice. Halve the segments. Mix them with the garlic, tomatoes, basil, olives and 4 tablespoons of the oil, season to taste with salt and pepper and set aside to infuse.

2 Wash and pat dry the fish and pull out any small bones with a pair of tweezers. Brush with the remaining oil and coat well with the jerk seasoning.

3 Heat a large, heavy-based pan and fry the cod fillets, skin-side down, for 5 minutes. Turn them over and cook for a further 3 minutes. Transfer to a low oven at 150°C (300°F), Gas Mark 2, to rest for about 5 minutes. Garnish the fish with basil and serve with the salsa and a green salad, if liked.

Scallops with Ginger and Asparagus

A simple sophisticated dish using the finest ingredients. You can't go wrong as long as you don't overcook the scallops.

Preparation time 10 minutes **Cooking time** 10 minutes **Serves** 4

12 fresh scallops

2 spring onions, finely sliced

finely grated rind of 1 lime

1 tbsp ginger cordial

2 tbsp extra virgin olive oil, plus extra for drizzling

250 g (8 oz) thin asparagus spears

juice of ½ lime

salt and pepper

a few mixed salad leaves, to serve

few chervil sprigs, to garnish

1 Discard the coral and the tough muscle from the side of each scallop. Wash the scallops and pat dry. Cut each one in half and place them in a bowl.

2 Mix together the spring onions, lime rind, ginger cordial and half the oil, and season to taste with salt and pepper. Pour this dressing over the scallops and set aside to marinate for 15 minutes.

3 Meanwhile, steam the asparagus spears for 5–8 minutes, until tender. Toss them with the remaining oil and the lime juice. Season to taste with salt and pepper and keep warm.

4 Heat a large nonstick frying pan until hot, add the scallops and fry for 1 minute on each side, until golden and just cooked through. Add the marinade juices.

5 Arrange the asparagus spears, salad leaves and chervil on plates with the scallops and any pan juices and serve.

Crème Caramel

The simple baked egg custard, a universal favourite, becomes a memorably sophisticated dessert in this classic treatment.

Preparation time 15 minutes, plus chilling   **Cooking time** 50 minutes **Serves** 4

500 ml (17 fl oz) milk

1 vanilla pod, split in half lengthways

4 eggs

50 g (2 oz) caster sugar

mint sprigs, to decorate

Caramel
50 g (2 oz) granulated sugar

1 tbsp water

1 tsp lemon juice

1 Put the milk and vanilla pod into a heavy saucepan and bring to the boil. Remove from the heat and leave for 5 minutes to infuse. Place the eggs and sugar in a bowl and whisk until thoroughly combined. Discard the vanilla pod and whisk the milk into the egg and sugar mixture.

2 While the milk is infusing, make the caramel. Put the sugar, water and lemon juice into a small saucepan and cook over a moderate heat, stirring well until the sugar dissolves. When it turns a rich golden caramel colour, remove the pan from the heat immediately.

3 Pour the caramel into 4 small moulds or a 1 litre (1¾ pint) charlotte mould. Rotate the moulds quickly so that the caramel coats the base and sides evenly.

4 Strain the custard through a fine sieve. Pour into the moulds and stand them in a bain marie or roasting tin half-filled with water. Cook in a preheated oven at 150°C (300°F), Gas Mark 2, for about 45 minutes, or until set. Leave to cool and then chill in the refrigerator before unmoulding. To unmould, dip the base of the moulds into a bowl of hot water for 30 seconds and then turn the custards out on to a serving plate. Decorate with a sprig of mint.

Sweet Wonton Mille-feuilles

These lovely sweet canapés are perfect for drinks parties or for serving after a meal. Wonton wrappers are available from Asian stores and large supermarkets. These are wonderful with a glass of Champagne.

Preparation time 8 minutes, plus cooling **Cooking time** 3 minutes **Makes** 12

25 g (1 oz) unsalted butter

2 tbsp caster sugar

½ tsp ground cinnamon

9 wonton wrappers

125 g (4 oz) mascarpone cheese

1–2 tbsp icing sugar, plus extra for dusting

1 tsp lemon juice

125 g (4 oz) strawberries, hulled and sliced

1 Melt the butter and mix together the caster sugar and cinnamon. Cut the wonton wrappers into quarters, brush them with the melted butter and coat with a layer of the spiced sugar.

2 Place them on a baking sheet and bake in a preheated oven at 200°C (400°F), Gas Mark 6, for 2–3 minutes, until crisp and golden. Transfer to a wire rack to cool.

3 Beat the mascarpone with the icing sugar and lemon juice and spread a little over 12 of the crisp wontons. Top with half of the strawberry slices. Repeat the process with the wontons and remaining mascarpone and strawberries for the second layer. Place the remaining wontons on top and dust with a little extra icing sugar. Serve with glasses of Champagne, if liked.

After-work suppers

If you work full time, producing an enjoyable and balanced meal every night is quite a feat. Unless you are super-human, you just won't fancy a long spell in the kitchen – here's how to avoid it.

Be realistic

Don't try to produce a gourmet meal every night. Be realistic about what you can tackle when you get home. If you have the ingredients for something complicated and don't fancy making it, you will end up with a takeaway and the food will waste. Not every meal has to set the world on fire – there is something comforting about the same old favourites. Have a repertoire of meals that can comfortably be tackled when you are tired, and stick to it. This is especially true if you are cooking for other members of the family. Don't be talked into taking on more than you want or can cope with.

Slow and gentle

Some people find cooking therapeutic. Slowly stirring a risotto or keeping an eye on a roasting chicken is one thing, but making pastry is quite something else, even if it takes the same amount of time to get the dinner on the table. So afterwork suppers are not just about fast food. The meal doesn't have to cook quickly, it's the fiddly preparation you want to avoid. If you choose something that goes in the oven with little fuss, and cooks for an hour or so, it won't be a hardship to sit down with a glass of wine while you wait.

Quick cooking

The other approach to a meal after work is the quick supper which is ready, from refrigerator to plate, in minutes. This might be a dish of pasta with a fresh tomato and herb dressing, a fillet of fish with steamed vegetables, or stir-fried noodles. Some people like to spend time over the weekend cooking casseroles and bakes then simply reheat them when they get in from work. This requires planning, however, and not everyone wants to spend their weekends in the kitchen.

Planning

Aim to go shopping once a week, and be organized about what you are going to cook each night, so the right ingredients are always to hand. There is nothing more irritating than sorting through the cupboards and trying to make a meal out of what you find.

Pre-work preparation

Before you go to work, double check you have all the ingredients you need and that they are defrosted. If you are going to be in late, think about putting the dinner on the timer. Most ovens have a timing facility, so you could put in jacket potatoes or a casserole to be cooked ready for when you get in. Electric slow cookers will cook a casserole or stew at a low temperature all day, using little power. The results are delicious – and imagine the aroma that will greet you as you come through the door.

Emergency meals

Keep in some emergency rations in case you have unexpected guests and there's nothing to eat. This may be a tub of frozen sauce to go with pasta, a portion or two of lasagne in the freezer, or some dried wild mushrooms for an impromptu risotto.

Meals in minutes

- Fresh fettucine tossed with chopped fresh tomatoes, a splash of olive oil and basil.
- Pan-fried chicken livers with chopped rosemary and a splash of sherry on a bed of mixed leaves, served with crusty bread.
- Mixed bean salad with canned beans, herbs, chopped onion and canned tuna or boiled egg. Dress with oil and vinegar.
- Tabbouleh made with instant bulgar wheat, chopped herbs, tomatoes and cucumber. Serve with cooked meat or fish if you like.
- Poached smoked haddock on a bed of wilted spinach, with a tub of supermarket fresh cheese sauce and brown bread.
- Egg noodles, served with tiger prawns pan-fried with spring onions, mangetout, ginger and soy sauce.
- Frittata made with chunks of leftover boiled potato, spring onions and frozen peas.
- A salad of watercress and rocket, topped with a poached egg, fried lardons and vinaigrette. Serve with focaccia.
- Jacket potato with a tasty filling.

Pasta with Radicchio and Cheese Crumbs

A simple but unusual pasta dish with tender radicchio and shallots complemented by crunchy golden breadcrumbs.

Preparation time 5 minutes **Cooking time** 25 minutes **Serves** 2

175 g (6 oz) dried spaghetti

65 g (2½ oz) butter

25 g (1 oz) fresh white breadcrumbs

15 g (½ oz) grated Parmesan cheese

2 shallots, finely chopped

1 garlic clove, sliced

1 head radicchio, shredded

dash of lemon juice

salt and pepper

1 Cook the pasta in a large pan of lightly salted boiling water for 10–12 minutes, until tender but still firm to the bite. Drain the pasta, reserving 2 tablespoons of the cooking liquid.

2 Meanwhile, melt half the butter in a frying pan and fry the breadcrumbs, stirring frequently, for about 5 minutes, until evenly golden and crisp. Transfer the crumbs to a bowl, cool slightly and add the Parmesan.

3 Heat the remaining butter in a wok or large saucepan and fry the shallots and garlic, stirring occasionally, for 5 minutes, until softened. Add the radicchio with a little lemon juice and season to taste with salt and pepper. Stir over a low heat for about 2 minutes, until the radicchio has wilted. Add the pasta, toss until heated through and serve topped with the cheese crumbs.

2 tbsp extra virgin olive oil

175 g (6 oz) lean lamb, finely chopped

1 large onion, chopped

3 garlic cloves, crushed

1 red chilli, deseeded and finely chopped

1½ tsp ground cumin

1½ tsp ground coriander

1½ tsp ground allspice

875 g (1¾ lb) canned chopped tomatoes

2 tbsp tomato purée

900 ml (1½ pints) Vegetable Stock (see page 161)

400 g (13 oz) can chickpeas, drained and rinsed

2 tbsp chopped parsley

1 tbsp chopped mint

50 g (2 oz) couscous

about 2 tsp sugar

salt and pepper

Lamb Soup with Chickpeas and Couscous

A fragrant main-course soup which involves little preparation. Relax with a drink and savour the aroma while it slowly cooks.

Preparation time 15 minutes **Cooking time** about 1 hour **Serves** 6

1 Heat the oil in a large, heavy-bottomed saucepan. Add the lamb to the pan and brown quickly. Using a slotted spoon, remove the lamb and place it on kitchen paper to drain.

2 Stir the onion into the pan and cook until soft and browned, adding the garlic and chilli when the onion is almost cooked. Add the cumin, coriander and the allspice and stir for 1 minute.

3 Return the lamb to the pan and add the canned tomatoes, tomato purée, stock and chickpeas. Stir well then cover the pan and simmer very gently for about 45 minutes until the lamb is tender.

4 Stir the parsley, mint and couscous into the soup, cover and remove from the heat. Leave to stand for 5 minutes. Add the sugar and salt and pepper to taste.

Steamed Chicken with Pak Choi and Ginger

A quick-cook dish bursting with flavours. If you don't have the time or inclination, serve the chicken without the salsa.

Preparation time 12 minutes, plus marinating **Cooking time** 11 minutes **Serves** 2

1 Combine the ginger, garlic, soy sauce, tangerine syrup, mirin, sugar and five-spice powder in a bowl. Place the chicken in a shallow, heatproof dish, pour in the mixture and turn to coat thoroughly. Set aside to marinate for 10 minutes.

2 Meanwhile, make the ginger salsa. Mix together the ginger, chilli, coriander leaves, sesame oil and lime juice and season to taste with salt and pepper.

3 Place the chicken with the marinade on a plate in a bamboo steamer and cook for 8 minutes. Remove the chicken from the dish and keep warm. Steam the pak choi in the cooking juices for 2–3 minutes. Serve the chicken and pak choi with the salsa, garnished with coriander sprigs.

1 cm (½ inch) piece of fresh root ginger, peeled and grated

1 small garlic clove, crushed

1 tbsp dark soy sauce

1 tbsp tangerine syrup

1½ tsp mirin

1 tsp sugar

pinch of Chinese five-spice powder

2 skinless chicken breast fillets

2 pak choi, halved

coriander sprigs, to garnish

GINGER SALSA
2.5 cm (1 inch) piece of stem ginger, peeled and very finely shredded

1 red chilli, deseeded and finely chopped

a few coriander leaves, chopped

1 tsp sesame oil

juice of ½ lime

salt and pepper

Stocks and supplies

Everyone knows the scenario: you are hungry, it's dinner time but you haven't been shopping. If you follow the advice below, you should have a range of ingredients in the storecupboard just waiting for you to whip up a perfectly respectable meal.

Staples

Starchy staples form the base of most meals and happily they also store well. Keep a selection of the following in your storecupboard:

Rice Stock risotto, long-grain and basmati rice for risottos, pilafs, kedgeree and as an accompaniment.

Couscous, bulgar wheat and other grains These can be used as an accompaniment to moist dishes or as a base for a salad like tabbouleh.

Dried pasta Stock long pasta such as spaghetti or fettucine, plus some shorter varieties like penne.

Noodles Dried noodles are a good storecupboard stand-by and cook quickly. Even quicker are the long-life, moist, ready-to-eat noodles in plastic packets.

Flour Keep in strong bread flour, self-raising and plain for impromptu bread making, pizza bases, pancakes, cakes and muffins.

Dried pulses These are very versatile ingredients. They do, however, get drier and tougher with age so don't keep them for too long.

> ### TOP TIP
> Canned chopped tomatoes are absolutely invaluable, so keep a few tins in store. They can form the base of a rich sauce for pasta or for pouring over grilled meat or fish, they are great for adding a rich flavour or bulking out casseroles and stews, as well as creating spicy soups or curries.

Above Rice is a great storecupboard stand-by. It is perfect for pilafs, risottos and accompanying curries and casseroles.

Canned goods

Canned foods stay fresh for a long time, so stock up on some tins. Some canned foods are more appealing than others. The good ones are tomatoes, beans and pulses of all kinds, coconut milk, water chestnuts, pineapple chunks for both savoury and sweet dishes, sweetcorn and olives.

Canned fish of all varieties also make a useful standby. Try tuna, sardines, mackerel fillets, clams, mussels, octopus or squid in oil or ink sauce, anchovies and smoked oysters. All of these are delicious with pasta, as pizza toppings, stirred into soups or risottos, or as part of a salad.

Bottles, jars and packets

You can never have too many flavouring ingredients to add character to your meals. Be sure to stock a good selection of spices for curries, rice dishes, soups and stews. Buy them in small quantities because they lose their flavour quite quickly.

Make sure you also have dried and prepared mustard, horseradish, Worcestershire sauce, mayonnaise, wine vinegar, soy sauce, Thai fish sauce, and dried chilli flakes.

A variety of different oils is also useful for creating meals of all kinds – have in store some vegetable or groundnut oil, olive oil, sesame oil and perhaps some walnut oil for dressings.

Exciting extras

Keep some interesting ingredients at the back of the cupboard for when you fancy something tasty. Here are some ideas:

- a can of smoked oysters – eat them as a nibble with a glass of wine or toss into a pasta sauce for a sensational flavour.
- a jar of caviar or, for smaller budgets, lumpfish roe.
- some jars of antipasti in oil, such as marinated peppers, wild mushrooms, artichoke hearts and sun-dried tomatoes.
- a packet of dried wild mushrooms – morels are the best.
- some high-quality dried pasta flavoured with squid ink.
- smoked tuna in a can or jar.
- a jar of cherries marinated in Kirsch.
- some good-quality dark chocolate for grating over ice cream or an impromptu batch of brownies or chocolate cake.

Storecupboard salads

If you've got some salad leaves in the refrigerator, or a can of kidney beans or mixed beans in the cupboard, a few other flavoursome ingredients will turn them into an instant salad. Canned sweetcorn adds sweetness and bite, while a can or jar of artichoke hearts adds body and flavour. Marinated peppers in oil, capers and olives will also make great salad ingredients.

Consider adding some canned fish, such as tuna, mackerel fillets or chopped salty anchovy fillets. Dress the whole lot with a little vinaigrette and tuck in.

Be inventive

If you've come to make a dish and don't have all the ingredients you need, check the cupboards and freezer – is there something else you could substitute instead? You may even discover a better combination than the original you had planned.

The freezer

For many of us, the freezer is an extension of the storecupboard. Much of what we buy in the supermarket is put straight into the freezer for storage until we need it. A freezer can store a much wider range of foods than a basic cupboard, including homemade or shop-bought meals ready for defrosting and reheating.

Try to keep a range of ingredients in the freezer, from which you can make meals. Meat and fish of all kinds freeze really well, though some of the more delicate shellfish, such as lobster, crab and scallops, can go rather watery and tasteless.

Keep a pack or two of minced beef or lamb, some chicken joints perhaps, a couple of whole herring or mackerel for a tasty supper, plus a bag of raw tiger prawns for a quick treat.

Most hard cheeses respond well to freezing, and even some of the soft cheeses come out fine. A block of Cheddar and a piece of Emmenthal will always be useful for an impromptu sandwich, macaroni cheese, or cheesy pancakes. Butter and margarine also freeze well, so you need never run out. Buy in bags of frozen fruit and vegetables as these are always useful.

Foods that don't freeze well

Some foods can be frozen and thawed more successfully than others. The following foods do not respond well to freezing: eggs, cream, bananas, avocado, fruits with a high water content, such as oranges, celery, boiled potatoes (mash them first), salad vegetables, tomatoes (unless they are cooked), custard, jelly, yogurt, soured cream, meringue, icing or mayonnaise.

TOP TIP

The freezer is great for storing leftovers for another day. You may not fancy having the same meal again straightaway, so if you cook too much, put the extra into the freezer rather than the refrigerator, and you can have it when you do want it.

Did you know?

Foods that have been defrosted should be used up quickly. Don't leave them lying around at room temperature, and never refreeze food that has already been frozen. The only exception is if you have cooked the food after defrosting. For example, minced beef that was frozen and thawed can be refrozen if it has been cooked in a Bolognese sauce, or a frozen and thawed chicken can be refrozen if it has been roasted first.

Pasta with Puttanesca Sauce

4 tbsp olive oil

1 onion, finely chopped

3 garlic cloves, crushed

large pinch of dried chilli flakes

6 canned anchovy fillets, drained and chopped

2 x 400 g (13 oz) cans chopped tomatoes

½ tsp caster sugar

75 g (3 oz) black olives, pitted and finely chopped

small handful of basil leaves

2 tbsp capers, rinsed and drained

salt

To serve
freshly grated Parmesan cheese (optional)

pasta

This intense Italian tomato sauce has plenty of flavour thanks to the black olives, anchovies and chillies. Rich and thick, it's great tossed with almost any pasta, especially spaghetti, for a delicious quick supper dish. Scatter with Parmesan cheese if you have some.

Preparation time 15 minutes **Cooking time** 15 minutes **Serves** 4

1 Heat the oil in a heavy-based saucepan. Add the onion and fry gently for 3–4 minutes until softened. Add the garlic and chilli and cook for a further minute.

2 Add the anchovy fillets, tomatoes, sugar and black olives, and bring to the boil. Reduce the heat and simmer gently for 10 minutes until the sauce has thickened.

3 Add the basil leaves, capers and a little salt and stir through for 1 minute. Serve hot over pasta, sprinkled with Parmesan cheese, if liked.

Individual Macaroni Cheeses

250 g (8 oz) macaroni

4 rashers smoked back bacon, diced

1 garlic clove, crushed

150 ml (¼ pint) single cream

150 ml (¼ pint) milk

pinch of freshly grated nutmeg

175 g (6 oz) hard cheese, such as Cheddar or Gruyére, grated

4 tbsp chopped basil

salt and pepper

If you haven't got any cream in the refrigerator, use all milk instead. This makes a warm and satisfying undemanding supper dish for any occasion.

Preparation time 5 minutes **Cooking time** 20 minutes **Serves** 4

1 Cook the macaroni in a pan of lightly salted, boiling water for 10–12 minutes, until tender but still firm to the bite. Drain and place in a large bowl.

2 Meanwhile, dry-fry the bacon in a small frying pan until browned but not crisp. Add the garlic, fry for 1 minute, then add the cream and milk and season with a little nutmeg. Bring just to boiling point.

3 Stir in 125 g (4 oz) of the cheese and all the basil, remove the sauce from the heat and stir gently until the cheese melts. Season to taste with salt and pepper and stir into the macaroni.

4 Spoon into individual gratin dishes, top with the remaining cheese and bake in a preheated oven at 230°C (450°F), Gas Mark 8, for 10 minutes, until golden.

2 tbsp olive oil

1 onion, chopped

1 garlic clove, crushed

1 tsp hot chilli powder

1 tsp ground coriander

½ tsp ground cumin

400 g (13 oz) can red kidney beans, drained

400 g (13 oz) can chopped tomatoes

600 ml (1 pint) Vegetable Stock (see page 161)

12 tortilla chips

50 g (2 oz) Cheddar cheese, grated

salt and pepper

soured cream, to serve (optional)

Chilli Bean Soup

This warming and spicy concoction makes a great starter or light lunch. Keep the ingredients in the cupboard just in case.

Preparation time 8 minutes **Cooking time** 22 minutes **Serves** 3–4

1 Heat the oil in a saucepan and fry the onion, garlic, chilli powder, coriander and cumin, stirring frequently, for 5 minutes, until the onion has softened. Add the beans, tomatoes and stock and season to taste with salt and pepper.

2 Bring the soup to the boil, cover and simmer for 15 minutes. Transfer to a food processor or blender and process until fairly smooth. Pour into heatproof bowls.

3 Place the tortilla chips on top of the soup, scatter over the grated cheese and grill the bowls of soup for 1–2 minutes, until the cheese has melted. Serve immediately with soured cream.

Nutrition for all

As well as offering protection against colds and more serious illnesses, eating a healthy diet has other beneficial effects. It can make you feel good from within and generally more optimistic about life. It should also give you more energy, and take away that sluggish, lacklustre feeling caused by eating too much junk food.

A healthy diet

A healthy diet is primarily about balance. Our bodies need certain amounts of carbohydrates, proteins, fats, vitamins and minerals in order to function properly and, by eating sensibly, this is easy to achieve. With busy lifestyles and stressful jobs, it is all too easy to neglect our diet. However, it is well worth taking the time to think about what you eat, since a sensible diet will boost energy and vitality and doesn't necessarily mean hours of preparation and cooking.

Guidelines for healthy eating

Healthy eating does not mean compromising on enjoyable foods or cutting out treats, it simply means that you should be aware of the food that you eat and follow a few simple guidelines.

1 Eat a variety of different foods There is no one food that will provide all the nutrients you need. For this reason it is important to eat a wide variety of foods from all of the main food groups.

2 Maintain a healthy weight Body weight is the result of the balance between energy taken in, usually measured in calories, and the amount used up. Those who consume more calories than they use gain weight. The more physically active you are, the greater your energy need, so a healthy balance of food and exercise is the best plan.

3 Eat foods rich in starch and fibre Starchy foods are valuable sources of fibre and can be used in many different ways. For a well-balanced diet, you should include a starchy food at two, or preferably three, meals daily. At a main meal, most of the space on the plate should be taken up with a starchy food and vegetables, with the amount of meat or fish being quite small in proportion.

4 Eat plenty of fruit and vegetables These contain vitamins and minerals that help to keep you healthy. They may also protect you from diseases such as coronary heart disease, and some forms of cancer. Aim to eat five portions of fruit and vegetables a day, excluding potatoes.

5 Cut down on foods containing fat There are several kinds of fat which have different effects on our bodies. Fat helps to make our diets more palatable and some fats are a good source of important nutrients, so a certain amount is essential. In particular, we need small amounts of 'essential fatty acids' which our bodies cannot manufacture themselves. Evidence shows that too high a proportion of saturated or hydrogenated fat in the diet can increase the risk of coronary heart disease.

6 Restrict your use of salt Salt affects the balance of fluid in the body and raises blood pressure. It draws water out of body cells, drying tissues including the skin. So limit your intake by not adding salt to foods and by eating salty foods only sparingly.

7 Limit your consumption of sugary foods and drinks Most of us enjoy the taste of sweet things. Sugar provides energy in the form of calories, but very little in the way of other nutrients, and it upsets your body's blood sugar levels. It is, therefore, sensible to cut right down on your intake of sugar, to maintain long-term health.

8 If you drink alcohol, drink sensibly Research has shown that a certain amount of alcohol may improve some aspects of our health. However, moderation is essential as there are also risks associated with alcohol.

Cooking methods

Healthy eating is as much about how you cook as what you cook. Two main principles are to retain nutrients and reduce fat.

- As a general rule, cook fruits and vegetables as little as possible or not at all.
- Add as little oil or fat to foods as possible.
- Boil, steam or poach foods, rather than frying or roasting with oil.
- Grill meat, rather than frying.
- Remove any visible oil or fat from food before serving.
- Steam vegetables instead of boiling.
- Tear up leaf vegetables rather than slicing them with a knife to retain nutrients.

The food pyramid

This is all about eating a wide variety of foods, from each of the major food groups. The pyramid is made up of these groups. Eating foods from each section of the pyramid every day, in the proportions shown, will provide a balance of the necessary nutrients.

Level 1

Sugars and fats

Foods containing sugars and fats are at the top of the pyramid and so should be eaten in the smallest quantities. They include butter, cooking oils, oil-based dressings, ice cream, pastries, confectionery and certain soft drinks, which should be eaten sparingly as they are high in fat or refined carbohydrate such as sugar and honey.
Eat 1 serving per day

Level 2

Protein and dairy foods

The next step of the pyramid contains protein and dairy foods. Protein can come from animal sources (meat, fish, eggs, milk, cheese and yogurt); or vegetable sources such as beans and lentils and seeds. Meat, fish and alternatives provide protein, iron, zinc, magnesium and some B vitamins, especially B$_{12}$. Milk and dairy foods supply our bodies with protein, calcium and zinc, and vitamins B$_{12}$, B$_2$, A and D. Try to choose lean cuts of meat and low-fat dairy products to avoid too high an intake of fat.
Eat 2–3 servings per day

Level 3

Fruit and vegetables

Fruit and vegetables form the next step of the pyramid. These provide fibre and some carbohydrates, as well as many of the vitamins and minerals that are essential for our bodies to function efficiently. It is best to eat fruits and vegetables when fresh, although certain varieties are fine frozen, too. Canned produce and dried fruit also provide some of the nutrients needed.
Eat at least 5 servings per day

Level 4

Starchy foods

The large base section of the pyramid contains the staple, starchy, carbohydrate foods that should provide the major source of energy in the diet. These include cereals (such as wheat, rye, oats, barley, millet), rice and products made from them, such as bread, pasta, noodles, cornmeal and breakfast cereals. Other staple carbohydrate foods in this group include potatoes, yams and other starchy vegetables. All the foods – the more unrefined, the better – in this group are rich in nutrients – supplying fibre, B vitamins and some calcium and iron.
Eat 4–5 servings per day

When disaster strikes

When disaster strikes in the kitchen, the cardinal rule is DON'T PANIC. It is only food after all, and there is usually something you can do to rectify the situation if you follow the tips below.

Lumpy sauces

If a sauce develops lumps, beat it well with a whisk. If that doesn't help, either process it in a blender or food processor until smooth, or pass it through a fine sieve.

Curdled mayonnaise

Mayonnaise can curdle if the eggs and oil are at different temperatures, so eggs for mayonnaise should be at room temperature. If you see it starting to curdle, beat in a few drops of boiling water, which may smooth it. Alternatively, break another egg yolk into a clean bowl, beat well and gradually add the curdled mixture to the egg yolk.

Too much fat

The easiest way to skim fat from the top of stocks, soups and stews, without waiting for them to get cold is to first take off as much as you can with a metal spoon. Next cut a piece of absorbent kitchen paper into strips and draw each piece gently across the surface of the liquid. Carry on in this manner until all the fat has been absorbed.

Burnt saucepans

If your risotto, stew or sauce sticks to the bottom of the saucepan and burns, don't stir it! Remove it from the heat immediately and taste the food. If it tastes burnt, throw it away. If it tastes okay, tip the contents into another pan, leaving the burnt bits in the first pan. Don't be tempted to scrape around the pan to get it all out.

Curdled hollandaise sauce

If your hollandaise starts to separate, put a spoonful of vinegar into a clean bowl and whisk in the sauce very slowly until it thickens.

Stop it sticking

Watch rice and pasta carefully as they are cooking to prevent them drying out, and top up with more boiling water if necessary. If they are inclined to stick together, stir a tablespoon of olive oil into the cooking liquid.

Too much seasoning

If your sauce, soup or stew is too salty, add some cubes of peeled potato and boil them in the liquid until soft. They should take away some of the salt. If you have added too much pepper, there is not a lot you can do except to replace half of the liquid with stock or water.

Curdled custard

Don't panic if the custard overheats and starts to separate. Quickly stop the cooking by plunging the base of the saucepan into a bowl of ice-cold water (already in the sink just in case) and whisking the custard vigorously with a balloon whisk. Alternatively, pour the custard into a food processor and blend until smooth, then strain it through a fine sieve. Hopefully the custard will look silky smooth once more; if not, you may have to admit defeat and throw it away.

Below Rather than throwing away a cake that spent too long in the oven, disguise the colour by sprinkling with icing sugar.

Burnt cakes

If the tops of your cakes are too brown, slice off the burnt bits after cooling and coat the cake in chocolate or icing to cover it. Or simply sift some icing sugar over the top.

Unwilling egg whites

No matter how much you beat, sometimes egg whites will only produce a few bubbles, rather than a fluffy mass. Check the eggs: newly laid eggs will not whisk easily – they are much better after four or five days. Also check your equipment: a scrupulously clean bowl and whisk are essential, since the smallest speck of grease or egg yolk will prevent the whites whisking well. A pinch of salt may help to increase the volume.

Broken meringue

If you were planning a beautiful pavlova but the meringues have fallen apart when you tried to take them off the baking sheet, break them into pieces and fold them into the whipped cream with the chopped fruit. Serve the mixture in pretty glasses or bowls.

Wet pastry

If you add too much water when making pastry, it will be hard when you cook it. If your pastry feels too damp, don't just add more flour or the proportions will be wrong. Rub a little more flour and fat together in a clean bowl and add that to the pastry. Knead again.

Unexpected guests

If you are suddenly faced with an extra guest for dinner, just pad out the meal you were originally planning. Serve an extra accompaniment to supplement the main dish (think pasta, bread, another vegetable, pastry, rice or a salad), or make an impromptu starter or nibbles before the meal. If you have exactly the right number of chicken portions or steaks, for example, cut the meat into strips or chunks and cook it for less time.

Badly behaved cakes

If your cake sinks in the middle, leave it to cool and then cut out the centre with a circular pastry cutter to make a ring shape. Ice or decorate in the normal way. If the cake has an awkward peak in the middle, simply slice it off when the cake has cooled to make icing and decorating easier.

Mistiming dinner

If dinner is running late, there is not much you can do except wait. There is no point eating it before it is

Above Broken meringues can be transformed into a crunchy, creamy dessert when mixed with whipped cream and fruit.

done, much better to wait and have it perfect. Above all, don't worry – the longer people have to wait, the hungrier they get and the more they enjoy the food! In the meantime, serve some nibbles to keep everyone happy. Get out a jar of olives, open a bag of crisps, cut some cucumber and carrot batons and serve them with taramasalata or hummus or serve radishes with salt for dipping – use whatever you have.

Unrectifiable disasters

If all is lost – black pastry or totally soggy spaghetti, for example – there are other choices. Firstly you could cook some more, although this will obviously depend on whether you have any more ingredients. Otherwise you could cook something else, which is where a well-stocked storecupboard comes in. However, if you don't have time for either of these options then it is always a good idea to have a back-up in case of disaster. It might be a tub of good ice cream, some fresh pasta and tomato sauce in the freezer, or some tubs of fresh soup. Coolly put plan B into action and your guests need never know. If, however, you are completely stuck and the cupboard is bare, then there is always the option of getting a take-away. Even if you are entertaining, fish and chips can be quite fun. Just come clean, have a laugh about your disaster, and enjoy the rest of the evening.

Cooking terms explained

Here is an glossary of cookery terms – some familiar, some more obscure – that you may come across.

Al dente
The Italians say that pasta is ready to eat when it is 'al dente' – which, when literally translated, means 'firm to the bite'.

Antipasti
Italian hors d'oeuvres. The Italian translation is 'before the meal' and it usually means an assortment of cold meats, vegetables and cheeses, which are often marinated.

Arborio
The Italian rice used in making risotto. It is similar in shape to pudding rice, but never quite softens in the middle.

Au gratin
A cheese and breadcrumb topping, browned under the grill.

Bain-marie
A large, water-filled pan or tin in which smaller dishes are set for cooking when an indirect, gentle heat is required.

Bake blind
To part-bake an unfilled pastry case by pricking the base with a fork, covering with greaseproof paper or foil and filling with ceramic or dried beans.

Balsamic vinegar
Italian vinegar that has been aged in oak casks for anything up to 20 years. It is dark in colour, with an intense, slightly sweet flavour.

Barbecue
To cook over glowing coals.

Bard
To cover or wrap lean meats in a sheet of fat to prevent drying out.

Baste
To spoon pan juices (usually fat-based) over meat or vegetables to moisten during cooking.

Beignets
Fritters.

Beurre manié
Flour and butter worked into a paste, then used to thicken soups, stew juices and so on.

Beurre noir
Butter heated to a light brown colour, usually served with fish.

Bind
To hold dry ingredients together with egg or some other liquid.

Bisque
Smooth and thickened shellfish soup.

Blanch
To immerse food briefly in boiling water to soften, remove skin, parcook, set a colour, or remove a strong taste.

Bouillon
Broth or unclarified stock obtained from boiling meat or vegetables.

Bouquet garni
Classically made up of a bay leaf, a sprig of thyme and 2–3 parsley sprigs, which are either bound together with string or tied into a small muslin bag. It is used to flavour almost any savoury dish that needs long cooking, and is removed before the dish is served.

Braise
To cook food very slowly in a small amount of liquid in a pan or pot with a tight-fitting lid, after initial browning.

Brochette
Skewered meat, fish or vegetables, then grilled, griddled or pan-fried.

Buckwheat
Small, triangular-shaped grain, milled into either flour or grains.

Bulgar wheat
Cracked wheat that has been partially processed. Sometimes sold as cracked wheat and used extensively in Middle Eastern cooking.

Butterfly
To slit a piece of food in half horizontally, almost cutting through so that when opened it resembles butterfly wings. Often used for king prawns, chops and thick fillets of fish.

Canapé
Small appetizer of pastry, biscuits or similar with a savoury topping.

Capers
Small buds of a flowering shrub grown in the Mediterranean. As they are normally pickled in brine or salted, they should be washed and dried before use.

Casserole
Ovenproof cooking pot with a lid.

Cassis
A fruit liqueur or syrup made from blackcurrants.

Cassoulet
A French dish which consists of haricot beans cooked in a stewpot with pork, other meat and poultry, seasoning and a gratin topping. Sausages, duck and goose portions are often added.

Caramelize
To cook sugar or sugar syrup to the caramel stage. The term is also used when grilling a sugar topping until brown.

Ceps (dried)
Dried mushrooms that need reconstituting in boiling water before using. Also known as porcini, which is their Italian name.

Clarify
To melt and strain butter of its milk particles and impurities; to clear stocks by filtering.

Cocotte
A small ovenproof dish without a lid.

Compôte
Fresh or dried fruit served cold in a syrup.

Consommé
Concentrated clear meat or poultry stock.

Coulis
A thin liquid purée, usually of fresh or cooked fruit or vegetables, which can be poured.

Court-bouillon
Aromatic liquid used for poaching fish or shellfish.

Couscous
This is actually a type of pasta although it is treated like a grain and is pre-soaked before cooking to soften it. It is often used in North African or Middle Eastern cooking.

Crackling
The crisp cooked rind of a joint of pork.

Cream
To beat butter and sugar together until it is pale with a thick consistency.

Croûte
A slice of fried or toasted bread on which food is served.

Croûton
Small slices or dice of fried or occasionally toasted bread used as a garnish.

Crudités
Raw vegetables such as carrot, cucumber and celery, usually cut into sticks or slices and eaten with a dipping sauce.

Curdle
To cause milk or sauce to separate into solid and liquid. Often used to describe any mixture that separates.

Deglaze
To free congealed cooking juices and sediments from the bottom of a roasting tin or pan by adding water, stock or wine and stirring over heat. The juices may be used to make gravy or added to a sauce.

Degrease
To skim grease from the surface of a liquid.

Demi-glace
A rich brown sauce.

Devilled
A food seasoned with a hot-tasting sauce and grilled or fried.

Dredge
To sprinkle the surface of food with flour, icing sugar and so on.

Dress
To pluck, draw and truss poultry or game birds; or to put dressing on a salad and toss.

Dropping consistency
The stage reached when a spoonful of a mixture held upside down will drop off the spoon reluctantly.

Empanada
A South American pastry turnover stuffed with a mixture of chopped meat and onions.

Emulsion
A milky liquid prepared by mixing liquids that are not soluble, such as oil and water.

En croûte
To cook food in a pastry case.

En papillote
To cook food enclosed in baking paper.

Entrée
In Europe, a dish served before the main course, now often referring to the main course itself.

Escalope
A thin slice of meat from the fillet or leg.

Fines herbes
A mixture of finely chopped fresh herbs. Traditionally these are chervil, chives, parsley and tarragon.

Flake
To separate cooked meat or fish into small pieces.

Flamber
To pour warmed spirit, often brandy, over food and set it alight which helps to burn off the alcohol and add flavour.

Florentine
A dish that is made with spinach.

Flute
To make decorative indentations in the edges of pastry pies.

Fold in
To combine two mixtures gently with a metal spoon to retain their lightness.

Freezer burn
Appears as brown or greyish-white patches on the surface of frozen food. It is caused by extreme dehydration and is often seen on meat, poultry and fish.

Fumet
A strong, well-reduced stock made from fish or meat.

Galette
Any sweet or savoury mixture that is shaped in a flat round.

Garam masala
A ready-made spice powder made up of several different Indian spices.

Garnish
To decorate or embellish a savoury dish.

Glaze
A mixture that is brushed on the surface of food to give colour and shine.

Gnocchi
These are little Italian dumplings made from mashed potatoes, potato flour, polenta or wheat flour. They are usually poached in boiling water to cook.

Goujons
Small strips of meat or fish, coated and deep-fried.

Hollandaise
A rich emulsion sauce made with egg yolks and butter.

Hors d'oeuvres
The first course, or savoury morsels served with drinks.

Hull
To remove the green calyx from fruit.

Infuse
To steep or flavour by leaving an aromatic ingredient in a hot liquid.

Julienne
Matchstick strips of vegetables, citrus rind or meat, used as a garnish.

Kibbled
Coarsely chopped, used mainly for wheat.

Knead
To work dough by stretching and folding it to distribute the yeast and give a springy consistency.

Knocking back
To punch or knead air from yeast dough after rising.

Knock up
To slightly separate the layers of raw puff pastry with the blade of a knife, to help rising during cooking.

Lard
To thread strips of fat (usually pork) into lean meat to moisten it.

Lardons
Small strips or cubes of pork or bacon fat, used to flavour or garnish a dish.

Liaison
Ingredients used to bind or thicken soups, sauces or other liquids.

Macerate
To steep raw food, usually fruit, in sugar syrup or alcohol.

Magret
A boned breast of duck, presented with the skin and underlying layer of fat attached.

Marinade
The liquid in which food is marinated.

Marinate
To soak raw food (meat, fish or vegetables) in liquid, often wine or oil, to tenderize and give flavour.

Medallions
Small rounds of meat, evenly cut.

Mousseline
A delicate mixture made from poultry or fish, and served hot or cold.

Niçoise
Food cooked or served with tomato, garlic, French beans, anchovies and olives.

Noisette
Boneless rack of lamb, rolled and cut into rounds; surrounded by a thin band of fat.

Pan-frying
Uses a heavy-based, heated pan and the food cooks in its own juices.

Parboil
To boil until partially cooked.

Pare
To peel or trim.

Passata
Sieved tomatoes.

Pâte
The French for pastry dough.

Pâté
A savoury paste of liver, pork, game and so on.

Pâtisserie
A French cake shop or sweet cakes and pastries.

Paupiette
Slices of meat or fish rolled around stuffing.

Poach
To cook by simmering very gently in liquid.

Polenta
The Italian name for corn meal.

Praline
Caramelized sugar and browned almonds mixed together.

Prove
To allow yeast dough to rise before baking.

Pulses
The dried seeds of members of the bean and pea families.

Purée
Cooked food, mashed, blended or sieved until smooth.

Quenelles
Light fish or meat dumplings, usually poached.

Ragoût
A stew.

Ramekins
Small ovenproof dishes, usually made of porcelain.

Reduce
To concentrate – or thicken – a liquid, by boiling it rapidly to decrease its volume.

Refresh
To rinse freshly cooked food under cold running water or by plunging into iced water to stop the cooking process and to set the colour, used particularly for vegetables.

Relax or rest
In pastry to allow the gluten in the flour to contract after rolling out; to allow the starch cells in the flour of a batter to expand.

Render
To melt and strain solid animal fat.

Roux
A basic liaison of melted fat (usually butter) and flour, cooked as a thickening for sauces or soups.

Rub in
To mix fat into flour, using the fingertips, to give a mixture resembling fine breadcrumbs.

Sabayon
A frothy sweet sauce of whipped egg yolks, sugar, wine and liqueur.

Salsa
In Mexico this usually applies to uncooked sauces served as a dip or accompaniment. Mexican salsas are usually made from chillies and tomatoes; in Italy the term is often used for pasta sauces.

Sauté
A method of frying that uses very little fat; the food is moved constantly throughout the process to prevent it sticking to the pan and burning.

Scald
To heat liquid, usually milk to just below boiling point. Also to rinse with boiling water.

Score
To make shallow or deep cuts over the surface of meat or fish before cooking to allow the heat to penetrate evenly.

Seal or sear
Sealing the surface of food, to retain the juices, goodness and flavour.

Seasoned flour
Flour with salt and pepper added.

Simmer
To cook food gently in liquid at just below boiling point.

Skim
To remove any scum or fat from the surface of a liquid with a metal spoon or small ladle.

Spatchcock
A chicken or poussin split open with poultry shears and spread out flat before cooking.

Steam
To cook food in the steam above boiling water, in a perforated dish or a special steamer.

Steep
To soak in warm or cold liquid in order to soften food and draw out strong flavours. Or to moisten cakes with a liqueur or syrup.

Stew
To cook meat, fish or vegetables slowly in a liquid in a closed dish or pan in the oven or on the hob.

Stir-fry
An Oriental cooking method in which food is lightly cooked in a little oil over a high heat with constant stirring.

Sun-dried tomatoes
These are a form of preserved tomato. They have a concentrated flavour and are usually preserved in oil.

Suprême
A choice piece of meat, usually a breast of poultry, and also a rich, creamy white sauce.

Sweat
To cook food, usually vegetables, gently in a little fat over a very low heat until the juices run.

Tempura
A Japanese style of deep-frying pieces of meat, fish, poultry and vegetables in a light batter. These are served with a dipping sauce of soy sauce.

Terrine
A pâté or minced mixture cooked in a loaf-shaped dish.

Tortillas
These are a flat type of bread unique to Mexico and are made from dried corn flour or from wheat flour. They are the basis for many Mexican dishes such as tacos and enchiladas.

Truss
To tie a joint or bird with string before cooking.

Vanilla sugar
Caster sugar flavoured with pure vanilla extract or essence. This can be made by adding a vanilla pod to a jar of caster sugar.

Vinaigrette
A salad dressing made with olive oil and vinegar or lemon juice.

Well
The hollow made in a pile or bowl of flour into which liquid, fat, etc. are added prior to mixing.

Zest
The thin outer layer of citrus fruit containing the citrus oil; the rind.

Index

Acknowledgements

Executive Editor: Sarah Ford
Editor: Alice Bowden
Executive Art Editor: Karen Sawyer
Design: One 2 Six Creative
Senior Production Controller: Martin Crowshaw
Picture Library Assistant: Sophie Delpech

PICTURE CREDITS
Special Photography: ©Octopus Publishing Group Limited/ Stephen Conroy.

DK Images/Dave King 72.
Getty Images/Antonio Di Ciacca 224 top; /Amy Neunsinger 202.
Octopus Publishing Group Limited 72; /Frank Adam 14 top right, 126/Clive Bozzard-Hill 53 bottom right, 212 top; /Jean Cazals 219; /Gus Filgate 176, 177, 211; /GGS Photographic 138; /Jeremy Hopley 86, 87; /David Jordan 38 top right, 42 top centre left, 139 top, 165, 229, 247 top left, 247 top right, 247 bottom right, 247 bottom left, 247 bottom centre left, 247 bottom centre right, 247 top centre right, 247 top centre left; /Sandra Lane 10 top left, 10 bottom right, 10 bottom left, 13 bottom right, 13 top centre left, 18 bottom right, 18 bottom left, 21 top left, 21 top right, 21 bottom left, 21 bottom centre left, 21 bottom centre right, 21 top centre right, 21 top centre left, 45 bottom left, 58 top right, 88, 102 bottom left; /William Lingwood 6, 14 bottom left, 17 bottom centre right, 37 bottom centre right, 41 bottom left, 42 bottom centre left, 49 bottom left, 49 bottom centre right, 57 top left, 58 top left, 65, 139 bottom, 171 top, 179, 225; /David Loftus 18 top right, 34 bottom left, 41 top left, 45 bottom right, 49 top centre left, 57 top centre right, 78, 113, 125, 204, 205, 214; /Jonathan Lovekin 82, 82 bottom right, 82 bottom centre; /James Merrell 140, 141 bottom; /Neil Mersh 14 top centre left, 42 top left, 42 bottom centre right, 213 bottom centre right; /Peter Myers 53 top right, 153; /Lis Parsons 7, 13 top right, 14 bottom right, 14 bottom centre right, 17 top right, 18 top centre, 104, 184, 186, 213 bottom right; /William Reavell 2 left, 5 right, 8 centre left, 8 centre right, 13 bottom left, 13 bottom centre left, 13 bottom centre right, 17 top left, 17 bottom centre left, 30 top left, 34 bottom right, 38 top left, 42 top right, 42 bottom left, 42 top centre right, 43 bottom right, 46 top left, 46 top right, 46 bottom right, 46 bottom left, 46 bottom centre right, 46 top centre right, 46 top centre left, 47 bottom centre left, 49 bottom right, 53 bottom centre right, 57 top centre left, 60 centre right, 97, 99, 100, 101, 105, 110, 111, 114, 115, 116, 120, 123, 136 right, 143, 161, 163, 198 left, 198 centre left, 201, 203, 208, 209, 215, 216, 224 bottom, 226, 230, 240; /Gareth Sambidge 10 top right, 14 bottom centre left, 141 top; /Simon Smith 1, 2 right, 2 centre left, 5 centre left, 13 top centre right, 45 top left, 57 top right, 57 bottom left, 60 left, 60 centre left, 62, 63, 64 left, 64 right, 70 bottom right, 70 bottom left, 70 bottom centre, 71, 73, 75 left, 75 right, 77, 80, 81, 83 top, 83 bottom, 84, 90, 91, 92, 94, 102 bottom right, 102 bottom centre left, 102 bottom centre right, 103, 118, 119, 127, 128, 129, 162, 174 bottom right, 174 bottom left, 174 bottom centre, 180, 187, 188, 189, 198 centre right, 207, 213 bottom centre left; /Ian Wallace 13 top left, 17 bottom right, 17 bottom left, 17 top centre right, 17 top centre left, 21 bottom right, 37 top left, 38 bottom right, 38 bottom left, 41 top right, 41 bottom right, 45 top right, 45 bottom left, 45 top centre right, 45 top centre left, 49 top left, 49 top centre right, 53 top left, 57 bottom centre right, 66, 67, 69, 85, 89, 96, 98, 107, 108, 109, 117, 121, 122, 130, 133, 149, 150, 164, 178, 212 centre, 212 bottom, 220, 228, 231 top, 231 bottom, 232, 233, 234, 235, 237, 239, 241, 242, 245; /Philip Webb 79, 93, 106, 175.